THE MANAGEMENT OF INTERNATIONAL ACQUISITIONS

The Management of International Acquisitions

JOHN CHILD, DAVID FAULKNER, AND ROBERT PITKETHLY

OXFORD

UNIVERSITY PRESS

OXFORD
UNIVERSITY PRESS

Great Clarendon Street, Oxford OX2 6DP

Oxford University Press is a department of the University of Oxford.
It furthers the University's objective of excellence in research, scholarship,
and education by publishing worldwide in

Oxford New York

Athens Auckland Bangkok Bogotá Buenos Aires Calcutta
Cape Town Chennai Dar es Salaam Delhi Florence Hong Kong Istanbul
Karachi Kuala Lumpur Madrid Melbourne Mexico City Mumbai
Nairobi Paris São Paulo Shanghai Singapore Taipei Tokyo Toronto Warsaw
with associated companies in Berlin Ibadan

Oxford is a registered trade mark of Oxford University Press
in the UK and in certain other countries

Published in the United States
by Oxford University Press Inc., New York

© J. Child, D. Faulkner, and R. Pitkethly, 2001

British Library Cataloguing in Publication Data

Data available

Library of Congress Cataloging in Publication Data

Child, John, 1940–
The management of international acquisitions: realizing their potential
value/John Child, David Faulkner, and Robert Pitkethly.
p.cm
Includes bibliographical references and index.
1. Consolidation and merger of corporations.   2. Industrial concentration.
I. Faulkner, David, 1938–   II. Pitkethly, Robert.   III. Title.
HD2746.5 .C457 2001   658.1´8—dc21   00-050503

ISBN 0–19–829632–0

3 5 7 9 10 8 6 4 2

Typeset by Florence Production Ltd,
Stoodleigh, Devon EX16 9PN
Printed in Great Britain
on acid-free paper by
Biddles Ltd., Guildford & King's Lynn

ACKNOWLEDGEMENTS

Many people have lent their time and support to this book. It would have been impossible without the participation of more than two hundred companies in the research that informs it. We are extremely grateful to the managers who took the time and trouble to complete and return our questionnaires. Special thanks are due to those who allowed us subsequently to visit their companies and to engage with them at length about their experience of post-acquisition management.

The research was funded by the Economic and Social Research Council (ESRC) under the auspices of its Centre for Business Research in the University of Cambridge. We owe a considerable debt to the Centre's director, Professor Alan Hughes, for the support and sound advice he lent to our work throughout. The administrative services provided by the Centre were also invaluable in the smooth running of the project and these were always offered with kindness and good humour.

When the research was undertaken, all three authors were faculty members of the Judge Institute of Management Studies at the University of Cambridge. Subsequently, David Faulkner and Robert Pitkethly took up positions at the Said Business School in Oxford, while John Child now holds the Chair of Commerce at the University of Birmingham. We owe a debt to various academic colleagues, at both Cambridge and Oxford, for their comments and discourses on the subject of post-acquisition management which have informed our understanding. In particular we should like to thank Andrew Brown, Mark de Rond, Roberto Duarte, Sally Heavens, Guido Mollering, Christos Pitelis, Oliver Schacht, and Malcolm Warner. Sally Heavens has also provided significant editorial input during the writing of this book, with the assistance of funding from the Said Business School. On the administrative side, Mary Beveridge, secretary of the Judge Institute, was indefatigable in making all kinds of necessary arrangements. Elizabeth Briggs, as PA to John Child, handled many of the day-to-day communications with the companies participating in the project, and later helped with the transcription of taped interviews and feedback to companies. That things went as smoothly as they did is due in no small measure to Elizabeth and Mary.

Last, but not least, we could not have persevered without the forbearance and love of our families. Even though we were investigating and writing on a subject that we believe is of the utmost significance in the contemporary world, without their support we might well have faltered before the task was completed.

John Child
David Faulkner
Robert Pitkethly
Cambridge and Oxford
July 2000

CONTENTS

LIST OF FIGURES

LIST OF TABLES

1

Introduction

Mergers and acquisitions (M&As) are a predominant feature of the international business system as companies attempt to strengthen their market positions and exploit new market opportunities. New announcements are made every day in the business press and each year sets a new record for the total value of M&As, especially those across national borders.

Despite this frenzy, there is a huge gap between the added value expected, or at least claimed, from M&A and the benefits usually realized. In the case of acquisitions, it has often been pointed out that the shareholders of acquired companies are more likely to gain from the deal than are those of the acquiring company. There is growing appreciation that much of the challenge in realizing value from M&A depends on how things are managed after the deal.

Management is therefore one of the three keywords which describe the focus of this book. The other two are *international* and *acquisitions*. The book is concerned with acquisitions across national borders. It addresses post-acquisition management in terms of the changes brought about and the processes involved. The consequences that post-acquisition management has for performance are a major concern.

The book's source of original data on these issues comes from a study of acquisitions made in the UK by companies from the countries that have in recent years generally contributed the largest sources of foreign direct investment (FDI) in the world: the USA, Japan, France, and Germany. The player missing from this list is the UK itself, and a further selection of domestic acquisitions by UK companies within the UK is also included, largely for purposes of comparison. Over 200 acquisitions were surveyed by questionnaire, and further material of a case study nature was collected through visits to 40 of these companies.

The decision to focus on cross-border acquisitions was made with several considerations in mind. First, acquisitions were selected because the problems of managing them usually present a greater challenge than in mergers, given the fear and resistance that often characterize the staff of the company that is taken over. Secondly, acquiring companies have a choice whether to integrate their new subsidiaries and introduce new practices; whereas mergers normally aim to create a new unified corporation. Thirdly, the management of cross-border acquisitions has to cope with differences in national as well as organizational culture. Such acquisitions therefore promise to shed light on the practical significance of cultural differences. Fourthly, comparing companies within the same country acquired by companies of different nationality permits an examination of whether the changes subsequently introduced demonstrate distinct national patterns of management. The UK control group is included to highlight the potential contrast between national profiles of post-acquisition change and those changes introduced to suit the UK environment. Finally, the anticipated presence of national patterns of management raises the practical question of whether any particular approach has more favourable consequences for performance than others.

Many acquisitions fail, and the key question is whether this is inevitably so. The investigations reported in this book indicate that failure is less likely if certain policies are followed. They also suggest that in some areas of management practice, post-acquisition policies can be tailored to suit the acquiring company's national style of management.

Summary of main findings

The research carried out for this book leads to a number of main findings, which may be summarized as follows:

- parent companies can play a significant role in improving the performance of their acquisitions;
- the optimum approach to post-acquisition performance requires a blend of international 'best practice' with other practices reflecting the acquirer's national traditions;
- acquisitions are vehicles for standardization in some aspects of management practice and for reproducing national differences in others;
- convergence is therefore apparent in some areas of management, especially cost control, operations, and HRM;
- an approach to integrating and controlling the acquisition should be identified that accords with the strategic objectives of the purchase and that recognizes relative competencies between the parent and subsidiary companies;
- open communication, staff involvement, and the creation of a generally non-restrictive atmosphere are especially important as keys to success in managing knowledge-based acquisitions where human capabilities are particularly vital;
- the clear communication of intentions towards change in an acquisition is preferable to an approach that is unclear or hesitant and hence generates uncertainties, especially in situations requiring a turnaround in performance;
- the single most important requirement for acquisition success may be the confidence to pursue a consistent post-acquisition policy, based on a clear vision that

can be informed by national preferences, especially when that policy is in tune with basic business common sense regarding customer awareness and the breaking down of organizational inefficiencies.

The successful approach that Cisco Systems has developed in its many acquisitions exemplifies a number of these conclusions, especially those concerning the clear communication of intentions and the management of staff. Cisco's approach is outlined in Box 1.1.

Box 1.1. Cisco's Successful Approach to Acquisitions

Cisco Systems Inc. ranked number one in the United States when consultant Best Practices surveyed its clients about successful M&A policies. The company had acquired 51 companies over the 6½-year period to the year 2000, and was increasing its pace with the intention of making as many as 25 acquisitions in that year alone.

Cisco plans its handling of acquisitions with great care. When it bought Cerent Corp., a fibre optics equipment maker, in 1999, it mobilized a transition team to oversee every detail of the acquired company's assimilation. The team spent many hours working out the company's intention for Cerent employees, 'mapping' each of them into a Cisco job. When Cisco formally took control, every member of the Cerent staff had a title, bonus plan, health plan, and direct link to Cisco's internal website. They also benefited from the good price Cisco paid for the Cerent stock they held.

In addition to providing significant employee benefits, a routine feature of Cisco's acquisition procedure is to guarantee job security for at least a year, so as to allay uncertainty. It provides its newly acquired employees with detailed information about Cisco, including phone numbers and e-mail addresses of Cisco executives. It takes pains to open up communications. In the case of the Cerent acquisition, Cisco hosted question-and-answer sessions for two days.

Cisco is primarily acquiring human capital and is therefore particularly concerned to 'keep those people whole', in other words to preserve their enthusiasm and commitment. It is also open about the mistakes it has made with some past acquisitions and how it intends to avoid them in the future.

Source: 'Cisco Sets Industry Standard for Mergers and Acquisitions', *Asian Wall Street Journal,* 3 Mar. 2000: 1 and 24.

A guide to the book

As mentioned, the issues concerning post-acquisition performance and the changes in management practice introduced by acquirers of different nationality provide the focus of the present book. It is organized into the following chapters:

Chapter 2 provides information on the scale and scope of M&A. The M&A boom is part and parcel of globalization and the chapter considers the main drivers behind this movement. Acquisitions are one of several strategic options for a firm to expand through integration with other companies. Cross-border acquisitions in pursuit of globalization raise questions about the reconciliation of different national approaches to management, and they provide opportunities to evaluate the performance impact of different national approaches within a given host economy.

Chapter 3 looks further into the issue of post-acquisition performance. It notes the disappointing performance that has characterized so many acquisitions. Pre-acquisition conditions predict acquisition performance only to a limited extent, and even then not consistently. This draws attention to the role of post-acquisition management, which has so far been given less attention than it deserves. The chapter reviews present knowledge about post-acquisition management. In so doing, it clarifies and justifies the prime focus of this book.

Chapter 4 reviews the theoretical background to the debate over the significance of national management practices as opposed to international norms of practice shaped by global forces transcending national boundaries. One set of influential perspectives stresses the formative influence of universal forces now at work in the global economy, whereas another grants explanatory primacy to national factors. The issues raised by these different perspectives are central to the question of whether acquisitions by companies of different nationalities are likely to bring in respectively different management practices rather than similar practices that reflect a growing convergence onto international 'best practice'.

Chapter 5 compares and contrasts the management practices of the five countries from which the acquirers covered in this book originate. It highlights those practices that appear to be consistently found among companies within the five countries or among multinational corporations having a home base there.

Chapter 6 describes the scope and methods of the original research undertaken for this book. It explains how the combination of a survey and case studies, employing primarily quantitative and qualitative methods respectively, should provide a credible picture of the impact of the foreign companies on their new British subsidiaries. The investigation of a number of UK acquisitions by UK companies as a control group is described and justified. The practical difficulties encountered in compiling reliable and comprehensive data on acquisitions in the UK point to the need for better information in this important policy area.

Chapter 7 combines survey and case study results to identify the major trends in post-acquisition management by country of acquirer. It distinguishes between the changes accompanying all or most of the acquisitions and those that are attributable to national effects among the acquiring companies.

Chapter 8 presents findings on the policies on control and integration between parent and subsidiary that were adopted following acquisition. It draws on both quantitative and qualitative parts of the research. The chapter closes with two case studies that contrast policies of high and low post-acquisition integration.

Chapter 9 takes a closer look at post-acquisition integration. It is concerned with how the ways of integrating acquisitions with parent companies relate to policies on control. Initial conditions, such as the performance of the subsidiary when acquired and the guiding philosophy of the acquiring firm, are also examined for the light they throw on integration policies.

Chapter 10 describes the change processes adopted by acquiring companies, and assesses how effective these were in bringing about improved performance from the acquired subsidiaries. It notes that acquirers' nationality is not necessarily the prime influence on their actions. The circumstances surrounding the purchase are also significant; for example, whether the company is making losses or not at the time of purchase.

Chapter 11 focuses on human resource management practices and communications. These are areas likely to be particularly sensitive to cultural influences. The common location of the acquisitions in the UK enables cultural effects to be more clearly identified, and this in turn throws light on how cultural differences were handled.

Chapter 12 looks at the impact that control, organization, and strategy have on post-acquisition performance. It examines performance changes in the light not only of changes made but also of potentially relevant contextual factors such as the performance of firms when acquired, their sectors, and size.

Chapter 13 offers four case studies that illustrate in greater detail the national differences in post-acquisition management identified in the previous chapters.

In conclusion, *Chapter 14* synthesizes the findings of the research and relates them to the basic issues of theory and practical policy identified in the earlier part of the book. In terms of theory, this chapter returns to arguments focused on the notions of globalization and convergence. In terms of policy, the chapter reviews the implications that the research carries for managing acquisitions in ways that lead to satisfactory performance.

2

Acquisitions in a Globally Competitive Landscape

This book focuses on the management of international acquisitions. These are takeovers of a company by another company that is located, or at least headquartered, in a different country. Acquisitions are usually categorized with mergers, both in published statistics and in popular discussion. Both are combinations of companies, but the atmosphere in which they are effected can differ considerably.

A merger is the result of a friendly arrangement between the management of companies that normally approximate in size or strength. The stock-holding in the newly combined enterprise is divided among the stockholders of the merging companies. By contrast, an acquisition is a takeover in which one company secures a sufficient proportion of another company's stock to control its decisions (Franks et al. 1985: 370). Acquisitions may be arranged on friendly terms, as when the owners of a small company seek to liquidate their capital or a diversified company wishes to divest a non-core business. Often, however, they occasion fierce battles between acquiring and target companies, and sometimes between rival bidders themselves. The sour climate engendered by this element of contest is one of the factors that make the management of acquisitions so difficult.

Merger and acquisition frenzy

Worldwide M&A activity in 1998 totalled over US $2,330 billion in terms of the stock values involved, or US $2,514 billion in transactions announced (Harris 1999; Melloan 1999). The pace continued to increase to a record estimated at US $1,166 billion in the first quarter of 2000 alone (Skapinker 2000). During the 1990s, the share of cross-border M&As ran at just over one quarter of the world total, in terms of both value and the number of deals (UNCTAD 2000: fig. IV.6). In 1999, cross-border M&A activity grew by more than one-third, to reach a total value of $720 billion (*The Economist* 2000). M&As of companies with their headquarters in the same country, though normally classified as domestic, often have cross-border features when they require the integration of operations located in different countries.

In 1998, the three countries with the largest selling values in cross-border M&As were the USA, the UK, and Germany—the same rank order as in 1997. British companies have for many years been consistently among the most popular targets for international acquisitions. About 40 per cent of the expenditure by US companies on international acquisitions in 1998—some $50 billion—went on the purchase of British firms. Preliminary United Nations figures show Britain in third place for 1999, being displaced by Sweden due partly to one-off receipts of $20 billion from the merger between Astra, the Swedish pharmaceuticals group, and the UK's Zeneca (*Financial Times* 2000).

On the purchasing (acquirer) side, the USA and UK together accounted for approximately one-half of the total value of all cross-border M&As in 1999, with the UK assuming the first position previously held by the USA. UK companies had previously come second to the United States in the period since 1993 (*The Economist* 1999; *Financial Times* 2000). German and French companies have consistently figured among the leading acquirers, with Japanese acquirers also featuring high in the list until the financial crisis of the mid-1990s (UNCTAD 1999: annex tables B.7 and B.8). M&As are therefore a major feature of international corporate life, and the UK is a particularly important location for them.

International mergers and acquisitions are a major vehicle for foreign direct investment (FDI) by companies. Most new FDI in 1998, especially between the USA and the European Union, was in the form of M&As. Cross-border M&As drove the large increases in FDI within the developed world as a whole (UNCTAD 1999). As the *World Investment Report 1999* notes, there are many factors that explain the current wave of merger and acquisition activity:

These include the opening of markets due to the liberalization of trade, investments and capital markets and to deregulation in a number of industries, and fiercer competitive pressures brought about by globalization and technological changes. Under these conditions, expanding firm size and managing a portfolio of locational assets becomes more important for firms, as it enables them to take advantage of resources and markets world-wide. (UNCTAD 1999: p. xxii)

The scale of cross-border M&A deals can be enormous. So-called 'mega deals' have a transactional value of more than US $1 billion. The number of cross-border mega deals has been rising steadily. In 1995 there were 35 such deals, 45 in 1996, 58 in 1997, and 89 in 1998. The two largest deals announced in 1998 were the acquisition of Amoco (US) by British Petroleum (UK) for $55 billion and the merger of the Chrysler Corporation (US) with Daimler-Benz

(Germany) in a deal worth $41 billion. In 1999, the acquisition of Air Touch (US) by Vodafone (UK) was worth almost $65 billion to create the world's largest mobile-phone operator. The combined company, Vodafone Airtouch, then went on to bid for Mannesmann, a German telecoms and construction company. The process of fighting a hostile takeover battle obliged Vodafone to raise its initial bid by $74 billion to a record-shattering $181 billion early in 2000.

It is very difficult to distinguish between a merger and an acquisition in the case of mega deals. Rather than involving monetary payments, which would be virtually impossible with the largest deals because of their sheer size, there have often been exchanges of stock between the two firms. These involve the issue of new stock by the acquiring firms to the shareholders of the acquired firms in return for the release of their stock.

Clearly M&As involve huge stakes and they are among the most important strategic decisions companies ever take. International M&As, however, are an integral part of an even more mega process, namely globalization. They are motivated by the globalization of markets and opportunities offered by the liberalization of trade. They are also motivated by the search for new sources of innovation and the unique competencies that sustain such innovation. At the same time, advances in communication technology ease the task of managing on a global scale the ever-larger companies that M&As help to create. As Samuelson (2000: 3) observes:

Behind the merger boom lies the growing corporate conviction that many markets have become truly global. By trying to maximize their presence in as many nations as possible, companies seek to achieve economies of scale—that is, to lower costs through higher sales and production volumes—and to stay abreast of technological changes that can now occur almost anywhere.

Globalization and the new competitive landscape

Globalization is the key feature of the new competitive landscape within which the M&A frenzy is taking place. It is important to bear in mind, however, that globalization is a trend and not necessarily an already extant condition. As Guillén (2001) points out, many unsubstantiated and sweeping claims have been made about globalization, and we should treat these with caution. In particular, globalization is not spreading evenly across the globe and it is more evident in certain areas of activity than in others (Castells 1996). Secondly, most cross-border integration, through both investment and trade, is actually focused on regional trade blocks (Rugman 2000). Nonetheless, whatever the exact spread of globalization or the balance between global and regional business, its connection with the rapidly growing trend of cross-border M&A remains essentially the same. We shall therefore use the term 'globalization' to refer to the trend towards cross-border economic and technological integration.

Globalization has been applied in a variety of ways to describe how the traditional divisions between world markets based on culture and taste are observed to be in decline as communications have improved, and as national trade barriers have been steadily falling through the activities of the World Trade Organization and regional agreements. Globalization is taking place through the international expansion of markets, through the impact of new communication technologies, and through growing economic interdependence with the liberalization of revenue, capital, and trade flows across borders. Globalization is therefore associated in many people's minds with a growing convergence in economic systems, cultures, and management practices.

As Govindarajan and Gupta (1998) point out, globalization can be defined in terms of different levels of focus. At a worldwide level, it refers to a growing economic interdependence among countries that is reflected in increasing cross-border flows of goods, services, capital, and know-how. At the second level, globalization refers to the interlinkages a specific country has with the rest of the world, or the extent to which the competitive position of companies within a specific industry is interdependent with that of companies in other countries. The third level is that of an individual company. Here, globalization refers to the extent to which a company has expanded its revenue and asset base across countries and engages in cross-border flows of capital, goods, and know-how across subsidiaries. The expansion of its revenue and asset base through international M&A increases the globalization of the acquiring company.

As far back as 1987, Peter Drucker with his usual prescience was writing in the *Wall Street Journal* that:

To maintain a leadership position in any one developed country a business increasingly has to attain and hold leadership positions in all developed countries world-wide. It has to be able to do research, to design, to develop, to engineer and to manufacture in any part of the developed world, and to export from any developed country to any other. It has to go transnational.

Today, this transnational imperative extends beyond developing countries to encompass the emerging markets of transition and developing countries. Given this strategic requirement and the time pressures to achieve it quickly, acquisitions often appear more attractive than arm's-length arrangements for purposes of strategic positioning and synergy capture. The homogenization of markets, and advances in IT support, are also expected to facilitate problems of managing the larger units created by M&A. International acquisitions are therefore seen to be inevitable in order to respond to the increasingly powerful drivers of globalization. These are market drivers, cost drivers, competitive drivers, and government drivers (Yip 1992).

Market drivers

Market drivers are the growth of common customer needs, the emergence of global customers, the development of global channels of distribution, and of marketing approaches that are transferable across cultural and geographical boundaries.

Levitt (1983) forecast the convergence of markets as a result of the development of economic and socio-cultural interdependencies across countries and economies. He argued that the new communication technologies are key to the growing homogenization of markets, reducing social, economic, and cultural differences, including old-established differences in national tastes or preferences. This process has forced companies to respond to growing similarities between consumer preferences. He also said quite simply that, if you can make a cheaper better product, cultural barriers will not prevent it becoming acceptable worldwide. The international success of the Japanese consumer electronics industry appears to support this claim.

There has been a long-standing debate about whether global markets are developing as tastes converge across the globe in a widening range of industries. Examples of such convergence include McDonald's burgers, designer jeans, and Coca-Cola. The debate centres on the desirability of standardization of products or services for broadly defined international market segments. This belief in a homogenization of tastes coexists with the view that fragmentation may more appropriately describe the trend in international consumer demand. A great deal of discussion has taken place over the opportunities for, and barriers to, such standardization (Kotler 1985; Quelch and Hoff 1986; Douglas and Wind 1987; Alden 1987).

The argument for global markets does not, however, necessarily signify the end of market segments. It can mean instead that they expand to worldwide proportions. The retail chain Benetton has built its whole strategy on these assumptions. In Benetton there is some adaptation of such things as colour choice for different domestic markets, but such adaptation occurs around the standardized core of Benetton's 'one united product' for its target market segment worldwide. It sells 'active leisurewear' globally to 15-to-24-year-olds.

Cross-border M&A provides many opportunities for achieving economies of scope from global marketing strategies. Branding provides a useful illustration of this potential. An increasing number of multinational corporations (MNCs) are standardizing their brands to send a consistent worldwide message and take greater advantage of media opportunities by promoting one brand, one packaging, and uniform positioning across markets. Rather than a patchwork quilt of local brands in local markets, the owners of international brands increasingly favour simplified international brand portfolios. Many local brands have been developed by high advertising spend over years and have established strong intangible switching costs among their local populations. Despite this, they are likely to die in the face of a determined global brand assault.

Focusing on fewer strong brands is seen as the best way of addressing fierce competition from other brands and private-label products, as well as getting the best value from expensive investments in advertising. Another way in which brand globalization is being felt is in the branding of companies themselves; a trend observable as companies become established as MNCs rather than just domestic market champions. Names that are felt to be too parochial or nationalistic are made more universally acceptable. Obvious candidates for such treatment have been previously state-owned enterprises, so that British Telecommunications became BT, British Petroleum became BP, and the Korean *chaebol* Lucky Goldstar became the internationally unexceptionable LG. Similarly, the name AXA was chosen to cloak the French origin of this insurance MNC and thereby make it more regionally and globally acceptable. This is the likely fate of many UK companies acquired by foreign multinationals.

Cost drivers

Globalization offers the advantage of economies of scale and standardization even for a segmented marketing strategy. In advertising costs, for example, PepsiCo's savings from not producing a separate film for individual national markets has been estimated at $10 million per year. This figure is increased when indirect costs are added, for instance the speed of implementing a campaign, fewer overseas marketing staff, and management time which can be utilized elsewhere.

International standardization of activities is established by practitioners at points in their value chain where advantages can be derived, even though there may not be a global operation across all functions. Benefits are possible from globalization in any or all of the following: design, purchasing, manufacturing operations, packaging, distribution, marketing, advertising, customer service, and software development. Globalization makes possible standardized facilities, methodologies, and procedures across locations. Companies may be able to benefit even if they are able to reconfigure in only one or two of these areas.

Potential cost advantages such as these are an important incentive to undertake cross-border M&As.

Competitive drivers

Yip (1992) identifies competitive drivers as the movement of competitor companies to compete worldwide rather then purely nationally, and their ability to develop global strategies. The extent of international consumer homogeneity is a central issue affecting the economics of all industries and therefore the most viable strategies of firms competing within those industries.

While there has been a clear trend towards world trade liberalization and the freer international movement of capital and technology, the thesis that competitive arenas are becoming more global is more questionable. The belief in consumer homogeneity is controversial and probably overstated. In many sectors, significant differences still exist between groups of consumers across national market boundaries and it has been argued by managers and academics alike (Kotler 1985; Alden 1987; Douglas and Wind 1987; Makhija et al. 1997) that the differences both within and across countries are far greater than any similarities. Secondly, there has been a growth of intra-country fragmentation, leading to increased segmentation of domestic markets. Thirdly, developments in factory automation allowing flexible, lower-cost, lower-volume, high-variety operations are challenging the standard assumptions of scale economy benefits by yielding variety at low cost. It can be argued therefore that such an approach to global strategies is oversimplified, focusing on the benefits of standardization when the emphasis internationally is more complex, often encompassing global, regional, and local approaches simultaneously.

A contingent approach has long been recommended to allow flexibility between the two extremes of full global standardization and complete local market responsiveness. Indeed, the two may be used simultaneously to achieve the advantages to be had from global structuring of part of the product/service offering, whilst adapting or fine-tuning other parts of the same offering to closely match the needs of a particular local market. This process of combining the advantages of both global and local operations has become known as 'glocalization'.

The experience of Kentucky Fried Chicken, an American international fast food chain, illustrates the point. After its initial entry into the Japanese market, KFC soon realized the need to make three specific changes to its international strategy; first, the product was of the wrong shape and size, since the Japanese prefer morsel-sized food; second, the locations of the outlets had to be moved into crowded city eating areas and away from independent sites;

third, contracts for supply of appropriate quality chickens had to be negotiated locally, although KFC provided all technical advice and standards.
Following these adaptations of product and site, KFC has been successful in
Japan. Similarly, McDonald's hamburger restaurants now serve Teriyaki
burgers in Tokyo and wine in Lyon. Each of these local market adaptations of
the core offering was critical to success, with the global strategy remaining
unchanged in its essentials. It is debatable therefore to what extent these
companies are pursuing 'global' or 'regional' strategies.

Whether competitive drivers are thought to be global, regional, or national
has considerable implications for a company's post-acquisition policy. A
perception that the company's competitive arenas are global, or at least
regional, in scope should encourage it to integrate acquired companies to
ensure their maximum conformity and contribution to a common strategy.
By contrast, a perception that the company's competitive arenas are nationally or even intra-nationally segmented is consistent with a policy of low
post-acquisition integration in order to allow the new subsidiary to extend
the company's competitive portfolio into a market and area of competence
distinct from its existing ones.

Government drivers

The most significant advantages of global trading are probably those associated with the size and spread of operations. Economies of scope and scale
allow for greater efficiency in current operations (Chandler 1990). Economies
of scale provide not just lower unit costs, but also potentially greater
bargaining power over all elements in the company's value chain. Economies
of scope can allow for the sharing of resources across products, markets, and
businesses. Such resources may be both tangible, such as buildings, technology, or sales forces, or intangible, such as expert knowledge, teamworking
skills, and brands.

Governments have come to recognize these economies, and they have
become an important force in the liberalization of trade policies across the
developed world. Protectionist governments employing anything other than
the infant industry argument are nowadays in a minority. Most accept, at least
in principle, the freer trade argument and its potential benefits. As Yip (1992)
observes, this has led to the development of compatible technical standards
across countries, together with common marketing regulations and a worldwide movement by governments to reduce trade barriers such as tariffs and
quotas, with the aim of encouraging world trade and hence globalization.
This may well be the most significant overall driving force behind the acceler-
ation of international M&A.

International M&As contribute towards globalization as well as being a response to it. There is a continuing interaction between the liberalization of trade and capital flows and the internationalization of production that is at the core of the globalization process. The internationalization of production is advancing mainly through M&As and strategic alliances. MNCs are key players in this process. They have pressed strongly for trade liberalization, and they have endeavoured to take advantage of new global opportunities in markets, sourcing, and innovation.

Multinationals are particularly concerned to secure a strategic and competitive position within the global economy. In almost every area of economic activity, corporations are now scrambling to establish themselves as global oligopolists. In this frantic race, various forms of integration with other companies offer the most rapid means for MNCs to move towards their strategic objective—through alliances, mergers, and acquisitions. The extent to which these corporations can secure an oligopolistic position through M&As varies greatly according to the number of new entrants and the pace at which new technology platforms are being introduced; there has been far less concentration in the knowledge-based sectors than in traditional manufacturing industries. Nonetheless, the opprobrium that attaches to oligopoly recalls the fact that acquisitions today are judged as much by their social effects as by the returns they promise to shareholders.

Acquisitions as a strategic option

Companies can grow through organic expansion or through various forms of external association with other companies. In conditions of rapid change, high innovation costs, and the scramble for strategic positioning in many sectors, expansion though external means has become an absolute necessity. The main options for external collaboration range according to the degree of integration between a company and the others that join it (Child and Faulkner 1998). Integration can be based on a number of factors: ownership, contractual agreement, 'lock in' through the commitment of highly specific assets, and common management structures.

Cooperative agreements are normally the least integrated and involve arm's-length relations between the partners. They are typically based on contractual agreements and their management requires little more than liaison between the partners. Joint ventures entail greater integration between the participating organizations. The joint venture or other combined unit will have its own management structure and hence the need to adopt a coherent set of management practices. It is not unusual for one company to be the lead partner and this solution is often favoured as a way of ensuring that the alliance has a common sense of direction and a unified management. Acquisitions and mergers aim at even more integration. A significant difference between a typical acquisition and a typical merger is that the latter aims at the total integration of two or more partners into a new unified corporation. By contrast, while some acquiring companies may choose to subsume their acquisition entirely within the parent organization, many continue to run them as subsidiaries. Acquisitions permit a degree of choice on the issue of integration that mergers normally do not.

While new cooperative agreements and joint ventures are being established all the time, there is a tendency for joint ventures and other alliances to become acquisitions after a period of years. It has been estimated that the median lifespan for alliances is only about seven years and that nearly 80 per cent of equity joint ventures—one of the most common alliance structures— ultimately end in one of the partners selling its stake (Bleeke and Ernst 1995). This sale is often to another partner. MNCs in particular generally seek to move joint ventures with local partners, which they originally established for purposes of market entry or to acquire specific knowledge, into subsidiaries. Many mergers also start off ostensibly as marriages of equals, with one partner subsequently becoming dominant. At the time of writing a joke is circulating in Germany about the merger in 1998 between Daimler-Benz and the Chrysler Corporation, in which signs of growing dominance by the first partner were already becoming apparent. The question is asked: 'what is the correct way to pronounce "Daimler-Chrysler"?' The answer is: 'Chrysler is silent.' Acquisitions are unequal partnerships. This may appear to be a contradiction in terms, but it does seem to reflect the kind of accommodation that so often evolves in other forms of collaboration in which partners in the first instance are formally equals.

Under modern competitive conditions, the unequal partnership characteristics of acquisitions can become a liability if careful attention is not paid to the way in which acquired companies are managed. Acquisitions are expected to derive benefits from the importation of new resources and superior practices into the acquired companies, together perhaps with more disciplined and focused managerial control. At the same time, companies do not necessarily spend large sums of their shareholders' money just to gain greater market share or impose stricter control over under-exploited assets. They may also be seeking to acquire highly effective intangible assets of creativity, know-how, and long-established relationships with customers and public bodies, in order to enhance their competitive capabilities. If the way post-acquisition management is handled causes these intangible assets to be damaged, or fails to give them space to perform, the realized value of an acquisition may be substantially less than was anticipated. Post-acquisition management is one of the main challenges in a world with so many acquisitions, the majority of which do not realize their anticipated benefits.

In the emerging world economy, the combination of new conditions of competition with the development of 'metanational' corporations (Doz et al. 2000) on the back of M&A and alliances is creating new challenges for management. These challenges centre on the continuing problem of how best to reconcile global advantages with local sensitivity, and international control and coordination with effective local sensing, knowledge sourcing, and initiative. They highlight the issues of post-acquisition management with which this book is concerned, including the way that change is handled in newly acquired subsidiaries, and the mode of control, communication, and integration that is applied to the relationship between the parent company and the acquired affiliate. Acquisition implies a redistribution of the legitimacy flow to a top-down mode, in favour of the acquiring company. This is the reverse of what an increasing number of MNCs are today seeking to achieve. The new challenge is seen to be one of effective polycentrism, distributive legitimacy, and the fostering of trust and mutual interdependence within a corporate system. In terms of management practice, this means denationalizing the corporate culture so that post-acquisition practices draw upon available strengths within the culture and experience of the acquired company that are shared within the parent corporation as a whole. The reconciliation of this aim with the imperative to establish control immediately after acquisition is clearly a delicate process that is difficult to achieve.

The nationality factor

The sensitivity of post-acquisition management is likely to increase when it is cross-border in scope, with acquirer and acquired coming from different countries, bearing different management philosophies and practices as a result. The debate continues as to whether there is a set of best practices in all areas of business or whether the observed methods of certain countries are best in certain situations or for certain functional areas, but not for others. The question of integration therefore involves considering not just 'how much?' but also 'on the basis of which practice?' It is of considerable importance to examine whether different cultural and managerial approaches can be applied with equally good results. From the perspective of anticipating the changes that might be introduced following an acquisition by a foreign company, it is also useful to ascertain the nature of any management practices that are associated with acquirer nationality.

Such complications can contribute to the fact that many acquisitions fail to achieve their expected potential. The failure of many M&As to improve productivity can often be attributed to the difficulties of combining different management styles and practices (UNCTAD 1999). The next chapter explores the significance for acquisition performance of these managerial factors, including national cultural differences.

Summary

The key points from this chapter are:

- There are more cross-border mergers and acquisitions than ever before.
- This movement is integral to the wider process of globalization.
- Mergers normally aim at the total integration of two or more companies; acquisitions range widely between total integration of acquired subsidiaries and the maintenance of the acquired company's identity.
- Acquisitions are one of several options for companies to achieve rapid expansion by forming new links between companies.
- In addition to establishing control after a takeover, MNCs also have to foster and draw upon the strengths of acquired companies.
- The mix of different management philosophies and practices in cross-border acquisitions adds to the challenge of managing them in ways that successfully balance the requirements of achieving control and synergy.

3

Post-acquisition Performance and Management

The challenge

On the surface, the scale and speed of mergers and acquisitions are breathtaking. Yet, impressive as the value of M&A transactions undoubtedly is, it is only the tip of a large and perilous iceberg. The success of a merger or acquisition depends on the ability to create added value after it has taken place. In practice, it has been estimated that in the medium term fewer than half of all mergers and acquisitions do actually add value. The shareholders whose company has been bought tend to end up richer, whereas the shareholders of the purchasing company rarely do. The *World Investment Report 1999* comments with some surprise that the current wave of mergers and acquisitions 'does not seem to be deterred by the relatively poor results that have been observed with respect to M&As' (UNCTAD 1999: p. xxii).

It is a challenge to reconcile the different systems and cultures even of two companies that have agreed amicably to merge on the basis of equality. It can become a formidable task, taking years of effort, to effect the changes intended for a company that has been acquired, often in hostile circumstances. Yet the rationale for the takeover of a company will often have been predicated on an ability to make such changes in turning around an under-performing organization and integrating it as necessary with the parent's activities.

Three major issues therefore recur in discussions of acquisition: value creation, post-acquisition management, and post-acquisition performance. Although all three issues are interrelated, each raises different questions. Strategic issues are prevalent in discussions of value creation. Post-acquisition management mainly concerns matters of organization. The analysis of post-acquisition performance involves both strategy and organization.

This chapter focuses on the performance problem and the bearing that post-acquisition management has on it. Post-acquisition management refers to the processes adopted to bring about changes in acquired companies, the type of changes introduced, and the measures taken to integrate and control the acquisitions. Later chapters examine these matters in greater detail.

The problem of post-acquisition performance

Value creation: the justification for acquisitions

Acquisitions are justified, especially to shareholders, in terms of the *potential value* they are anticipated to create. A number of specific motives may inform this anticipation. These include securing economies of scale or scope, increasing synergy through the combination of complementary assets, applying knowledge or skills from one organization to the other, and introducing greater control or discipline over a target company's management to secure better results. Other motives for undertaking acquisitions, which are not necessarily in the best interests of the acquirer's shareholders, may also apply. These include enhancing the standing of the company in terms of its size, increasing management's prestige or power, and reducing competition or other uncertainties in the external environment through an increase in market power or influence with public authorities (Napier 1989).

Strategic fit is the dominant theme in the literature on creating value from acquisitions, though organizational aspects are also taken into account. Shelton (1988: 279) states that 'value is created when these assets [of target and bidding firms] are used more effectively by the combined firms than by the target and bidder separated'. This implies that acquisitions of firms undertaking the same activities or ones supplementary to existing activities involving, for example, expansion into a new market should create more value than acquisitions of firms with non-related activities involving fundamentally different products, assets, or skills. Lubatkin (1988) discusses the strategy underlying mergers and concludes that a merger is worthwhile only if it contributes to the competitive advantage of the firm's business. Related mergers offer firms more options to make their business strategies more competitive than do unrelated mergers. The findings of research by Norburn and Schoenberg (1994) indicate that in practice the majority of companies make acquisitions that are related horizontally to existing product markets and focus upon small companies.

Potential value provides the economic logic for undertaking an acquisition. Post-acquisition performance can be evaluated in terms of the comparison between potential value and the *real value* actually created. The real value that acquisitions create has often fallen short of the potential value claimed for them. While the reasons for this can lie in a faulty strategic or financial logic, the challenge of post-acquisition management also appears to play an important role that is still not adequately understood.

A high proportion of acquisitions fail. Several studies suggest that the percentage is around 50 per cent. In the case of the UK, Kitchin (1974) stated that 47 per cent of acquisitions failed or were not worth undertaking, Hunt et al. (1986) suggested a failure rate of 45 per cent, and a survey by Coopers and Lybrand (1992) indicated that 54 per cent of acquisitions fail. More recently, Mark Sirower, an advisor to the Boston Consulting Group, was cited as concluding that about 65 per cent of acquisitions fail to benefit the acquiring companies whose shares subsequently under-perform their sector (Skapinker 2000).

There are two main approaches to assessing acquisition success. The first is in terms of shareholder value. Here evidence from both the UK and USA indicates that acquisitions create wealth for the acquired firms' shareholders rather than for those of the acquiring firm (Sudarsanam 1995). Studies of stock prices or other indicators of shareholder return indicate that acquiring company shareholders do not necessarily gain from acquisitions, especially in the early years (e.g. Agrawal et al. 1992; Hall and Norburn 1987; Loderer and Martin 1992).

The second is in terms of conventional business performance measures such as profitability and market share. Again, reviews of the evidence suggest that, on the whole, mergers and acquisitions lead to reductions in both acquirers' and acquired companies' profitability, and to declines in market share as well (Fowler and Schmidt 1988; Angwin 1999). Poor post-acquisition performance may also be indicated by high rates of subsequent divestment, though the decision to sell an acquisition could also signify an adjustment of strategic profile. Porter (1987) found that among thirty-three large US companies in the period 1950 to 1986, 56.5 per cent of acquisitions made by 1975 were subsequently divested, with the figure rising to almost three-quarters in the case of unrelated acquisitions. He commented that 'only the lawyers, investment bankers, and original sellers have prospered in most of these acquisitions, not the shareholders' (p. 46).

Reasons for acquisition failure

Various reasons are suggested why firms continue to make acquisitions when the likelihood of their benefiting appears quite small. Managers may make mistaken, over-optimistic, estimates of a proposed acquisition's value. They may be more motivated to maximize their wealth than that of shareholders, tempted by the rewards of empire-building. Larger company size is associated with improved benefits, opportunities for advancement, and personal prestige. As those concerned with the divorce of ownership from control warned many years ago (Berle and Means 1932), the ability of shareholders to monitor corporate managers decreases as companies become larger and more complex. Post-acquisition administrative problems may also be underestimated, since these are likely to rise significantly if an acquisition increases a company's complexity through diversification and is accompanied by resistance within the acquired company.

These reasons point to both pre- and post-acquisition factors that may account for the poor performance of many acquisitions. Angwin's (1999) review of the evidence concludes that pre-acquisition factors by no means provide a complete explanation. How acquisitions are funded and whether takeovers are hostile or friendly appear to make little difference to the returns received by acquiring company shareholders. Some strategic factors appear to improve the chances of acquisition success, while the evidence for others is inconsistent. Thus acquiring companies with a good performance track record tend to make more successful acquisitions. However, the evidence on a key strategic issue—whether the acquisition is in a related business—proves to be inconsistent.

The very limited extent to which pre-acquisition factors can predict acquisition performance indicates two possibilities. The first is that pre-acquisition conditions may be more complex than studies have allowed for. The significance of relatedness, for instance, may depend on the potential for technological and other synergies, and whether the acquiring company's management is skilled in realizing these. An acquiring company may, by contrast, possess more of a distinctive competence in effecting turnarounds or asset rationalization, in which case the relatedness of the acquired company's business is of less significance to shareholder returns. Realization of potential benefits from relatedness may also be qualified by factors such as the cultural distance between the acquiring and acquired companies. A large cultural distance may hamper efforts to introduce changes into the acquired company and to integrate it. Cross-border acquisitions may for this reason present a special challenge. Datta and Puia (1995) examined the extent to which shareholder value creation in cross-border acquisitions was dependent on the relatedness of acquiring and acquired companies, and also on the cultural distance between them. They concluded that, despite the increasing popularity of cross-border acquisitions, they do not on average create shareholder value. Higher cultural distances were associated with greater negative value creation. The researchers found that the impact of relatedness was not clear-cut, though they concluded that over a longer period of time related acquisitions tend to create more value.

The second possibility is that much of the disappointment with acquisition performance stems from post-acquisition factors. As Angwin comments (1999: 1/16), 'we need to re-focus our attention upon the post-acquisition phase as this clearly mediates as between pre-acquisition characteristics and post-acquisition performance'. The assumption here is that the real value of an acquisition is closely bound up with how successfully the acquisition is subsequently managed. Haspeslagh and Jemison note in this respect that 'although the strategic fit of an acquisition is the basis of the potential for value creation, it is managing the acquisition process well that underlies actual value creation' (1991: 164). They argue that value creation depends on how well acquired capabilities are put to use. The transfer of these capabilities after the acquisition presupposes actions and activities on the part of managers in both acquiring and acquired companies. These capabilities represent a potential but, once transferred, they still must be applied before they can lead to a competitive advantage.

From this capabilities-based perspective, the challenge is not just to acquire capabilities, but also *to preserve, to transfer,* and *to apply* them in order to enhance competitive advantage. All three of these operations—preservation, transfer, and application—are anchored in the organizational and cultural contexts of the acquiring and acquired firms. So, while value creation *potential* is a perception founded mainly on the degree of relatedness between acquired and acquiring companies, only the process of post-acquisition management can really *generate* value. This leads to the conclusion that:

relatedness gives an ex ante indication of potential sources of value creation, but it does not determine the nature, scope, and probability of actual value creation. Taking synergies from relatedness for granted is symptomatic of a more fundamental weakness of the strategic school: its disproportionate emphasis on the strategy task, leaving aside practical impediments to value creation such as interpersonal, inter-organizational, and intercultural friction. (Haspeslagh and Jemison 1991: 302)

Others have similarly concluded that attention needs to be given to the managerial and organizational factors that enable companies to realize value from their acquisitions. Schweiger and Weber (1989) recognize that the potential for achieving synergy, the strategic and operational advantages that neither firm can achieve on its own, is one of the major attractions of M&As. They affirm that top managers should be prepared to manage those factors that potentially contribute to success or failure. To the factors most taken into account—identification of strategic fit between the combining firms; determination of an appropriate purchase price; and actual achievement of fit through the integration of two firms—they add another which, in their opinion, is not carefully considered: organizational and human issues.

Markides and Oyon's (1998) work confirms that value creation depends partly on factors other than purely strategic ones. Their research indicates that cross-border acquisitions create more value for shareholders than do domestic acquisitions (a finding supported by Danbolt 1998), but that acquisitions in certain countries do not create value. While this latter finding requires further investigation, the authors suggest that it has more to do with features of the acquiring company and the acquisition itself than with the country where the acquisition takes place. This is consistent with the argument that managerial factors play an important part in the realization of value from acquisitions.

Post-acquisition management

Three issues come to the fore in post-acquisition management. The first is the degree and type of change introduced into the acquired company. This is concerned with the potential for acquisition to effect improvements through the introduction of new or modified management practices. Some of these changes may be associated with the second issue, which is the form of integration and control that the acquiring company seeks to introduce into its relationship with the acquired company. The third issue concerns the processes of post-acquisition change whereby new practices and an integration platform are introduced. Differences in the organizational and national cultures of the acquiring and acquired company have a close bearing both on their integration and on the process of change.

Post-acquisition change

The study of post-acquisition change has been rather fragmented. Most attention has been given to human resource issues, which include HR planning and downsizing, training, and changes to systems for communications and rewards (Napier 1989). There is remarkably little research into the other changes that are made following acquisitions. Angwin (1999) again provides a useful review. As might be expected, the turnover of top managers from acquired companies is appreciably higher than in other companies, even though some acquirers may wish to retain their experience and expertise. Walsh (1988), for instance, found that top management turnover following an acquisition is higher than the normal level and that senior executives are the first to leave. The first area of management practice to be integrated with that of the acquiring company is normally financial control. There is considerable evidence that acquiring companies impose financial control at the start of the post-acquisition phase. In addition to the introduction of changes in the financial area, studies have found that changes are often made to the top management team, to organizational structure, sales and marketing, production, technology, personnel, and reporting relationships. Changes to information systems have been less often reported though this is expected to be an area of increasing importance, especially when close integration of the acquired company is sought.

Angwin (1999) suggests that there are clear parallels between post-acquisition management and corporate turnarounds, and he draws upon turnaround studies such as Slatter (1984) and Grinyer et al. (1988) to identify the main areas of change involved. These are major changes in management, especially the CEO; stronger financial controls; intensive efforts to reduce production costs; an increased importance given to marketing, especially customer relations and a new product market focus; and debt reduction. These and other studies point quite strongly to the key role that the CEO of an acquired company can play in bringing about its transformation. The evidence also indicates that CEOs appointed from outside the acquired company will replace more subordinates and generally bring about more change than will insider CEOs who hold continuing appointments or come from other positions within the acquired firm.

Integration

The introduction of post-acquisition changes implies that there is a degree of integration with the parent company. However, the extent and form of integration can vary substantially. An informed judgement is required as to the appropriate degree and form of integration in the light of contingent circumstances. This is the reasoning behind Haspeslagh and Jemison's (1991) framework of post-acquisition integration, which remains the most influential analysis to date.

These authors identify two key dimensions that provide a basis for choosing a particular approach to post-acquisition integration. These are the need for strategic interdependence in order to secure value that would not exist if the firms operated separately, and the need for organizational autonomy. Strategic interdependence concerns the nature of 'strategic fit'. It arises when there are complementarities between acquiring and acquired firms, and there is potential benefit from transferring capabilities between them. The transfer of superior management practice to an acquired firm is an example. The 'cultural fit' between the firms is a major factor for deciding on the appropriate level of acquired company autonomy (Child and Faulkner 1998). One of the difficulties with making acquisitions work is that:

Strategic fit and organizational fit often point in different directions. In these instances, the challenge is to manage the organizational dimension in a way that acknowledges the strategic logic of interdependence, the autonomy needs of the acquired firm, and the need to treat each person involved with dignity, respect and fairness. (Haspeslagh and Jemison 1991: 241)

These two dimensions give rise to four types of post-acquisition integration. *Absorption* involves a high need for strategic interdependence in order to create the value expected, and a low need for organizational autonomy to achieve good results. *Preservation* is characterized by a low need for strategic interdependence among the two firms but a high need for organizational autonomy; here the primary task of management is to keep the source of the acquired benefits intact. *Symbiotic* integration involves a high need for strategic interdependence and a high need for organizational autonomy, because the acquired capabilities need to be preserved in an organizational context that is different from the acquirer's. The fourth logical combination is that of the *holding acquisition*, in which there is a low need for strategic interdependence and a low need for organizational autonomy. This combination would suit the case of value capture through holding an acquired company for trading benefits; in other cases it runs the risk of being unnecessarily demotivating for the acquired company and does not make much practical sense. Besides these two key needs, Haspeslagh and Jemison maintain that the quality and size of the acquired firm are also important in influencing the level of integration. In the course of this book, we shall find a further influence on integration in that it also varies according to the nationality of the acquiring company.

A number of studies have helped to flesh out the contingency approach to post-acquisition integration developed by Haspeslagh and Jemison. Pablo's (1994) research revealed that two factors accounted for nearly 75 per cent of the total explained variance in decisions on post-acquisition integration. These were (1) strategic task needs (successful sharing or exchange of the critical skills and resources that form the foundation for value creation) and (2) organizational task needs (preservation of any characteristics of an acquired firm that are a source of key strategic capabilities). Cultural and political factors accounted for the other 25 per cent of explained variance. The main theoretical contribution of this research, in Pablo's view, is to demonstrate that the level of post-acquisition integration is based on multiple decision criteria.

Lindgren and Spangberg (1981) maintain that the more related the acquisition, the higher is the degree of integration necessary in order to achieve the synergy needed to create benefits. Datta and Grant (1990: 39–40) found, as a complement to this, that the autonomy given to acquired firms' managements in unrelated acquisitions is typically greater than in related acquisitions, and that this autonomy is positively associated with acquisition success. Autonomy emerges as an important factor because it helps to maintain the levels of commitment, enthusiasm, and creativeness necessary in the acquired company to preserve its competitive advantage. There are some acquisitions from which value creation is sought through effecting a turnaround, or pursuing high growth prospects in an unrelated business, rather than through strategic or organizational integration (Anslinger and Copeland 1996). These acquisitions would benefit from a holding company mode of integration, though this does not necessarily mean a lack of intervention by the acquiring company in order to effect improvements in the performance of the acquired business. A low level of integration does not therefore equate to low intervention or control by the acquiring company.

Cultural differences

Cultural differences are another aspect of post-acquisition management. They are reflected in management practices and styles. They can result from either national or organizational cultures (Lindgren and Spangberg 1981; Buono et al. 1985; Marks and Mirvis 1992; Norburn and Schoenberg 1994; Chu 1996; Reece 1996; Carrington 1997). The effects of cultural differences can be present as early as the stage of negotiating an acquisition (Chu 1996), but they will be perceived more clearly during the period of post-acquisition management. Cultural difference should be taken into account in decisions on the desired level of post-acquisition integration. Haspeslagh and Jemison (1991: 142–4) comment that:

because we regard strategic capability transfer as the precursor to value creation, it is clearly vital to preserve the strategic capability that is to be transferred . . . the preservation of capabilities requires boundary protection and, hence, organizational autonomy. The important question, thus, is not how different the two cultures are, but whether maintaining that difference in the long term will serve a useful purpose.

The discussion of culture has focused the recognition that it can have potential disruptive consequences which have to be addressed if value is to be realized from acquisitions. According to Norburn and Schoenberg (1994), 65 per cent of those acquirers who had experienced serious problems with post-acquisition integration said that these difficulties had been due to cultural differences. Morosini and Singh's (1994) findings revealed that the interaction between post-acquisition strategy implemented by the acquirer and the seller's national cultural traits plays a significant role in performance following cross-border acquisitions. David and Singh (1993) argue that organizations which effectively respond to cultural and relative deprivation issues in post-acquisition management are the ones that can achieve the potential economic benefits.

While cross-border acquisitions are seen as the right way to build market share (Miles 1995; Svelicic and Rojec 1994), cultural differences imply that their management will be more difficult. A survey of top managers in larger European acquirers (Angwin and Savill 1997) indicated that 61 per cent of respondents believed cross-border acquisitions to be riskier than domestic ones. The sources of risk can be categorized as internal and external. Internal risks include culture, morale, and language. External risks include market conditions, politics, and regulation. The managers surveyed cited internal risk as the main reason for cross-border acquisitions being riskier than domestic ones.

Very et al. (1996) argue, however, that previous studies of the cultural factor are misleading because they assume that the difference between 'what was' in the acquired firm before the merger or acquisition and 'what is' after the event is a source of stress. In their view, 'acculturative stress' results when expectations of 'what ought to be' are not fulfilled. Acculturative stress is influenced by national culture difference, but not necessarily in the expected direction because some cultural differences can be a source of attraction rather than stress. Child and Faulkner (1998), for example, indicate that cross-national cultural differences can provide complementary resources for international strategic alliance partners as well as creating obstacles to cooperation. In fact, the cultural problems associated with combining organizations may be as severe in domestic as in cross-national settings due to strong organizational cultures and because the coupling between the units may be looser in the latter case. One would expect that when a high level of post-acquisition integration is sought, cultural differences would pose more of a problem. Datta (1991), however, found that compatibility of management styles was important to superior performance in acquisitions characterized by both high and low levels of post-acquisition operational integration. So the cultural issue appears to retain its significance under all circumstances.

If the potential effects of culture clash on post-acquisition outcomes seem clear, how to overcome the problem is less evident. According to Buono et al. (1985), culture change is among the most difficult things for human beings to achieve, since culture provides the foundation for personal identity and the conduct of one's life. Even if organizational, procedural, and other post-acquisition changes can be justified on rational grounds, they are resisted or even sabotaged because of threats to the pre-existing culture. Those who have to manage a culture clash will therefore be keenly interested in how to overcome the problems associated with it. Sebenius (1998) discussed the issue of different management styles with the CEO of an acquiring company. The CEO's view was that the negative impact of cultural differences may be overcome through creating a common language around a superordinate unifying goal. He commented on how a strategic conception has to predominate in this common language: 'We all shared a strategic vision of the central importance of efficiently structured size for competitive success in our industry' (p. 38).

The question of culture also draws attention to human resource management, and here the literature on post-acquisition management raises several questions. According to Lindgren and Spangberg (1981: 247) 'the most important factor when it comes to post-acquisition management seems to be the ability of managing people rather than systems and structure'. Schweiger and Weber (1989) investigated the relevance for managers of human resource issues considered during the pre-M&A planning and post-M&A implementation stages. In the first stage, the most relevant human resource issue was considered to be the characteristics of acquired managers, with particular reference to their capabilities. In the implementation stage, the main consideration was whether to leave the HRM policies of the acquired firm as they were or whether to adopt those of the acquiring firm.

Ulrich et al. (1989) argue from a case study that post-acquisition management should focus on three features: defining philosophy, design structure, and implementing the people-related aspects of the merger. Schweiger et al. (1987) identify five major areas of concern for people involved in acquisition operations: loss of identity, lack of information and anxiety, survival, lost talent, and family repercussions. Marks and Mirvis (1992), in turn, unveil some similar problems inherent to this phase: post-merger trauma, mythologizing old jobs, and job assignments. As a response to these problems, Schweiger and his colleagues (1987) argue that human resource management should focus on terminations and the merging of culture and reward systems. They see managers as having an important role in the solution of these problems, remaining committed to employees, being honest, showing understanding for employees' concerns, minimizing political behaviour, and so forth.

Towards a view on post-acquisition performance

One point of apparent agreement in discussions of the influences on post-acquisition performance is that it can only be accounted for by a combination of several factors. Thus Hitt et al. (1998) affirm that the success or otherwise of acquisitions is likely to result from a configuration of variables rather than any one factor. They identify six such variables: resource complementarities, friendliness of the process, low-to-moderate debt, change experience, emphasis on innovation, and focus on core business. Datta and Grant (1990) highlight the need for adopting a perspective that recognizes the role of factors associated with the assimilation of acquisitions. They argue that, along with strategic fit or relatedness, which has dominated the strategic management literature on acquisition performance, it is important for studies to incorp-orate factors related to post-acquisition managerial decisions and organiza-tional fit. The problems are to a large extent unique in each case and the specific situation may require different kinds of solution.

There is disagreement, however, about the weight that should be attached to different factors. The lack of consensus about the significance of strategic and organizational factors has encouraged the substitution of a process perspective for a factorial one. The process perspective 'retains the important role of issues of strategic fit and organizational fit, but it adds the considera-tion of how aspects of the acquisition decision making and integration processes can affect the final outcome' (Haspeslagh and Jemison 1991: 306).

This book focuses on the non-managerial and managerial factors that may impact on post-acquisition performance. Non-managerial factors include the size of acquiring and acquired companies, date of acquisition, profitability of the subsidiary at the time of its acquisition, sector, and nationality. Managerial factors include post-acquisition integration and changes in prac-tice. It may well be that there is no universally applicable way to manage a newly acquired company in order to create value. This would be the conclu-sion if investigation showed that acquiring firms were achieving performance improvements from their new subsidiaries through a number of different routes. We explore this possibility by examining national variation in post-acquisition policies and practices, and whether these have any different impact on the performance of acquired companies. Specifically, we examine the management of post-acquisition change among British companies acquired by companies from the four countries that have been the major investors in the UK since the mid-1980s: the USA, Japan, Germany, and France. We also include a sample of acquisitions by other UK companies for purposes of highlighting the foreign influence in changes introduced. Additional issues considered are how post-acquisition changes were brought about, the nature of control and integration in the relation between subsidiaries and parent companies, and policies related to HRM.

These are practical questions worthy of examination in their own right. In addition, this book can address broader issues because the scope of the research it reports covers acquiring firms from five different nationalities. Of particular concern is whether or not the management of international acqui-sitions demonstrates the presence of distinct national practices. Over the past twenty years, it has been argued forcefully that there are contrasting national systems of business and managerial practice which are strongly embedded in the specific cultural and institutional heritage of the home countries of busi-ness corporations. More recently a contrary view has been advanced, namely that the pressures of operating in a worldwide competitive environment, and the globalization of value chains among large transnational corporations, are encouraging the strategies and practices of those corporations to converge.

The debate continues, therefore, as to whether the advanced industrial countries tend to pursue different management practices and, if so, in what respects. As firms globalize through foreign direct investment, do the observed methods of certain countries appear to be better suited to certain situations and less appropriate in others? Does Japan, for example, possess the secret of effectiveness in operations management, while others such as the United States have something special to contribute in human resource management or the management of innovation? To what extent do firms when investing abroad adapt their practices to the host country or, alternatively transfer and implant them to advantage? And how much does it all matter? It may be that a given situation can be tackled with different cultural and managerial approaches with equally good results.

Summary

The key points from this chapter are:

- A high proportion of acquisitions fail—as many as 50 per cent.
- Pre-acquisition factors, such as the quality of the acquisition and its fit with the acquiring company's strategy, do not provide a complete explanation for acquisition performance.
- How an acquisition is managed determines whether its capabilities are put to good use; managerial factors therefore play an important part in the realization of value from acquisitions.
- Three issues are prominent in post-acquisition management: the nature of change introduced, the form of integration and control adopted in the relationship between acquired and acquirer companies, and the process whereby change is introduced.
- Cultural differences between acquirer and acquired companies may make managing the latter more difficult, though synergies are also possible.
- Attention to human resource issues is particularly important following an acquisition, the more so if cultural differences are involved.
- Acquisitions in the same country by companies of different nationality will indicate whether different national management approaches can give equally good results despite the variance in cultural distance.

4

Theoretical Perspectives

This chapter summarizes the continuing debate about the significance of national influences on management as opposed to those deriving from global forces transcending national boundaries. This debate informs the issue as to whether cross-border acquisitions promote greater convergence in management practice or, by contrast, reproduce different approaches to management within the companies they take over.

Contrasting theoretical perspectives

There is a fundamental divide among scholars of international business and management between those who argue that transnational forces carry increasing weight in the globalizing world of today and others who emphasize the continuing influence of nationality. The two theoretical approaches contrast in terms of their sensitivity to nations or regions as analytically significant contexts.[1]

The first category consists of perspectives that are not sensitive to particular nations or regions as special contexts but refer instead to universal rationales. These universals are seen to arise from ubiquitous economic and technological forces that are in turn motivated by universal human needs and drives. These generate certain operational contingencies that establish a functional imperative for organizational design and management process, regardless of national setting. By extension, increasing convergence between management practices is expected as countries develop industrial and post-industrial economies with similar political systems and personal lifestyles, a convergence that is seen to have accelerated under the impetus of late twentieth-century globalization. This first set of perspectives may therefore be called 'low context' in the sense that they do not grant national context

---

[1] The discussion in this chapter draws upon Child (2000). The two theoretical approaches are also analysed and informed by historical data on France, Germany, and Italy in Djelic (1998).

any analytical significance over and above the configuration of universals that happen to characterize a country at any point in its development.

The other category consists of theoretical perspectives that grant primacy to national cultures or institutional systems, when accounting for differences in organization. They all assume that systems of management and organization are embedded within national contexts that are identified as either cultural or institutional. Because they grant explanatory primacy to specifically national factors, they may be termed 'high-context' perspectives. They posit national uniqueness in organizational structures, systems, and behaviours, and expect national organizational differences to persist over time regardless of economic and technological development.[2]

Low-context perspectives

A common feature of low-context perspectives is that they minimize the impact of national distinctiveness. They contain a strong presumption of eventual convergence in management and organization as nations engage in an increasingly efficient global economy and become increasingly subject to the impact of technological change. These perspectives imply that, as new technologies break down barriers of communication and information, people will come to express similar demands for organization and work to be arranged in ways that meet their common psychological needs and aspirations. This encourages the search for new forms of organization that more effectively reconcile business efficiency and human needs. Economics, technology, and psychology thus figure prominently among the low-context perspectives.

Economic universalism

Economic theory centres on the allocation of scarce resources through the pursuit of utility via the market mechanism. By extension, it purports to explain the formal organization of economic activities by firms as a rational response to market conditions. For example, Chandler (1977) accounts for the rise of the modern 'multiunit business enterprise' by reference to the growth of markets, assisted by new production and transportation technologies, and the development of professional managers to coordinate activities previously

---

[2] This vivid terminology is employed by the Halls (1990) for distinguishing linguistic and other cultural differences that bear upon the nature of communication.

conducted in the market place (Biggart 1997). Williamson (1985) also refers to market factors as the primary condition for hierarchically controlled and coordinated firms to develop. These factors include the costs of coordinating market transactions and maintaining market contracts, as well as risks due to opportunism by market partners when the deal entails investing in specific-use assets. Most economists assume that their market-based theories are universally applicable and can account for which forms of business organization will be effective (that is, expected to survive in the long term), wherever the national location.

The credibility of economic universalism has grown since the advent of neo-liberal economics in Western countries and the introduction of economic reform in former state-socialist or state-militarist countries. It argues that, given the growth of the global economy and common human aspirations for betterment, 'free-market' economics will eventually prevail in all societies, and present a common context for management. Djelic (1998: 11) identifies this strand of the argument as the 'rationalization variant', whereby a set of global and universal ideologies ('sets of cultural rules') leads to an increasing similarity of managerial and organizational arrangements.

The economic perspective regards management and organization as micro-level phenomena. Economists therefore generally confine themselves to discussing broad alternative organizational choices such as that between U- and M-form structures (Williamson 1970), the organizational internalization of markets (Buckley and Casson 1976; Williamson 1985), and models for the organization of international business (Bartlett and Ghoshal 1989; Ghoshal and Westney 1993). Economic universalism continues to hold powerful sway in much contemporary work. For example, the debate on corporate governance is powerfully informed by agency theory and by criteria for efficient resource utilization including transparency and fiduciary accountability (Hawley and Williams 1996; Shleifer and Vishny 1997). Another example concerns one of the most far-reaching developments in cross-national organization, the internationalization of firms. The most sophisticated line of theorizing available to account for the stages through which activities are located abroad, and the choice of forms for organizing international operations, articulates these issues in terms of general principles governing risk, managerial exigency, and market opportunity (Johanson and Vahlne 1977; Kogut 1988).

Economic theory endeavours to apply principles in ways that rarely accord a positive value to national specifics. When these are taken into account, it tends to regard them as contingencies such as market imperfections that constrain economically optimum behaviour, or opportunism that generates economically dysfunctional behaviour. In other words, national conditions tend to be treated as constraints on the effective operation of the market system rather than as features that confer cultural preferences for, and differential degrees of institutional legitimacy on, particular ways of organizing.

Technology

Technological change and development has been regarded as the prime mover of capitalism (Schumpeter 1943; Toffler 1971). Moreover, as Dicken (1998: 145) notes, 'technology is, without doubt, one of the most important contributory factors underlying the internationalization and globalization of economic activity'. The impact of technology extends not only to the location of productive activities but also increasingly to the ways in which these can be managed. This development is associated with the contemporary 'shift from a technology based primarily on cheap inputs of energy to one predominantly based on cheap inputs of information derived from advances in microelectronic and telecommunications technology' (Freeman 1988: 10). With the increasing importance of this 'new technology', there is a convergence between the considerations advanced for management by information theorists and those advanced by students of technology.

Much of the literature on information and communications technologies claims that these technologies offer path-breaking new ways of handling information which have implications for the design of effective organizations (Fulk and DeSanctis 1995). It is argued, for example, that such technologies offer more effective ways of reconciling long-standing inherent managerial dilemmas such as the simultaneous need for control and flexible autonomy. Some elevate information to the spirit of the age, arguing that it carries a universal message for organization and management. An example is found in Applegate's (1995) work on 'designing and managing the information age organization'. She takes the view that advances in information technology, when coupled with changes in workforce capabilities, can address the problems that previously stood in the way of transformation from bureaucratic to organic, if not virtual, organizations. Given an increasingly competitive and fast-moving world economic environment, Applegate believes that advances in information technology and related conceptions of information, knowledge, and learning have created an irresistible movement towards new forms of organization.

If these IT solutions are so powerful, it follows that managers cannot neglect to apply the new technologies to their organization if they are to remain competitive. Insofar as solutions are being offered by technologists working from broadly similar design principles, this may well be a strong force for international convergence. An additional reason for anticipating increased similarity lies in the connectivity that modern information technologies provide around the world. This facility for disseminating and sharing information is also thought to promote homogeneity. In these ways, information theory—or at least the technological deterministic strand of it— also offers a low-context perspective.

As modern communication and information technologies spread ubiquitously, they become more integrated into the ways that, in contemporary organizations, information is processed, people communicate, and knowledge is managed. In other words, there is a rapidly increasing elision between the design of such technological systems and that of the management system itself. The key question that follows is whether preferences for particular forms of organization are now driving the use of technology or whether the technology itself impacts on management and organization.

Child and Loveridge (1990) concluded from studies of IT in European services that it remains an open question as to whether the application of new technology promotes similarities in organizing across different countries. This is because the issue is characterized by considerable design and negotiating latitude. Moreover, a relationship and elision between technology and organization do not necessarily denote causality. There is a long-standing dispute in organizational theory over this matter. Some have regarded technology in general, and production technology in particular, as constraining or even determining workplace organization and social relations (e.g. Woodward 1965; Hickson et al. 1974). The implication of this perspective is that, whatever the national setting, the adoption of a given technology will have the same consequences for the design of a viable organization and the way that social relations at work are structured (Child 1981). In other words, technological determinists argue that different production technologies determine particular organization structures and behaviours independently of the local context (Knights and Murray 1994). As Hickson and his colleagues claim, 'the technological equipment of an oil refinery requires much the same operatives and supervisors wherever it is' (1974: 64). Others have, by contrast, concluded from close examination of the adoption of particular forms of technology that the decisions made at the time reflected managerial preferences for increasing control over the work process rather than any technological imperative (e.g. Noble 1977).

One might have expected the greater inherent flexibility of the new technology to have softened the deterministic stance. Some observers, however, continue to embrace a position of technological determinism even though their message may now be an optimistic one emphasizing how new technology can assist people to realize their potential (cf. Zuboff 1988), rather than the earlier pessimistic message of alienation (cf. Blauner 1964). This leads

Dicken (1998: 145) to warn that 'it is all too easy to be seduced by the notion that technology "causes" a specific set of changes [and] makes particular structures and arrangements "inevitable"'.

Psychological universalism

This perspective assumes that all human beings have common needs and motivational structures. The desire to satisfy shared needs forms the basis for similar structures of individual motivation. Even some cross-cultural psychologists, who recognize that human behaviour varies across different cultural settings, remain chiefly concerned to pursue the discipline's aim of arriving at universal generalizations. Thus, they tend to regard the contextual specifics of different countries as anomalous rather than fundamental (Bond and Smith 1996). According to Poortinga (1992: 13), 'it is assumed that the same psychological processes are operating in all humans independent of culture'.

Many universal psychological theories and concepts, such as Maslow's (1943) 'need hierarchy' and Adams's (1965) 'equity theory', are now the standard fare in textbooks on management and organizational behaviour. This not only indicates their wide acceptance; it also serves to propagate them further. While such psychological theories differ in detail, they take individuals or groups as their focus, more or less in isolation from their cultural and social context. Thus people are regarded as essentially the same everywhere. They all need to eat, have security, enjoy social relations, and derive some meaning from their lives. Reducing the theoretical and methodological level to the individual encourages the assumption that all people share a similar set of needs. The more basic needs are taken to be biological and physiological in nature. They are not subject to a high degree of social definition; whether you have sufficient to eat and enjoy shelter and security are to a large extent common necessities.

The assumption of universal human needs has importantly informed the analysis of utility that underlies much economic theory. Psychological universalists see national differences in behaviour resulting from the differential impact of economic circumstances rather than from intrinsic human differences. This view carries clear implications for management. It suggests that consumers enjoying similar educational and living standards will have similar wants, and thus implies that the policies of companies aiming at given markets will need to converge. Within companies, psychological universalism has strong implications for the design of work organization as well as for control and reward systems. Thus for a developed country such as the UK, psychological theories converge in recommending less hierarchical structures and open communications in order to foster employee commitment and, through greater transparency, to facilitate goal acceptance and a feeling of equity.

Transnational effects

Low-context, universalistic arguments draw attention to the pressures of operating in a worldwide competitive environment, the pervasiveness of modern information technology, and the homogenization of needs and lifestyles between urbanized populations. The globalization of production among MNCs, largely in response to these trends, is said also to be working towards convergence in their strategies and practices (Dicken 1998). These are the most prominent firms in international M&A activity. M&A is therefore assumed to convey transnational rather than national 'effects'.

Calori and De Woot (1994: 53) note that some of the European company directors they interviewed perceived a narrowing of the gap between American, European, and Japanese management philosophies and practices, 'especially in multinational corporations which are in direct contact with the three continents'. This links directly to the thesis of convergence among MNCs, namely that 'leading corporations should gradually be losing their national characters and converging in their fundamental strategies and oper-ations' (Pauly and Reich 1997). MNCs are commonly defined as those with production facilities in two or more continents and with worldwide sourcing and/or distribution (Daniels and Radebaugh 1992).

The transnational effects argument is based on the premiss that 'the same challenges faced all managers everywhere as the world's increasingly linked economies sped toward the twenty-first century' (Bartlett and Ghoshal 1989: p. x). Or, as Ohmae has stated (1990: 94), 'Country of origin does not matter. Location of headquarters does not matter. The products for which you are responsible and the company you serve have become denationalized.' The model for the denationalized MNC has increasingly become that purveyed in the large US and international business schools from which the MNCs draw their career managers, and at which their senior executives attend pro-grammes on the latest thinking. Indeed, some such as Ferner and Quintanilla (1998) suggest that many MNCs from countries outside the UK and USA go through a process of 'Anglo-Saxonization' as their international activities expand. Nevertheless, these authors also conclude that there is clear evidence of a nationality effect as well.

An important component of the model is a long-term strategic orientation and, as indicated by Mintzberg's (1994) critique, one that has been predicated on strategic planning. Consistent with their size and with business school precepts, MNCs are expected to rely heavily on a high level of internal formalization. Formal accounting, HRM, market research, operations, and other systems are likely to be of a standardized nature, since MNCs seeking to benefit from global products or technologies, and having considerable ownership-specific advantages, are likely to derive considerable benefits from this policy. MNCs are also likely to place a heavy emphasis on training, especially managerial training. Their well-known support for business schools stems partly from a belief that they must develop a core of highly professional executives, sharing a similar corporate culture and managerial approach, in order to maintain sufficient integration and control across their worldwide operations. These managers are likely to be deployed by MNCs into the key positions within affiliates and joint ventures in order to ensure integration with corporate policies and procedures, especially in the first few years (Edstrom and Galbraith 1977). The emphasis among MNCs on globalization will be reflected in a high level of transactional integration between them and their affiliates.

The argument for transnational effects suggests that there will be many common features in the changes that international companies bring to their newly acquired UK subsidiaries. This would amount to a generalized *acquisition effect*. Acquisition presents opportunities for changes to be made. The rationale for many acquisitions is to exploit perceived opportunities for securing a greater return from assets, and this will establish an impetus for change in management practice within the subsidiary. In addition, new investment may be made in plant and information technology, and this will provide opportunities for new practices to be introduced. There is also likely to be something of a general 'new broom sweeps clean' effect. Secondly, cross-border acquisitions are more likely to be undertaken by companies aware of standard 'state-of-the-art' international best practice than are purely domestic acquisitions. For this reason, they may lead to the introduction of similar changes, regardless of acquirer nationality, in certain areas such as cost control where standard techniques are well developed.

High-context perspectives

Despite exposure to common contingencies in the world economy, Dicken concludes that 'the home-base characteristics invariably remain dominant' (Dicken 1998: 196–7). Recent comparative research suggests that national differences persist in the strategies, governance structures, and R&D systems of MNCs (Pauly and Reich 1997). This conclusion is consistent with high-context perspectives. These share the strong presumption that management practices have their own distinct national characteristics deriving from the cultural preferences and embedded institutions of different societies. The most influential theories thus refer to national culture and institutions respectively.

Cultural theory

Cultural theory places 'low-context' perspectives into their appropriate cultural setting. Economic utilities, personal motivations, and the ways in which information is interpreted and used are seen to be culture bound. As such, thinking and behaviour are seen to be governed by cultural values, which therefore differentiate management across nations and other social collectivities.

The cultural perspective has two main implications for post-acquisition change. First, it suggests significant differences in the management practices favoured by acquiring companies of different nationalities or cultural regions. It predicts that these differences will be particularly strong in culturally sensitive areas, such as time orientation and interpersonal relations. The management practices that fall within these areas include strategic time horizon, centralization of authority, modes of communication, and reward systems. Second, the studies reviewed in Chapter 3 suggest a correlation between problems in effecting post-acquisition change and the width of the cultural gap between the acquiring and acquired company. Cultural gaps can be bridged, however, and any potential problems they cause may either be exacerbated or mitigated by the approach adopted by the acquiring company towards sensitive issues such as rationalization and redundancy.

The two best-known cultural perspectives on management and organization are those of Hofstede (1980a, 1991) and Trompenaars (1993). While these two Dutchmen fiercely contest the validity of their respective cultural dimensions and methodologies, they agree on the following basic assumptions: cultural values are deep seated and enduring; they vary systematically between different societies; they condition what is acceptable organizational practice; and they predict inter-societal differences in economic performance (GDP).

The cultural perspective has for some time provided the dominant paradigm in comparative studies of organization. It is indicative that Hickson and Pugh (1995) chose to subtitle their review of the field 'The Impact of Societal Culture on Organizations around the Globe'. Even before Hofstede's seminal and unifying work, international studies of organization predominantly regarded culture as the key explanatory factor for cross-national differences, as reviews such as Roberts (1970) make clear. Attention to culture also has intuitive appeal to practising international managers, for whom it serves as a convenient reference for the many frustrations they can experience when working with people from other countries, the source of which they do not fully comprehend.

Despite its appeal and influence, many questions remain to be answered about the cultural perspective. The most fundamental concerns the theoretical status of culture. Is culture all pervasive, as Sorge (1982) argues, so that we need to reposition our economic and technological theories within a cultural space, as Boisot (1995) advocates for information theory?[3] In other words, does culture take primacy over other factors, not only in terms of predictive power but also in terms of structuring the systems of meaning and shaping the rationales that theories can legitimately employ? If so, then the validity of a comparative study of management across cultural boundaries employing concepts and equivalent operational measures derived from only one culture comes into question. The attraction of comparing the management practices introduced by firms of different cultural origin into the same national cultural milieu is that it reduces this problem of comparison.

Another problem is that, despite the attention of many scholars, there is still no adequate theory on the relevance of culture for management and organization. Key issues remain unclear; in particular, the organizational features shaped by culture, how they are so influenced, and the significance of culture compared to, for example, economic, technological, and political factors. A satisfactory theory would have to address two levels of analysis. The first concerns the independence of culture as an explanatory variable, and the extent to which cultures themselves are shaped by national economic, technological, and political factors through the mediation of lifestyle, mass media, access to global information, and government-sponsored ideology. Can culture be regarded as an independent, let alone dominant, force? The common assumption that national differences can simply be expressed in cultural terms, and that nation can be used as the unit of analysis for culture (Gannon 1994), remains an untested hypothesis. The second level concerns the identification of organizational attributes that are culture specific in the sense that they vary systematically between, and are sensitive to the impact of, cultures.

These considerations imply that:

A test of national differences which are culturally intrinsic would require an examination of whether organizational characteristics continue to differ across nations when contingencies and economic systems are similar or controlled, and a demonstration

---

[3] To quote Sorge (1982: 131): 'there is no "culture-free" context of organization, because even if organizational solutions or contexts are similar, they are always culturally constructed and very imperfectly interpreted as the reaction to a given constraint.'

that the remaining differences are explicable in terms of an adequate theory of national cultures. (Child 1981: 305)

The comparison of changes brought about by acquiring companies of different nationalities made in this book is one way of conducting a controlled test of national effects. The common location of the acquired companies within the UK, and the possibilities of examining those facing similar contingencies of size and sector, offer some control over the impact of economic system and other variables.

Cultural information theory is a variant of cultural theory. Information is a ubiquitous social phenomenon. Information theory takes the view that managing organizations primarily involves the processing and communication of information, whether this is in imparting a vision, reaching decisions, carrying out control and coordination, or managing knowledge. As a result, information theory is applied to a range of organizational levels, from strategic decision-making down to the information-processing capabilities of individuals. Information thus infuses management practice.

Among cultural information theorists, Boisot (1986) is particularly fruitful for a cross-national understanding of organizational forms. He identifies four institutionalized approaches to organizing transactions and relationships, in terms of their characteristic modes of information-processing. These modes are defined in terms of two primary dimensions of information: its codification and diffusion.[4] Boisot named the domain which these dimensions create the 'culture-space', on the basis that there are marked cultural and/or institutionalized preferences to be found in different nations for particular positions on the two dimensions. Thus the relatively open, transparent 'Anglo-Saxon' nations, with their highly codified legal and other systems, would be expected to favour a combination of high information codification and diffusion (availability). The four fundamental organizational forms to which this framework gives rise are bureaucracy, market, clan, and fief. On the assumption just made, Anglo-Saxon nations should exhibit a high preference for the organization of transactions through markets, and this is undoubtedly the case.

At the group or team level, information theory adopts a quite different focus depending on whether it is sensitive to the influence of cross-national culture or not. Abstracted from culture, emphasis is likely to be placed on the

---

[4] More recently, Boisot (1995) has added a third dimension: the extent to which information is concrete and situation specific rather than abstract and situation general. This third dimension is highly relevant for the transfer of organizational knowledge and practice across nations, where it is often not the specific concrete practices that can be successfully transferred but rather the more abstract principles informing them. These principles then require recontextualization, i.e., to be applied as new specific concrete practices that suit the new social context.

effective functioning of teams as information-processing units, employing procedures such as agreeing objectives, preparing briefing papers, recording the results of discussions, and accumulating a relevant knowledge base. The intention is to structure team process in ways that will encourage the transformation of available information, especially from tacit to explicit, and the codification of that explicit knowledge into a property available to the organization as a whole (Nonaka and Takeuchi 1995). If, however, information theory is sensitive to cultural influences, it will recognize that accepted modes of group functioning, including the conduct of meetings, vary considerably across cultures. It will therefore pay a great deal more attention to the social composition of groups or teams within organizations, and to the processes whereby they can find a commonly acceptable way of proceeding, communicating, and (eventually) sharing identity (Tjosvold 1991; Drummond 1997).

Institutional theory

The institutional perspective stresses that management and business have different institutional foundations from one society to another. Key institutions are the state, the legal system, the financial system, and the family. Taken together, such institutions constitute the distinctive social organization of a country and its economy. The forms these institutions take and their economic role are seen to shape different 'national business systems' or varieties of capitalism (Whitley 1992*a*, 1992*b*; Orru et al. 1997). Although the institutional perspective draws on a long sociological tradition, there remains little agreement about, or understanding of, the processes whereby institutions are formed and in turn impact on organizations (Tolbert and Zucker 1996). There is, however, much more consensus on the potential analytical power offered by the perspective.

Institutional theorists stress the historical embeddedness of social structures and processes. This carries two particularly significant implications for a cross-national analysis of management. First, 'institutional theory proposes that social and economic organization is informed by historically developed logics, which are changed only with difficulty' (Biggart and Guillén 1999: 742). In other words, institutions are likely to be 'sticky' in the face of economic and technological change. This means that, insofar as a country's constituent bodies (firms, public organizations, and so forth) are enabled, supported, and guided by national institutions, one would expect cross-national contrasts in the organizational responses to handling such change. Second, as Biggart and Guillén also note, the social organization of a country 'acts as a repository of useful resources or capabilities' (1999: 742). In other words, its social organization influences a country's ability to undertake certain kinds of production or other economic activity efficiently and effectively. National institutions such as education systems and the structure of social relations can, through their impact on the degree of ascription or achievement in society, impact on the ability of a country to base its economic wealth creation on innovation, say, rather than mass production. Institutionalists therefore argue that the conditions of economic survival through specialization around national strengths tend to preserve nationally distinctive patterns of management and organization, even within a fully open and globalized competitive system.

National effects

One of the implications following from the institutional perspective is complementary to that raised by cultural theory. Namely that the preferred management practices of acquiring companies will be shaped, at least in part, by the domestic national institutional contexts in which they are embedded. High-context perspectives therefore suggest that a *transfer of national practice effect* will be evident in the post-acquisition changes introduced by acquiring companies of different nationality. Another implication, however, is that the institutional environment of the host country for an acquisition may oblige acquiring firms to modify their preferred practices to suit the regulatory provisions, skill and educational levels, and other institutionally formed features of that country. To that extent, national differences in management practices among acquiring companies in areas such as employment, work organization, and marketing may be weakened in their application to acquired subsidiaries.

Relevance of theoretical perspectives to the impact of acquisition

Continuing debate

Until the 1980s, many students of management assumed that there were general principles that might be applied to situations, irrespective of the cultural heritage of the companies being studied (Hickson et al. 1974). The dominant view at the time was that the appropriate approach to management and to organization should be determined in the light of the prevailing circumstances, or 'contingencies', particularly those established by the market, the technology, and the scale of operation. National cultures and institutions were thought to be either of limited relevance or just one among several contingencies to which management practice had to be adjusted (Child 1981).

The view persists among some scholars that national differences are not particularly significant for the management of cross-border acquisitions. Hunt (1988) claims that almost all acquirers of whatever nationality adopt a 'hands-on' attitude towards structure, people, budgets, plans, and systems in the first year after an acquisition. Olie (1994) highlights leadership, appropriate organization structures, and compatibility of partner motives as the best predictors of merger success, rather than sensitivity to national practice. Similarly, Bartlett and Ghoshal (1989) in their description of the transnational corporation pay little attention to differing national managerial styles.

In the last two decades, however, there has been keen interest in national cultures and institutions, both of which have come to be seen as of critical importance for the development of management methods, strategies, and structures (Eltis 1996; UNCTAD 1995). There has been a growing body of research on national cultural differences relevant to management (e.g. Hofstede 1991; Hampden-Turner and Trompenaars 1993), and on the nature of management in different national business systems (e.g. Whitley 1992*a*, 1992*b*). This work leads to the expectation that the management practices introduced by owning companies of different nationalities will be quite distinctive. It introduces the possibility that an increasing number of companies face two distinct approaches to management—their own indigenous one, and that of the foreign partner or parent—as a result of being acquired by a foreign corporation.

An early example of work that isolated the nationality factor is seen in Dunning's (1958) pioneering research on American investment in British manufacturing. He concluded that most subsidiaries adopted substantially the same 'principles of management' as their US parent companies. Despite a long history of US investment in certain UK sectors since the last part of the nineteenth century, such as in the then newly developing electrical industries, Dunning did not find any appreciable adaptation to the local context of practices in areas such as control and operating methods. Perlmutter (1969), on the other hand, warned of the risk of ethnocentricity where the acquirer does not make any adaptation to local practice, and carries on behaving as though it is in its domestic market. Gates and Egelhoff (1986) identified the importance of MNCs' country of origin in their choice of control mechanisms over new acquisitions. Similarly, Calori et al. (1994) found that French companies exercise greater formal control over strategy and operations and less informal control through teamwork in their UK acquisitions than do American ones. They concluded that firms generally take their home practices with them when they undertake international acquisitions.

This line of research implies that inward FDI, through the control and influence it affords the foreign acquiring management, will stimulate the adoption of management practices consistent with those of the parent company. Acquisition as a vehicle for inward FDI provides a potentially powerful lever for the direct application of foreign management practice insofar as 100 per cent ownership legitimizes foreign owners' authority. It also encourages them to devote greater attention to their subsidiary, concomitant with their relative greater investment, than would be the case with joint ventures or other collaborative forms. Acquisitions offer weaker power bases for local management and employees to resist the introduction of new practices than do joint ventures or collaborations. Greenfield sites offer even less potential for resistance to the extent that both plant and workforce are introduced *de novo*, but they do not offer the possibility of a clear comparison with the practices prevailing before the application of FDI.

As Shrivastava (1986) points out, there are several areas in which a national influence on management practice might be evident, such as in accounting and budgeting systems, physical assets, product lines, production systems, and technologies; and most importantly at the level of managerial behaviour and corporate culture. Considerable attention has been paid to the impact on British and American industry of Japanese practices, especially operational methods. Oliver and Wilkinson (1992: 317) conclude that:

the survey data from both the 1987 and 1991 surveys reported here demonstrate a clear wish to move towards Japanese production methods on the part of UK companies as well as Japanese investors, and of themselves would suggest very substantial use of these methods.

UNCTAD, in its 1995 *World Investment Report*, carried a section reporting details of the favourable impact for production efficiency that has resulted from the implementation of Japanese methods through FDI. It noted that Japanese practices, especially operational methods centred around lean production and continuous improvement, have received the most attention by British and American companies. Oliver and Wilkinson (1992) caution that there was some evidence of a slowdown in the rate at which Japanese methods were being adopted by the early 1990s, and also that by then companies were reporting lower success rates with the implementation of such practices. There is clearly a need for further research into the possible impact of approaches emanating from Japanese and other national sources.

One of the more detailed studies has been that conducted by Abo and his colleagues into what they refer to as the Hybrid Factory (1994). Their book reports on how Japanese transplants in the USA are managed. In examining local US plants of Japanese companies, they conclude that 'it becomes clear that there is a dynamic interplay between two forces or tendencies: application of the Japanese system, and adaptation to local conditions. This is what makes our model a hybrid model' (Abo 1994: 36). Botti (1995) has also used a variant of this model to investigate Japanese transplants in Italy. The balance between the direct application of foreign management practices and their adaptation to local conditions leaves open the question of how far and in what manner FDI through M&A induces domestic changes.

The relevance of the national origin of the acquiring company in cross-border acquisitions is thus by now widely accepted. Previous research and discussion help us to consider how the waves of foreign investment into UK industry may have an impact on UK management practice and how this impact is realized. Eltis (1996), for one, concludes that British firms are producing closer to their technical potential as the result of learning from inward investors.

Three factors may bear upon changes in management practice within acquired subsidiaries. The first two, as already noted, are concomitants of acquisition itself. There may be a general *acquisition effect*. This effect is characteristic of acquisitions *per se* rather than reflecting any particular foreign approach to management and organization. The second effect is specific to the nationality of the new foreign owner and is the *transfer of national practice effect*. This takes the form of a transfer in management practice to domestic companies through the medium of foreign acquisition. It can also proceed through emulation within domestic companies, whether spurred by acquisition or not, as Oliver and Wilkinson (1992) noted in the case of Japanese-type production methods.

The third effect upon changes in management practice does not arise from acquisition itself. It derives from *general conditions affecting host country industry* during the period of study, be they the influence of new management ideas, the economic cycle of boom and recession, or the general institutional environment. These are changes that would have occurred anyway even in the absence of an acquisition. This effect is not specific to acquisitions since it bears upon all firms with equal potential. It poses a problem of separating out changes triggered specifically by acquisition from those that firms would have adopted anyway. In this book, we do not address the question of what changes might have happened independently of the impact of acquisition, though some of our case studies do illustrate the phenomenon.

These considerations draw attention to the questions of 'what is being transferred' from foreign investing companies, and 'what are we comparing?' (Morris and Wilkinson 1996: 727). The first question concerns the substantive characteristics of management practices that may be transferred. What differences in this respect might one expect to find between companies coming from each of the 'big four' foreign investing countries into the UK? The second question concerns the difference that FDI from specific national sources makes to the management practices introduced into UK subsidiaries, and how this compares to acquisition by domestic UK companies.

A provisional conclusion

The low-context perspective leans towards the conclusion that any impact inward FDI via acquisition may have on UK management will reflect the knowledge and experience that acquiring firms have of globally best management practice. Subject to their skills in implementing organizational change, the impact of acquiring firms from different countries should, on this argument, be more homogeneous than it is diverse. This homogeneity would reflect international practice rather than accommodation to the common features of the host country environment.

On the other hand, acquisition as a vehicle for inward FDI provides a potentially powerful lever for newly owning companies to apply their preferred management practices to their acquired companies. High-context theories draw attention to the ways these preferences are likely to be embedded in national cultures and institutions and hence to vary significantly between the countries of origin. Thus some hold that MNCs tend to use the organizational models most popularly espoused in the country where their corporate headquarters are located (Ruigrok and van Tulder 1995).

A provisional conclusion is that while low- and high-context theories appear to be irreconcilable, each may help to account for different post-acquisition changes in management practice. Some changes may be common to most acquisitions and reflect a global consensus on what constitutes good practice in a particular area such as cost control. Other post-acquisition developments, in areas such as HRM, may be more sensitive to the national context of the acquiring company initiating the changes and the approach to management characterizing that context.

The following chapter summarizes the conclusions of research into the management philosophies and practices that distinguish each of the nationalities addressed in this book.

Summary

This chapter has placed the issue of national approaches to management and their likely impact via acquisitions, into a broad theoretical context. Its key points are:

- There is continuing debate concerning the influence of nationality on management practice in a globalizing world.
- Some argue that transnational forces now carry greater weight; others emphasize the influence of nationality.
- One set of perspectives does not recognize nations or regions as significant contexts for the shaping of management practice, but refers instead to universal norms of practice arising from ubiquitous economic, technological, and psychological forces.
- This approach leads to the expectation that there is an 'acquisition effect' which is general in nature.
- Another set of perspectives grants primacy to national cultures or institutional systems, when accounting for differences in management practice.
- This approach leads to the expectation that there is a 'transfer of foreign practice effect' which reproduces national differences via acquisitions.
- While these appear to be irreconcilable theoretical approaches, each may help to account for different post-acquisition changes in management practice.

5

National Management Practices

The arguments for and against national effects on management practice, discussed in the previous chapter, place the issue into a broad theoretical context. The low-context perspectives caution against an uncritical assumption that national effects will necessarily prevail over other influences on post-acquisition changes in management practice. Bearing this caution in mind, this chapter examines the management practices associated with the major industrial countries considered in this book. Specifically, it reviews evidence on the salient characteristics of management practice in the five countries of origin of the acquiring companies investigated: USA, Japan, Germany, France, and the UK.

The only certainty about such national characterizations is that they are incomplete and all too often present oversimplified summaries of the diversity that exists within most countries associated with factors such as firm ownership, size, and sector (Lane 1989). Nevertheless, they are a distillation of conclusions drawn from research and discussion of national specifics, and they suggest the broad differences in post-acquisition management practice that might be expected to emerge from the present research (cf. Dosi and Kogut 1993). Space unfortunately does not permit us to examine the origins of such national differences, on which there is already a substantial literature (e.g. Chandler 1977; Locke 1989; Djelic 1998).

US management practice

The USA has come to represent a model of professional management across the world (Lawrence and Edwards 2000). American management is based on individualistic and rationalistic paradigms (Hampden-Turner and Trompenaars 1993; Hickson and Pugh 1995; Lawrence 1996a). Despite concerns in the 1950s over the development of 'Organization Man' (Whyte 1956), individualism in the form of entrepreneurship, risk-taking, and competitive success is prized in the American executive. In such an environment, colleagues are frequently thought of as competitors in the race for advancement and success, and some conflict between them is not regarded as abnormal (Lawrence 1996*b*). Promotion may be rapid, since tenure with the company may be short. Reward is primarily financial, with large performance-related bonuses the target. Termination, however, can be swift, and company loyalty therefore tends to be transient and not deeply felt (Ouchi 1981; Alston 1989). This management culture places a strong emphasis on achieving short-term financial results (Jacobs 1991), with many US companies being managed for the maximization of profits and the short-term satisfaction of shareholders (Calori and De Woot 1994; Lawrence 1996*a*). This tendency strengthened from the 1970s onward, as pressures in the financial system to generate higher short-term returns intensified demands on US companies to increase dividends (Lazonick and O'Sullivan 1996).

The rationalistic strain in American management practice is manifest in the attention given both to formalization and planning. Abo (1994) comments that in the USA engineers design a job in terms of tasks, with job descriptions created on the basis of these tasks. This is a legacy from Fordism and the scientific management systems of Taylor. It leads to a high degree of workplace specialization and formalization throughout the company (Inkson et al. 1970; Child and Ellis 1973). Jamieson (1980) concludes from a comparison of US companies operating in the UK with indigenous British companies that the former are distinguished by their high degree of formalization (though not formality). This is evidenced in several areas of management, including systematic financial planning and budgetary control, formal selection procedures, job descriptions and management development programmes in the HRM area, and systematic, data-based market assessments. Lawrence (1996*b*) draws similar contrasts between American and British management. He concludes that American management is rationalistic in its approach, using strategic planning, standard procedures, and formalization to a greater extent than is typically found in the UK. Nevertheless, despite these differences, British management practice has more in common with the American than it does with that of any other European country (Lawrence and Edwards 2000). It is not surprising that larger US firms attach importance to the MBA for corporate advancement, since it is par excellence the training ground for this approach (Locke 1989).

In sectors where large firms dominate, the multidivisional structure came to be favoured (Chandler 1986; Fligstein 1990). This concept of American managerial capitalism involves direction from the top by a management team armed with the necessary information and sophisticated management systems. Through these means, it has the power to control activities that are delegated within a divisional structure. US firms have been seen to favour a high degree of integration between corporate and subsidiary levels based on sophisticated reporting systems (Harrigan 1986; Bower 1986).

Although major exceptions exist to the general pattern just depicted, exceptions which have been lauded (e.g. Peters and Waterman 1982), the management practice particularly associated with many US companies comprises:

- short-term financial orientation;
- rewards related to specific performance indicators;
- high rate of job change and inter-company mobility;
- rationalistic approach: emphasis on analysis and planning;
- reliance on formalization and systems;
- delegation down extended hierarchies;
- high level of integration between corporate and subsidiary levels.

Japanese management practice

Most discussion of Japanese management practice has focused on operations, specifically production and supply. In the early 1950s, some major Japanese companies enthusiastically adopted the idea of total quality control (TQC) from the United States, and Toyota developed methods of just-in-time (JIT) production which later developed into the concept of 'lean production'. TQC and JIT, combined with aspects of 'worker empowerment' such as multi-skilling, job rotation, teamwork, employee involvement through quality circles, and *kaizen* (continuous improvement), constitute the core of the so-called Japanese management system (e.g. Elger and Smith 1994; Oliver and Wilkinson 1992; Morris and Wilkinson 1996). Nevertheless, this system is by no means completely adopted within Japan (Fruin and Nishiguchi 1993; Whittaker 1993).

Abo (1994) describes the Japanese management system as very flexible with few rigid job demarcations. Teamworking is fostered. There is a use of implicit control based on a shared corporate norms and understanding. The whole workforce is constantly encouraged to improve its skills, and there is considerable investment in internal training (Alston 1989; Pascale and Athos 1981). Rewards are generally based on a combination of seniority and evaluation by superiors rather than on specific performance indicators. Promotion tends to be very slow through a seniority system and, at least in the major corporations, jobs held by men are expected to reflect long-term mutual obligations (Ouchi 1981; McMillan 1996). Though this 'salaryman' system is now under threat (Nakamoto 1997), it was in place among most larger Japanese parent firms during the period of the present study.

The emphasis on collective loyalty and training facilitates knowledge creation as a continuing process, by encouraging the sharing of collective wisdom and its effective communication throughout the company (Nonaka and Takeuchi 1995). Nevertheless, despite the *ringi* system of circulating papers for comment, final approval is often very centralized (Lincoln 1993). Japanese subsidiaries in the UK have been found to be more tightly controlled by their parents than American-owned subsidiaries, with a much higher proportion of expatriates (Dunning 1993*a*; also Yoneyama 1994).

Externally, major corporations are the hubs of supplier *keiretsu* characterized by long-term relations, computer integration, and technical cooperation, though these do not necessarily involve single-sourcing (Gerlach 1992; Fruin and Nishiguchi 1993). The value that the Japanese place on cooperative activity extends to external networks of suppliers and customers.

The major Japanese companies have a long-term orientation reflected in the emphasis on strategic goals rather than solely financial ones, as well as in their long-term employment practices (though the latter have recently come under pressure in Japan itself). Japanese managers see growth rather than bottom-line profit as their priority, based on the achievement of customer value and superior quality (Abegglen and Stalk 1985; McMillan 1996).

The management practice particularly associated with Japanese companies thus features:

- long-term perspective;
- emphasis on strategic rather than financial goals;
- priority to growth;
- commitment to long-term employment;
- rewards based primarily on seniority and superior's evaluation;
- internal training and seniority system;
- heavy investment in training;
- flexible tasks;
- low specialization;
- stress on teamwork and knowledge-sharing;
- emphasis on lean production and continuous improvement;
- collective orientation;
- decision formulation and knowledge creation via collective participation and responsibility;
- centralized final approval of decisions;
- close relations with suppliers and customers;
- high corporate/subsidiary integration, via secondment and personal contact.

German management practice

There is some disagreement between investigators over the key characteristics of (West) German management. These may reflect differences in sampling, such as large versus *Mittelstand* firms (Lane 1989), and methodology (Ebster-Grosz and Pugh 1996), as well as the tension between two traditions of bureaucratic and craft organization (Lane 1997). Some of the difficulty in pinning down the characteristics of German management practice lies in the fact that, by some standards, they are poorly developed especially in regard to formulating objectives and engaging in strategic thinking. This is illustrated by the problems BMW got into with its acquisition of Rover. On balance, though, Lawrence and Edwards (2000: 120) conclude that although 'the Germans have to some extent exempted themselves from the rules of business and management, [they have] still won'.

There are, nevertheless, three identifiable values underlying German management practice, namely: (i) a long-term view especially of investment in human and technical resources (Hickson and Pugh 1995; Glunk et al. 1997); (ii) a strong technical emphasis associated with competition through quality and innovation rather than price (Maurice et al. 1980; Ebster-Grosz and Pugh 1996, Marr 1996; Lane 1997); (iii) an emphasis on stability or high uncertainty avoidance (Hofstede 1980*a*).

The relatively long-term view adopted by many German companies is reflected in the high proportion of post-tax profits which they choose to retain in the business rather than distribute as dividends—a figure of 60 per cent in 1993, which incidentally is similar to that found among Japanese companies—and also an internationally high percentage of revenue spent on R&D (Hickson and Pugh 1995; Glunk et al. 1997; Lane 1997). Banks and industry are strongly interwoven and support from the former assists companies to take decisions for the long term (Lane 1995). There is not necessarily, however, the same kind of long-term employment commitment that has characterized larger Japanese companies, although German managers do on average appear to stay with their firms longer than their UK counterparts (Stewart et al. 1994; Glunk et al. 1997; Lane 1997).

Lane comments that the German 'system of education and training . . . puts a strong emphasis on skill development at all levels and responsiveness to industrial needs', and contrasts the production orientation of the German system with the financier-dominated British industrial model (1995: 3). A strong technical emphasis is manifest in the generally high level of technical training offered to managers and employees, and the much less well-defined boundary between managers and technical specialists than is typically found in US and UK firms (Child et al. 1983; Glunk et al. 1997). German manufacturing also is characterized by a high-quality engineering emphasis (Warner and Campbell 1993; Marr 1996). German managers generally enjoy a thorough training in a defined area of competence and, in that respect, they are specialist rather than generalist, at least compared to Japan. However, their engineering training is broadly conceived, combining for instance a knowledge of design and production engineering, and this makes it possible for many 'staff' functions to be integrated into 'line' management in German companies (Lane 1989). German companies, for these reasons, tend to be run with a flat organizational pyramid due to the technical competence of their managers (Maurice et al. 1980; Marr 1996).

Culturally, the Germans emerge from surveys as tending towards high levels of uncertainty avoidance (Hofstede 1991). They value stability, which may explain their apparent emphasis on rules and control (Hampden-Turner and Trompenaars 1993). German organizations tend to exhibit a high level of formality, as in the importance attached to job descriptions, production planning and control, and clear-cut procedures (Horowitz 1980; Glunk et al. 1997). As Hickson and Pugh (1995: 97) observe, 'one of the most characteristic aspects of the German culture, which certainly strikes an outsider, is their way of managing uncertainty through an emphasis on planning and orderliness'. This penchant for order, however, is manifest according to some writers in organizational structures rather than in processes (e.g. Stewart et al. 1994). Lane (1989, 1997), indeed, argues that a flexible, participative approach to coordination typically coexists with formalization in German firms.

Formal arrangements for participation in German industry are institutionalized by law. Works councils provide a basis for information and participation. There are many checks and balances in the German system against a manager's freedom of action, and there are even two boards of directors, an executive board and a supervisory board representing both employee and shareholder, in larger firms (Marr 1996). As with the Japanese, loyalty is stressed, and in-house training emphasized. These arrangements point to quite a strong collective and communitarian orientation. Germans are said to prefer group participation and collective action, in contrast to Anglo-Saxon individualism (Hampden-Turner and Trompenaars 1993). It has also been claimed that German managers and staff have a strong sense of identity with, and loyalty to, their companies, and that this is reciprocated (Calori and De Woot 1994).

In short, although the picture of German management practice is not so clear-cut as that of American and Japanese management, its main contours comprise:

- long-term business orientation;
- tendency to production improvement rather than short-term profit distribution;
- often a fairly long-term orientation towards employment;
- strong technical and production emphasis;
- substantial investment in training;
- tendency for managers and staff to remain within one functional area;

- formalization, especially emphasis on operational planning, procedures, and rules;
- preference for participative collective action.

French management practice

Hampden-Turner and Trompenaars (1993: 333) comment that 'France defies easy categorization. It requires a sense of irony, for which the French are famous, to make sense of seemingly contradictory results'. Contradictions exist in French history and culture between equality and hierarchy, liberty and dependence, fraternity and vested interests ('droits acquis') (Barsoux and Lawrence 1990).

If this is correct, it might prove equally difficult to identify a characteristically French set of management practices. French companies are, comments Sorge (1993), a contradictory mixture of feudal-paternal and rational-legal-bureaucratic in atmosphere. Lane (1989) similarly concludes that French managements apply two difficult-to-harmonize control strategies in combination: personal centralized control and bureaucratic control. French managers and employees appear to welcome a clear-cut line of authority within which to work, and they score quite highly on Hofstede's scale of power distance (Hofstede 1991). Others have argued, nevertheless, that they are not authoritarian in the sense of maintaining personal distance between organizational levels (Hampden-Turner and Trompenaars 1993; d'Iribarne 1994).

Actions are taken and decisions made on a relatively individualistic basis, though decision-making is concentrated towards the top of hierarchies (Horowitz 1980; Hickson and Pugh 1995; Szarka 1996). Acquisitions tend to be based on strategic rather than short-term financial considerations. This emphasis is often phrased in a quasi-military language in which the contestants adopt, by analogy, the stance of the great generals and marshals (Barsoux and Lawrence 1990). This is, however, the strategy of personal leadership rather than long-range planning, to which French companies are averse (Lane 1989).

Research by Maurice et al. (1980), comparing French with West German and UK manufacturing firms, found that in France there are usually more levels in the hierarchy, and there is a high lateral differentiation of organizations into departments, work groups, and jobs. French hierarchies tend to be more top heavy, with up to twice as many supervisors and managers as in German firms. Below the top leaders, the French *cadres* form a distinct managerial status group in French industry, clearly demarcated from ordinary employees. Calori and De Woot (1994) add to this hierarchical characterization by noting that French companies have a far higher number of organizational levels and a lower level of participation than German or other northern European countries. Tall French hierarchies bring with them large pay differentials, with correspondingly higher levels of industrial grievance (Gallie 1983).

French organizations also have more non-managerial white-collar specialists in either commercial-cum-administrative or technical functions, which reflects a tendency to separate technical, planning, administrative, and supervisory tasks from execution and operational ones (Sorge 1993). In order to manage this segmented and complex operation efficiently, French organizations tend to make extensive use of written rules, instructions, and communications in a 'bureaucratic' fashion (cf. Crozier 1964). As a result, the French, Sorge (1993) claims, are very good at producing a high-quality homogeneous product on a large scale, but less good where flexibility is required. Despite this extensive use of the written word, there is some evidence to suggest that French managers are not so rigid in their adherence to rules as are German managers. Horovitz (1980) suggests that the French use procedures as a 'policing device' rather than for control in the cybernetic sense. Moreover, d'Iribarne (1994) maintains that the internal differentiation of French organizations is based not so much on bureaucracy as on a more traditional sense of occupational stratification and its attendant rights and duties.

With the qualifications offered, we may summarize the management practice particularly associated with French companies as comprising:

- strategic rather than financial orientation, though not necessarily based on long-term planning;
- tall organizational hierarchies, with a relatively large managerial component;
- high degree of specialization;
- widespread use of written media;
- individual rather than collective working and decision-making, though the latter tends to be centralized;
- combination of personal centralized and bureaucratic control strategies.

UK management practice

There are considerable sectoral differences in British management practices. Partly because of the more pluralistic institutional context in the UK, there are greater variations in, for instance, training and human resource management policies across firms and industries than might be expected in, for example, Germany. Also the period since the mid-1980s has witnessed considerable changes in UK management practice, under pressure from international competition and encouraged by government policies under Margaret Thatcher and her successors. The following is therefore a necessarily broad-brush characterization.

UK management practice has tended to reflect the fact that industry, in particular engineering, carries low status in Britain and is supposedly conservative (Lane 1997). This has led to a low emphasis on quality, at least until world competition made quality a necessity, and to a lower level of education amongst British managers generally when compared with their counterparts in other industrial countries (Handy et al. 1988). The dominant influence of the City has encouraged a short-term financial emphasis rather than a strategic one, and the short-termism of UK management has been frequently cited, both in academic studies (e.g. Lane 1995) and by those working in industry (cf. Marsh 1995).

While UK management practice is said to share some features with that of the USA and other so-called 'Anglo-Saxon' countries (e.g. Hickson and Pugh 1995), others have identified distinct UK features. Systems and standard operating procedures (SOPs) are less significant than in the USA (Lawrence 1996b). This gives rise to a relative informality in communication and reporting within UK companies, including looser control over subsidiaries, even to the extent that ambiguity and 'fudging' are permitted in order to maintain personal comfort and avoid confrontation. Lane (1997) comments that while British firms tend to have more written operating rules than German firms, these are less likely to be followed. The committee is the main vehicle for drawing people together and making formal decisions, but this is not usually as task oriented as the US system of task forces or teams. Compared with US companies, less faith tends to be placed in the value of analysis and planning within UK management. Strategy is regarded as an inherent and emergent rather than as an objectively analytical phenomenon (Lawrence 1996c).

There is a relatively high level of mobility among UK managers, both between organizations and between functions within a company. Nicholson and West (1988) found that about 75 per cent of all job changes among UK managers involved a change of functional area. UK management practice, in this way and others, evidences a belief in the virtues of generalism rather than specialism, a feature which contrasts particularly with German practice (Lane 1997). In many companies, this is reflected in relatively large general management superstructures (Lawrence 1996b). Another feature is that, in recent years, increasing emphasis has been placed on performance-related pay in the UK (Kessler 1996).

The management practice particularly associated with British companies thus comprises:

- short-term financial orientation;
- large general management superstructures;

- fairly low integration of corporate and subsidiary levels;
- low level of functional specialization;
- high mobility of managers between functions;
- use of formal meetings, especially committees;
- interactive informality—limited formal and paper-based reporting;
- limited importance attached to systems and SOPs;
- increasing emphasis on performance-related pay.

A note on comparisons from China

The considerable investment by foreign firms of various nationalities in China during the past twenty years provides a common ground on which to compare both their practices and their insistence in applying them. Evidence from foreign joint ventures in China supports some of the distinctions that we have drawn between the management approaches of firms with different nationality. For instance, Firth (1996) found that the nationality of the foreign partner is a significant factor affecting the use of management accounting techniques in Sino-foreign joint ventures. US partners, compared to their counterparts from Japan, are more insistent on implementing accounting techniques and systems that match those of their domestic operations. Ireland (1991) found that US firms make a significant effort to introduce their formalized management approach to joint ventures in China, whereas Japanese firms are more cautious about imposing their own practices. European ventures in China tend to adopt a mixed management approach in which their styles and those of Chinese partners are blended. Thus, firms of different nationality may differ not only in the practices they introduce but also in their insistence that their own approaches be adopted by their affiliates.

A note of caution, however, comes from comparisons that Child and Yan (2001) made between American, Japanese, European, and overseas Chinese joint ventures in China. They found that there were few effects on joint venture strategy and management practice stemming from parent company nationality, whereas the impact of whether those parent companies were multinationals or not was wide ranging.

Summary

Table 5.1. summarizes and compares the key management practices that the review of research suggests are particularly associated with the five nationalities considered. It has to be stressed again that some evidence is incomplete and contradictory, especially for French and German practice.

Table 5.1. Summary of management practices associated with firm nationality

	Strategic orientation	Organization	Formalization	Integration of subsidiaries[a]	Job features	Rewards
USA	Short term, financial	Tall but recently delayered; delegated management	High formalization, advanced systems, use of planning	High, via reporting and other systems	High mobility	Performance related
Japan	Long term, strategic; close network links	Centralized, but participative; stress on teamwork and normative consensus	Low, but with systems for training and knowledge-sharing	High, via secondment and personal contact	Low mobility; long-term employment commitment; strong training emphasis	Based on seniority and superior's evaluation; low differentials
Germany	Long term, especially towards production improvement	Flat, stress on formal position combined with participation	Officially high, but relatively flexible process	Evidence not clear; probably medium	Low mobility; emphasis on specialism and qualification	Largely skill based

| France | Strategic, but not necessarily long term | Tall and stratified; low participation | High; bureaucratic | Evidence suggests high | Medium mobility; emphasis on specialism | High differentials based on hierarchical position |
| UK | Short term, financial | Large management component | Medium; procedures and plans followed flexibly | Low to medium | High mobility; emphasis on generalism rather than specialism | Increasingly performance related |

[a] In the early stages of internationalization, European MNCs tended to rely on informal controls over foreign affiliates, based on personal relationships and being implicit rather than formalized. However, as the number, age, size, and geographical dispersal of their foreign subsidiaries increased, enhanced integration through explicit formal control mechanisms became more apparent (Hedlund 1986).

6

Scope and Methods

This chapter describes the scope of the research undertaken for this book and the methods employed. The initial aim was to study a sufficiently large number of acquisitions to obtain a broad picture of the nature of acquisition by companies from different countries. The research then moved on to developing a series of more detailed case studies to get a better understanding of the processes and contingent circumstances behind these acquisitions. A combination of quantitative and qualitative methods aims to provide a credible picture of the impact of foreign companies on their British acquisitions.

Research that seeks to explore the post-acquisition management of UK companies by their foreign parents faces problems both of scope and method. Can the extent of the population of relevant acquisitions be determined and how can it be sampled? Once a sample has been obtained, how should the potential impact on acquired companies be measured or assessed? In the case of the present investigation, both sampling and measurement pose particular problems, though they are not insuperable. Each offers some lessons for conducting research of this nature.

Scope

Population

It would have been very convenient for this investigation if there had been some easily accessible, reliable record of all UK companies acquired by foreign parents. All that would have remained would have been to decide which of them to include in the research sample and how the study was to be carried out. Unfortunately, such a conveniently available record does not exist. No official comprehensive records of acquisitions of UK companies by foreign companies are publicly available, nor is there any unofficial set of records that can be guaranteed to be comprehensive.

The solution adopted in this research has been in the first instance to try to identify as many acquisitions of UK companies by foreign companies as possible. The sources used in identifying relevant acquisitions include the

British press and Reuters Textline database, activities recorded by the Invest in Britain Bureau of the DTI, and those recorded by the Central Statistical Office. Publications such as *Acquisitions Monthly* were also consulted.

While this multi-pronged approach to identifying relevant acquisitions is unlikely to have captured all of them, it is reasonably certain that a representative sample of relevant acquisitions has been isolated as a starting point for the study. It is worth pointing out, however, that the eclectic nature of the sources used to identify relevant acquisitions and the ensuing difficulties in making contact emphasize that, in future, it would be of great assistance if some official, comprehensive database of UK acquisitions were to be available.

Survey sample

The aim of the present research is to study the impact on UK management practices resulting from foreign acquisition, with reference to the countries principally supplying inward FDI. The first step was therefore to determine which countries were the largest sources of inward FDI over the ten years investigated between the mid-1980s and mid-1990s.

Table 6.1 summarizes the amount of direct investment into the UK over this period, as estimated by the DTI's Invest in Britain Bureau. Although the UK has been a major host economy for inward FDI throughout the twentieth century (Jones 1993), the scale of inward FDI since the mid-1980s has been large and growing. In recent years, the UK has been the most popular destination in Europe for overseas investors. In 1996, foreign acquisitions of UK firms exceeded the total value for all other European Union countries combined and was topped worldwide as a takeover target only by the USA (KPMG 1997).

In most years during that period, companies from the USA, Japan, Germany, and France have been the largest national sources of FDI into the UK and mostly in that rank order. In certain years, countries such as Canada and the Netherlands have exceeded the value of FDI from one or more of the top four countries, but this has not been sustained year on year. In the years shown, the proportion of total inward FDI accounted for by the top four countries has been overwhelming, ranging between 70.8 per cent and 80.9 per cent of the total.

In view of this history, it was decided to confine the investigation to acquisitions made by US, Japanese, German, and French companies. Furthermore, only acquisitions occurring in the period between 1 January 1985 and 31 December 1994 were sampled. This procedure had the advantage, first, of including only FDI cases where reasonable recall of the pre- and post-acquisition situations was possible. Secondly, it meant that only acquisitions

Table 6.1.   Main sources of direct investment into the UK, 1986–1995 (£m)

	1986/7	1988/9	1990/1	1992/3	1994/5
USA	594.2	1,502.4	1,002.3	1,213.1	2,876.9
Japan	443.9	293.9	1,085.0	109.1	1,156.7
Germany	58.3	174.9	544.4	402.3	1,535.4
France	80.9	215.5	198.8	59.2	1,188.2
TOTAL	1,537.7	2,891.2	3,876.9	2,520.2	8,351.3
% of total	76.6	75.6	73.0	70.8	80.9

Note: Countries of origin: years to March (£m).

Source: Invest in Britain Bureau.

more than two years old were included, so that changes would have had a chance to be implemented. The addition of the UK as one of the acquirer countries allowed for the possibility of distinguishing between general acquisition effects and those specifically associated with the foreign nationality of acquirers.

A collation of data from several sources indicates the number of FDI-related activities (projects) by US, Japanese, German, and French companies. The sources used are activities recorded in the British press and recorded on the Reuters Textline database, activities recorded by the Invest in Britain Bureau of the DTI, and activities recorded by the Central Statistical Office. An analysis from these sources was conducted by the authors in 1995, covering the period 1 January 1985 to 31 December 1994. This identified a total of 1,422 independent activities during the period which took the form of new acquisitions, joint venture formations, collaborations, or consortia involving foreign investment, but excluded greenfield developments or expansions of existing facilities.[1] The proportion of these activities accounted for by the top four foreign-investing countries is shown in Table 6.2.

A dominant 79 per cent of all deals involved merger or acquisition activity (N=1,122), and a further 10 per cent the purchase of a majority or minority stake. Thus it would seem that, whatever the evidence for the fast growth of genuinely consensual alliances, powerful companies still prefer outright purchase or an equity stake in their partner, if they can achieve it. Of the other

---

[1] These sources are unlikely to be comprehensive. In particular, smaller deals are likely to go unnoticed by the British press and unrecorded by the DTI and CSO. The actual level of activity will therefore certainly be higher than that captured by the above sources. However, it is believed that the relative size of the number of activities by type, nationality, and industry will reflect the overall picture, and these are the only data readily accessible to researchers.

Table 6.2. Proportion of inward FDI activities by leading national sources

Nationality of foreign investor	Number of activities[a]	Percentage of total
USA	861	60.5
Japan	240	16.9
Germany	176	12.4
France	139	9.8

[a] Excludes 6 consortia which involved partners from more than one of the four countries.

cooperative forms, joint ventures accounted for 5.5 per cent of all deals, collaborations 3.4 per cent, and consortia 2.1 per cent. The relative importance of the types by value is not known, since the value figures for the deals were rarely declared in the press. However, the commonly held impression that US companies prefer wherever possible to have an ownership rather than an alliance relationship seems to be borne out by the figures. Eighty-six per cent of the US deals were acquisitions; but only 75 per cent of the German deals, 68 per cent of the Japanese, and 60 per cent of the French.

Most categories of industry have been affected by the influx of FDI, but the largest industries by number of deals have been in information technology, mechanical and instrument engineering, the financial services industry, business services, and chemical and pharmaceutical industries. Although individual countries show some differences in their sector patterns of investment, these differences are smaller than the similarities. The trend of investment over the decade surveyed is, on the whole, similar for the four inward FDI countries surveyed. It built steadily during the late 1980s only to decline sharply as world recession forced companies to concentrate on their domestic survival, and the declining level of world trade reduced the attractiveness of opportunities for foreign investment. The post-1990 fall was most marked among Japanese investments. It is the deals recorded in the database summarized above that provide the opportunity to establish the nature and extent of the impact of foreign management on UK management practice.

The list of 1,122 acquisitions identified was subsequently augmented by 148 further relevant acquisitions from data in the journal *Acquisitions Monthly*; the same journal also furnished information on UK–UK acquisitions during the period of study.

From the list of acquisitions, a nationally stratified sample of fifty companies was selected for use in the pilot survey. The response rate from this mailing was 36 per cent which, together with comparable data from the ten initial interview-administered questionnaires, gave 28 usable questionnaires.

The split among nationalities of these replies was Japanese nine, US five, French five, German nine. The success of this stage prompted the move to a fuller survey.

As mentioned above, there were many companies in the population for which it proved impossible to gain sufficiently precise identification, despite considerable searching. There had, for example, often been name changes to parents and/or subsidiaries. It was eventually possible, however, to mail questionnaires to a further 844 companies, of which 576 had US, Japanese, French, and German acquirers, and 268 had UK acquirers. We requested that a named manager should complete the questionnaires. We normally approached the managing director of the acquired subsidiary in order to obtain a view on change across the full range of management practices, or another senior manager if the MD did not have sufficient experience of the period since acquisition. The response, plus the pilot questionnaires and the comparable data from the initial ten questionnaires, gave a total of 201 usable questionnaire replies, or 22.2 per cent of all administered. The usable questionnaires were split amongst the nationalities as follows: US 69, Japanese 29, French 32, German 21, UK 50. It is worth noting that the overall reply rate to the questionnaire mailing was 41.8 per cent. In addition to the 201 usable replies, we received 40 refusals and 112 replies indicating that the company for some reason fell outside the scope of the intended sample. The unusable replies came from companies acquired outside the time period, or of nationality other than one of the five in question, or which proved not to involve a straightforward acquisition. Their high number again illustrates the difficulties of identifying relevant acquisitions from publicly available data.

Checks for bias

Checks were made for potential sources of bias that could distort comparisons by nationality of acquiring company. Respondents divided fairly evenly between those who had joined the subsidiary before acquisition (52 per cent) and those who joined after (48 per cent). As expected, there was a tendency for those appointed after acquisition to perceive both that more change had taken place and that the parent company had exerted greater influence. They also tended to take a more positive view of post-acquisition profitability, though not sales. This bias was, however, only significant in 28 per cent of items for the strength of change, 18 per cent of items for the direction of change, and 12 per cent of items for acquirer influence. It accounted on average for a difference of 0.18 within the 7.0 range of possible scores on the scale of post-acquisition profitability. There was some skew in the distribution of pre- and post-acquisition appointees by acquirer nationality, with Japanese, French, and UK acquirers having larger numbers of post-acquisition appointees responding than the norm. This means that the assessments of change and acquirer influence may be somewhat inflated for these nationalities.

Other checks revealed that there was no association between acquirer nationality and two other potential sources of bias: subsidiary profitability at time of acquisition, and size of acquired company. While acquirer nationality was not evenly distributed across sectors classified as high-technology manufacturing, low-technology manufacturing, and service, sector itself was not a predictor of variations in either change or acquirer influence, except for certain operations management techniques which did not apply to all service companies. US acquirers tended to have fewer years elapsing between acquisition and response to the questionnaire compared with other nationalities, but this time lapse did not correlate with reports on the direction or strength of change, with perceived acquirer influence on change, or with reported post-acquisition performance. There was also no bias between responses to the pilot questionnaire and the full questionnaire regarding integration, of either strategic or operational control, the changes that had taken place, or acquiring company influence on them. Finally, although only 84 per cent of respondents answered the post-acquisition performance evaluation questions, there was no association between response/non-response to these questions and their reports about the changes that had taken place or about acquiring company influence on them.

Case studies

In addition to the questionnaire survey, a series of interviews was conducted with senior managers of acquired companies in order to provide a more detailed understanding of the processes and contingent circumstances behind these acquisitions. This provided useful confirmation of a number of the survey findings as well as illustrations of them.

The same list of potentially relevant examples of FDI prepared for the questionnaire survey, with data from the Central Statistical Office, Reuters, Predicasts, DTI, the journal *Acquisitions Monthly*, and other sources, was used. Interviews were held with companies selected from among those acquired by a US, French, German, or Japanese parent and providing usable questionnaire replies. Forty out of seventy-nine companies asked (50.6 per cent) agreed to interview, and were divided equally among the four nationalities. Ten of the interviews were those carried out as part of the pilot process. Interviewed companies were spread over the whole of the United Kingdom, with the exception of Wales and Northern Ireland. Seventy per cent of companies interviewed were in the manufacturing sector and 30 per cent in service industries. The average numbers of employees of the subsidiary companies replying to the survey and of the subsidiary companies interviewed are shown in Table 6.3. There are no statistically significant differences between the two sets of averages.

In order to minimize bias that could result from the range of interviewees selected, the interviews focused on change events and minimized more judgemental and qualitative questions. The persons interviewed were the managing director, chief executive, or chairman of the subsidiary in thirty-three of the forty companies. Only three of these had been appointed from the parent company. It should also be noted that thirty-eight of the forty interviewees were British and therefore that the research must be viewed within a British frame of reference.

The sample was made deliberately heterogeneous in nature in order to ensure that, if national patterns of behaviour did emerge from such a sample, there might be a prima facie conjecture made that such behaviour had some consistency over a wide range of contingencies. The range of industries covered in the survey was extremely wide and this was also a characteristic of the case study sample, as shown in Table 6.4.

Table 6.3. Survey: average number of employees in companies surveyed and interviewed

Parent nationality	Of companies replying to survey	Of companies interviewed	t-test p value
US	681 (69)	1,499 (10)	0.39
French	593 (32)	983 (10)	0.46
German	441 (21)	208 (10)	0.30
Japanese	628 (29)	970 (10)	0.51
OVERALL	618 (151)	931 (40)	0.25

Note: Figures in parentheses are the numbers of companies participating.

Table 6.4. Case studies: spread of interviewed acquisitions between sectors of industry

	US	Japanese	French	German
High-tech	3	3	2	2
Services	4	1	3	1
Manufacturing	3	6	5	7

Among the case studies, Japanese and German companies acquired more traditional manufacturing companies and US and French companies more service companies, but all three categories were adequately covered to mini-mize the risk of skew in the results.

The companies interviewed are thus reasonably representative of the sample surveyed using questionnaires save for the exclusion of UK companies acquired by UK companies. These latter were not included in the selection of case studies since the cross-national interactions occurring in the transfer process between companies intended for study would obviously not be present in UK–UK cases.

The prior international experience of the acquirers varied from high to negligible, the size of the acquirers from medium-sized domestic companies to major MNCs, and the condition of the acquirees from strongly loss making to very profitable. Furthermore, the risk that MNCs would import practices from experience gained in other countries, and thus distort the attempt to identify specifically national practices amongst the acquirers as suggested by Buckley and Ghauri (1999), was minimized by ensuring that MNCs were not overly dominant in the case study sample, as shown in Table 6.5. In the survey sample, no more than 8 per cent of acquirers appeared in the *Fortune Magazine Global 100* although many more of course did in the *Fortune Magazine Global 500*. A further factor, however, is that almost all of these companies were MNCs with recognizable base-country origins. Thus Mitsubishi is clearly a Japanese MNC and Siemens a German MNC. The strong influence of the management practices of their country of origin can therefore be readily assumed.

A further possible distorting factor might be the variety of different motives for making the acquisitions. Dunning (1993*a*: 56–61) suggests four principal motives for foreign acquisition: (1) resource-seeking; (2) market access; (3) efficiency; and (4) strategic asset- or new capability-seeking. This was also investigated in the interviews, and it was judged that the strongest motive for the acquisitions concerned was the desire for greater market access, usually as part of a globalization strategy (Table 6.6). Another important motive, how-ever, was the acquisition of strategic assets and new capabilities. Furthermore, some motives could only be categorized as 'other', such as the purchase of

Table 6.5. Case studies: spread of acquirers between MNCs and nationals

	US	Japanese	French	German
MNCs	4	5	7	4
National companies	6	5	3	6

Table 6.6.   Case studies:[a] motives for acquisitions amongst companies interviewed

	US	Japanese	French	German
Resource-seeking	0	1	2	1
New market access	5	8	7	6
Efficiency	0	0	1	2
Gain strategic assets or new capabilities	4	1	5	5
Other	2	1	0	0

[a] The total exceeds 40 since some acquisitions were judged to have more than one motive.

a UK perfume company by a US company for clearly idiosyncratic reasons of the CEO.

Thus the forty case study companies covered a wide range of manufacturing and service industries, the prior international experience of the acquirers varied from high to negligible, the size of the acquirers varied from medium-sized domestic companies to major MNC, and the condition of the acquirees varied from strongly loss making to very profitable.

Method

Having identified a sample of acquisitions to study, the second problem is how to study that sample. Here the dilemma is the eternal one facing any management research; whether quantitative or qualitative methods provide a better window on reality. The present research has tried to reconcile the two methodologies to some extent by including both qualitative and quantitative elements of analysis. Considerations of time and expense have necessarily meant, however, that the number of companies studied using quantitative postal questionnaires greatly exceeds those studied by means of interviews conducted on site. Interviews with companies have also been necessarily limited in their extent. Nonetheless, the interviews do provide a useful illustration and confirmation of the results of the overall survey.

The survey

The main instrument for collecting the quantitative data in the survey was a postal questionnaire. A draft of this questionnaire was developed through interviews in ten companies and, in the light of this feedback, some minor changes were made. The resulting schedule was pilot tested on a sample of fifty companies. Piloting did not indicate the need for any substantial modifications, and the questionnaire was then used in the main survey of acquired companies.

The questionnaire aimed to address the range of nationality-specific topics identified in the previous discussion of national management characteristics, as well as areas where change might be expected following an acquisition. The headings and examples of subjects covered in questions are as shown in Table 6.7.

In order to assess performance since acquisition, respondents were asked whether, to the best of their knowledge, their company's position vis-à-vis its main competitors had improved or worsened since its acquisition with respect to its profitability and sales. They answered along seven-point scales.

In addition, respondents were asked some more open-ended questions to identify the greatest changes they perceived had taken place and that had the most impact on the company. Information was also collected about the profitability of the company when taken over, the size and growth of sales and turnover, senior managerial appointments, and some basic details regarding the respondent's job title and time spent with the company.

A key feature of the questions was the distinction between the direction and strength of post-acquisition change and the degree of influence of the new parent company in bringing about that change. There were forty-eight items on change and forty on parent influence. Most questions occurred as pairs of questions relating the change and influence involved in a particular issue since acquisition. Both were scored using Likert-type scales. For the degree of parent influence these ranged from 0 representing 'none' to 5 representing 'very great' influence. The scale used for change ranged from -3 to $+3$, giving

Table 6.7. Examples of questionnaire subjects

Headings	Examples of subjects covered by questions
Company philosophy	Style and culture, strategic vs. financial orientation
Strategy	Prime orientation, time horizon
Organization structure	Hierarchy, basic configuration
Control	Key positions, decision-making
Communication	Openness, formality
Finance	Financial planning, financial control
Human resource management	Promotion, training, job rotation
Sales and marketing	Distribution, marketing information
R&D/product development	Team-based vs. sequential
Operations	Use of IT, operations management techniques
Procurement	Multi- vs. single sourcing

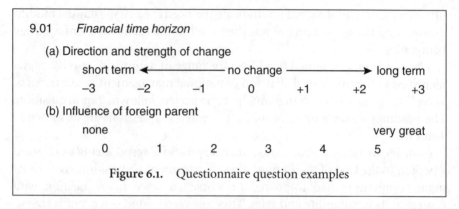

9.01   *Financial time horizon*

(a) Direction and strength of change

short term ◄─────────── no change ───────────► long term

   −3   −2   −1   0   +1   +2   +3

(b) Influence of foreign parent

   none   very great

    0   1   2   3   4   5

Figure 6.1.   Questionnaire question examples

seven possible replies. An example is the question relating to Financial Time Horizon shown in Fig. 6.1.

To check for potential bias caused by the association of positive scores with particular replies, some pairs of replies were reversed after the pilot survey. There was no significant[2] difference found in the results compared to those of the pilot survey replies.

Case studies

Site visits were made to all but one of the case study companies. Most information was collected through interview with a senior manager in the acquired company who was present during the period of post-acquisition change and who also had a broad knowledge of all relevant events. The interview schedule itself covered a wide range of management practices. Background information on the story behind the acquisition was also gathered. Respondents were asked open-ended questions about which changes they felt had been the greatest and had had the most impact on the company. The interviews involved questions under the following headings:

1. General background to the acquisition: reasons and consequences.
2. Background to major changes and influences:
     2.1. discussion of two/three major areas of change;
     2.2. patterns of influence;
     2.3. integration.
3. Impact of acquisition on performance:
     3.1. What have been the main benefits of the acquisition?

---

[2] In this book the word 'significant' refers to *statistical* significance, namely the probability that a relationship has not occurred by chance. Unless noted otherwise, significant means a p value of 0.05 or less.

3.2. What have been the main disadvantages of the acquisition?

3.3. How has the acquisition contributed to profitability and growth?

In each case the interviews lasted for at least an hour and each was tape recorded with the interviewees' permission. Table 6.8 summarizes key features of the people interviewed.

Details of the companies interviewed, their parent companies, industries, and the condition of the acquired company on acquisition, as well as the codes by which they are referred to throughout this book, are given in Tables 6.9 to 6.12. Where a distinction needs to be drawn between the UK company that is acquired and the foreign parent company, the former is designated by the suffix -UK.

It is appreciated that single-interview qualitative research has an inherent risk of bias (Bowman and Ambrosini 1997) and, if conducted with executives at different levels in the hierarchy, may give inconsistent results where judgements are required. The status of the chosen interviewee was highly consistent. Moreover, the results of the interviews can be compared with those of the questionnaire for the same company to provide some confirmation.

Table 6.8. Case studies: interviewee and company characteristics

No. of interviewees	French	German	Japanese	US	Total	Per cent of total
Subsidiary CEO/chair	7	9	8	9	33	83
Other directors	3	1	2	1	7	17
TOTAL	10	10	10	10	40	100
Appointed from parent	0	3	0	2	5	13
Appointed from subsidiary	10	7	10	8	35	88
Joined company before acquisition	8	7	8	7	30	75
Average no. of years since acquisition	7.4	5.6	7.2	5.5	6.4	
Average no. of subsidiary employees	983	212	922	1,213	833	

Table 6.9. Case studies: US acquisitions

Acquirer	Acquiree	Acquiree industry	Acquiree condition
US1 Major MNC (H)	Small family co.	Medical implants	Just profitable
US2 Large national retailer (L)	Perfumier	Cosmetics	Losses
US3 Major transport co. (H)	4 local transport cos.	Courier	Losses
US4 Major MNC (H)	Specialist Mfg. co.	Automobiles	Losses
US5 Major int'l. consultancy (H)	National IT consultancy	IT consultancy	Profitable
US6 Large national high-tech co. (L)	High-tech defence co.	Electronics	Profitable
US7 Major MNC (H)	National FM co.	Facilities Mgt.	Profitable
US8 Major MNC (H)	Small Mfg. co.	Synthetic fibres	Just profitable
US9 Large national co. (H)	Specialist start-up	Insurance	Profitable
US10 Large int'l. co. (H)	Small national co.	Engineering	Just profitable

Notes: International experience: H = high, M = medium, L = low; information gleaned from the interviews.

Table 6.10. Case studies: Japanese acquisitions

Acquirer	Acquiree	Acquiree industry	Acquiree condition
J1 Major national co. (L)	Small family co.	Engineering	Losses
J2 Major national co. (L)	Ex-sub. of MNC	Engineering	Losses
J3 Major national co. (L)	Old branded co.	Household goods	Losses
J4 Major MNC (M)	National branded co.	Computers	Losses
J5 Large domestic bank (L)	City merchant bank	Banking	Losses
J6 MNC (H)	Medium Eng. co.	Engineering	Just profitable
J7 MNC (H)	National branded co.	Men's clothing	Just profitable
J8 Major int'l. co. (M)	Ex-Scandinavian sub co.	Polymers	Losses
J9 Major MNC (H)	Old manufacturing co.	Engineering	Just profitable
J10 Large national family co. (L)	Old ex-sub. of US	Pharmaceuticals	Just profitable

Table 6.11. Case studies: French acquisitions

Acquirer	Acquiree	Acquiree industry	Acquiree condition
F1 Major MNC (M)	2 small private cos.	Defence	Losses
F2 Large MN bank (H)	City firm	Banking	Losses
F3 Small Parisian bank (L)	City firm	Banking	Just profitable
F4 Major domestic co. (L)	Domestic co.	Engineering	Profitable
F5 Major MNC (H)	Small domestic co.	Marketing	Just profitable
F6 MNC (H)	IT consultancy co.	IT consultancy	Profitable
F7 MNC (H)	Brand name co.	Adhesives	Losses
F8 Major MNC (H)	Regional co.	Water	Profitable
F9 Family co. (L)	Ex-sub. of UK plc	Pharmaceuticals	Profitable
F10 Major MNC (H)	2 regional cos.	Water	Profitable

Table 6.12. Case studies: German acquisitions

Acquirer	Acquiree	Acquiree industry	Acquiree condition
G1 Major MNC (H)	Family co.	Pharmaceutical	Profitable
G2 Large national co. (L)	Small regional co.	Engineering	Losses
G3 Major *Landesbank* (H)	City bank	Banking	Just profitable
G4 Major MNC (H)	Specialist Manf'r.	High-tech medical	Just profitable
G5 Major MNC (M)	Truck agency	Automobiles	Losses
G6 MNC (H)	Small family co.	Fire security	Just profitable
G7 Medium national co. (L)	Small local co.	Furniture	Losses
G8 Medium national co. (L)	Med. national	Trailers	Profitable
G9 Major MNC (H)	Small family co.	Chemicals	Profitable
G10 Domestic co. (L)	Small national co.	Construction	Profitable

Summary

The questionnaire-based survey and the interview-based case study research enabled a wide and credible picture to be built up of the impact of foreign companies on their new British subsidiaries. As the results presented in following chapters show, the data collection methods used have enabled many statistically sound conclusions to be reached and supplemented with representative examples drawn from the interview programme. Together with the existing literature on the subject, this facilitates the successful triangulation of the field of study. Moreover, the case studies permit a more in-depth appreciation of the processes of post-acquisition change and the factors impacting on this.

7

Trends in Post-acquisition Management

This chapter analyses trends in post-acquisition management practice according to the nationality of the acquiring company. It draws on evidence from both sources described in Chapter 6, namely the survey of 201 acquisitions and the more qualitative interviews in a subset of 40 of these acquisitions.

Acquisitions as levers for change

Companies acquired by French and US companies generally reported the greatest degree of post-acquisition change, and those acquired by German companies the least change. The differences in the reported levels of influence which acquiring companies from different national groups had on the changes reported in response to acquisitions were quite marked in a number of ways. French and US acquirers exercised significantly more influence on their new subsidiaries than Japanese and German acquirers. In certain areas there were major differences between parent company influence, which were very unlikely to have occurred by chance. In human resource management and marketing, US acquirers tended to exercise the greatest influence, closely followed by French acquirers. In the areas of organization, supply, and strategy, French acquirers tended to have exercised the greatest influence, closely followed by US parent companies. In each of these areas, Japanese and German acquirers exercised less influence. National differences in influence for company philosophy, communications, and operations were smaller, and were more likely to have occurred by chance; that is, the results did not reach the 95 per cent level of statistical confidence.

The acquisition effect supposes that the very fact of acquisition in itself has a significant impact on changes in management practice through the influence exercised by the acquiring company. Managers in the subsidiaries generally reported that being acquired had been a lever for change. Table 7.1 lists the correlations between aggregations of the moduli of post-acquisition change reported by respondents and their perceptions of the parent

Table 7.1. Correlations between the overall level of change and reported influence of acquiring company[a]

Category	N	Correlation	p
Total sample	124	0.52	0.000
US acquisitions	43	0.58	0.000
French acquisitions	19	0.66	0.001
German acquisitions	9	0.58	0.050
Japanese acquisitions	17	0.42	0.047
UK acquisitions	36	0.45	0.003

[a] Overall level of change = sum of the moduli of change on all items except for job rotation, type of planning, R&D/development of products and services, and operations. Influence of acquiring company = sum of influence scores for the same items.

company's influence on each change. The indicators of both change and influence relate to all those areas of management covered by the survey except for development of new products and services, and operations.[1]

Across the sample as a whole, approximately one-quarter of the variation in the degree of post-acquisition change was ascribed to the influence of the foreign parent. However, this proportion varied considerably according to the acquiring company's nationality. As Table 7.1 indicates, the correlations between perceived parent company influence and the degree of change in the acquired firm were noticeably higher in the case of US, French, and German companies than they were among companies with Japanese and UK parents.

Investigation of the reported acquisition and transfer of practice effects together requires a closer look at the data with reference to three specific questions. First, were there some areas of management practice in which little change was reported, suggesting that these may be relatively immune from either effect? Second, were there some areas in which changes were reported that were similar across acquirer nationalities? This would suggest that the very fact of the acquisition taking place acted as a vehicle for promoting general trends in management fashion. Third, were there areas of practice in which acquisition appears to have had an impact, and where the practices being transferred clearly differed by nationality of acquirer?

---

[1] Some participating companies, particularly in the service sector, did not regard the questions on development and operations as relevant, and these questions have been omitted in order to avoid losing too many cases from the analysis. Other cases with any missing data have also been omitted from this analysis.

Limits to the nationality effect

Little change

While, as Haspeslagh and Jemison (1991) found in their research, there were few acquisitions which had a total lack of integration with the new parent, there were several examples where the acquisition of a new subsidiary led to little change, as shown in Table 7.2.

Managers in the companies where this occurred suggested three main reasons for a reluctance on the part of the new owner to impose its presence on its acquisition. One was that some acquiring companies assumed that their new subsidiary understood its business better than the parent and so left it alone. The second was where the company was acquired for reasons unrelated to the mission or corporate strategy of the acquiring company; for instance, companies acquired as a by-product of the acquisition of the company's former parent group. The third reason was where the acquiring company recognized that it could learn from the new subsidiary in specific areas, was concerned to preserve the relevant skills in the subsidiary, and was therefore not willing to take the risk involved in meddling with the management of its new acquisition.

For example, a major German safety equipment manufacturer acquired a small entrepreneurial firm in the same line of business. Unusually the entrepreneur remained with the company, the MD of the German parent saying: 'We don't want you to change. Stay the way you are, because you have the ability to move in a market place more than we can.' A high-tech UK instrument company acquired by a German competitor with a larger global presence was also left alone by its new parent.

Table 7.2.   Areas of management practice: little reported post-acquisition change[a]

Job rotation of managers between different functions
Scientific or technically qualified staff as a percentage of total employment
Emphasis on formal qualifications for selection and advancement
Employment philosoph—recruitment and termination: short term vs. long term
Approach to promotion: slow vs. rapid
Methods of distribution: subcontracted vs. internal
Customer involvement in marketing decisions
Emphasis on managing the total supply chain
Degree of outsourcing
Range of suppliers (single source/multi-source)

[a] In these areas of management practice, the average modulus of change was less than 1 on a scale from 0 to 3.

Where little change occurred, this often appeared to be encouraged by the acceptance and trust that the subsidiary's management gained in the eyes of the new parent's management. An overall lack of change following an acquisition may thus be due to several factors which range from plain ignorance or apathy to a shrewd appreciation that the new subsidiary has much that it can teach the parent if it is 'preserved' sufficiently to allow the skill transfer.

Another reason for little change resulting from an acquisition may be a reluctance on the part of the new parent to act due to cultural factors. This leads to the risk that leaving a new subsidiary alone in the hope of preserving its good side may neglect the possibility of achieving useful synergies in other areas. In one acquisition of a UK pharmaceutical company by a Japanese company the UK managing director observed that: 'The slight negative is . . . that perhaps we could have made faster improvement in our business or development of our business with more interchange of ideas and operations between the two companies.'

Similar changes

Changes which are similar across all acquisitions may be categorized into three main areas; underlying change which would have occurred anyway, change catalysed by acquisition which also probably would have occurred anyway but somewhat more slowly, and finally change due to the acquisition but without distinction of parent nationality. These similar changes are listed in Table 7.3.

Change that was likely to have occurred anyway, even in the absence of an acquisition, was initiated by the subsidiary's management. It usually reflected general trends in management within the UK. As one manager of a UK firm acquired by a German company said, 'We have adopted a lot of new production and process techniques, but not as a result of the link-up with our new parent.' An American firm, US2, acquired a small UK toiletries manufacturer but took little interest in it. Despite this, the subsidiary initiated a wide range of changes over the following years. It adopted more formal planning systems, became more professional at marketing, learnt to communicate with employees in a more open way, installed several forms of automation, increased its outsourcing, lengthened its time horizon, improved its cost control, and increased formal training. But it claimed that 'there has been no effective influence on us by US2 at all'. The interviews also confirmed the existence of several areas where the survey found significant change but no significant differences between nationalities, e.g. in the adoption of new IT systems.

Acquiring companies of whatever nationality generally pay attention to image projection. This was often marked by something more than just a

Table 7.3.   Changes in management practice: no discrimination by nationality[a]

Area of change	Direction of change
Strategy: competing on price; offering unique products/ services; development of new products/services	More emphasis
Amount of training	More
Reward systems: performance oriented vs. annual increments	Performance oriented
Level of image projection	Higher
Communication philosophy: open vs. need to know	More open
R&D/product development: team based vs. sequential	Team based
Use of automation and IT	More
Cost control	More
Operations: employee responsibility for quality; continuous improvement; group working/work teams	More

[a] In these areas of management practice, the average modulus of change was greater than 1 on a scale of 0 to 3, but the probability of any differences between national categories of acquirer arising from chance was greater than 5%.

change of name of the subsidiary. It varied from a complete rebranding to the addition of a minor logo on the bottom of the letterhead. A UK insurance-related company was acquired by a far larger US group with a global reputation in the new but specialist field it was operating in. This association, and what amounted to a seal of approval from the larger company, greatly assisted the subsidiary in breaking into some highly conservative markets. With smaller acquiring companies a wish to build a global reputation often fuelled efforts to rebrand newly acquired subsidiaries. The other almost universal forms of change occurred in operations, cost control, technology, and some aspects of HRM.

Acquisition also had a strong effect on the confidence felt in a company by its customers, suppliers, bankers, and other associates. In order to keep the company trading successfully, substantially more in the way of financial support than is at first apparent was often found to be necessary. Foreign firms eager to preserve their investment and with strong finances are more likely to meet such demanding financial needs than a UK acquirer or MBO team, and this did indeed prove often to be the case.

The nationality effect

The third form of change is that which appears to relate closely to the nationality of the acquirers. Table 7.4 provides a general summary of those areas of post-acquisition change in management practice in which clear differences were apparent between the national acquirer categories. We will look at each nationality of acquirer in turn.

US acquirers

We noted earlier the distinctiveness of the American approach to management. It has attracted considerable attention and has had extensive influence

Table 7.4.　Areas of management practice: clear differences according to acquirer nationality[a]

Area of practice	Nature of difference
Formal meetings	German acquirers: fewer Other acquirers: more
CEO appointed by acquiring company	UK acquirers: 78% of cases US acquirers: 53% of cases Other acquirers: under 50% of cases
Sales and marketing director appointed by acquiring company	US acquirers: more likely than others
Managers without mainline functional portfolio appointed by acquiring company	Japanese acquirers: more likely than others
Capital expenditure requires final approval by parent company	US acquirers: 75% of cases Other acquirers: 89% or more of cases
Use of financial control systems	French, US, and UK acquirers: considerably more German and Japanese acquirers: somewhat less use
Communication mechanisms	German acquirers: less formal; others (esp. US) more formal
Primary orientation of the subsidiary	Japanese and German acquirers: more strategic UK and US acquirers: more financial

[a] These are areas of management practice for which differences according to acquirer nationality *across the sample as a whole* had no more than a 5% likelihood of occurring by chance.

around the world. Much in keeping with the stereotype, companies acquired by US parents when compared to the rest of the survey sample reported moves towards a shorter planning time horizon and a more short-term employment philosophy. They tended to retain a larger managerial super-structure, and to have more frequent managerial job rotation between functional areas. US-acquired companies had relatively more senior manage-rial posts in their UK subsidiaries held by people from the parent company. On the other hand, and perhaps as a result, the subsidiaries tended to have more autonomy over capital expenditure and changes in strategy. There was evidence of greater formalization being introduced than in other national groups, notably in the methods of securing market intelligence, the use of financial control systems, and the exercise of internal communications. US-acquired companies also tended to increase their use of systematic training through courses, rather than doing it on the job.

All the distinctive features of US management practice identified in the literature were evident in the comparison of US acquisitions with others, with one main exception. This was the introduction of performance-related reward systems, which all the national acquirer groups did to more or less the same extent. The strength with which the apparently typical American pattern of management practice is reproduced in their UK acquisitions is undoubtedly enhanced by the greater influence that US acquirers were reported to exercise. The American mode of post-acquisition management appears to be hands on, forceful, and distinctive.

These survey findings were reflected in the interviews. The American manager appointed to run a diversified US manufacturer's acquisition said: 'By linking in to US1 worldwide, all the necessary skills and facilities became available to the new acquisition.' In this case the company was very much 'absorbed' in Haspeslagh and Jemison's (1991) terminology. The US parent's mission statement hangs in every office, the structure was integrated into US1 Europe, course-based training has increased, open communication is com-pulsory, and a sophisticated planning system has been introduced. Compared to the pre-acquisition situation, there is more teamworking, a higher turn-over of personnel, more surface informality, and market-driven rather than R&D-driven attitudes.

Greater emphasis on financial control and on shorter financial time horizons is also typical of the US subsidiaries visited. The demand for continuous financial returns by US companies facing quarterly reporting constraints is well nigh universal, and well documented elsewhere. According to the UK managing director of US10 this has given rise to a style of man-agement depending very much on trust, but with a heavy emphasis on performance:

The relationship with the American CEO was one of trust. He left us to get on with it but he made himself familiar with the operation and went around the branches and at the end of the day he asked, 'Is this British management delivering that which we require?' If it was, he didn't interfere.

Very often along with the financial controls came a requirement for consistency with the corporate profile, sometimes tempered by a realization that in some cases there had to be a balance between instilling big company values and preserving the small company's entrepreneurial spirit and flexibility. That was not to say that US parents were very formal, but, as one MD of a US multinational manufacturing company's subsidiary US8 recalls:

I was at the site when the takeover took place and the CEO of US8 came over and said, 'Call me Hank.' . . . On the one hand, there's a high degree of informality but also a very high degree of toughness and an insistence on conformity. You've got to conform or you're dead.

The toughness mentioned above also extended to employee relations and this went along with the moves by US companies towards short-term employment philosophy and the shorter planning time horizons mentioned earlier. At the same time the disparate size of some US parent companies relative to their UK subsidiaries meant that very significant investments are still made in the subsidiaries. The managing director of US8 also said that the main benefit of the acquisition of his company was that 'our company was going down the tubes fast. US8 has been very successful in turning around the business and putting in huge sums of money.'

Virtually all the distinctive features of US management practice identified in the literature were thus evident in the comparison of US acquisitions with others. The strength with which the American stereotype emerges is undoubtedly enhanced by the greater influence that US acquirers were reported to exercise.

Japanese acquirers

In the survey, the companies acquired by Japanese parents reported the introduction of a number of changes that distinguish them from the rest of the sample. Relative to the other national groups, Japanese acquirers tended to introduce a stronger strategic orientation, with a longer-term financial time horizon and less emphasis on the use of financial control systems. Their employment philosophy on recruitment and termination was similarly longer term in the Japanese-acquired firms. Japanese acquirers also favoured longer tenure within the same management function (less managerial job rotation) than did the other nationalities. The Japanese long-term, strategic, and collective orientation was clearly apparent and consistent with conventional characterizations. As one managing director of a pharmaceutical company's subsidiary (J10) said: 'There is a feeling that we should know what we need to do and that we don't need to go to [our parent] for counsel. But they do know what is going on and they have been very supportive.'

A 'soft' relationship-based approach was encouraged in companies acquired by the Japanese. Compared to the rest of the sample, they tended to implement a greater shift towards collective managerial decision-making, favouring a bottom-up approach, and generally permitting rather more decision-making autonomy to their new subsidiaries. The MD of a UK consumer products company (J3) commented that 'I've been surprised how hands off they have been, contrary to the popular perception about wearing boiler-suits and so forth. We've had none of that.' However, when approval was required from Japan, this could be very slow in coming. The Japanese also tended to be very detailed in their planning techniques and, once agreed, expected plans to be achieved.

An emphasis on relationship was also evident in the approach to gaining market intelligence and customer orientation introduced by Japanese acquirers. They attached more value to personal contacts than did the other national groups. Consistent with the generally lower influence they were perceived to have exercised in bringing about post-acquisition change, Japanese companies introduced significantly more non-portfolio staff, or 'advisers'. It became clear from subsequent interviews that these advisers often have considerable technical experience. They normally have no formal role, however, and their contribution to the subsidiary depends considerably on the relationships that British managers develop with them.

The ways in which Japanese acquirers stand out compared to the other national groups support some but not all of the normal characterizations of Japanese management practice. Their long-term and strategic orientations, and preference for collective and relationship-based action, were clearly apparent and consistent with such characterizations. On the other hand, despite reports that Japanese companies generally adjust their HRM practices to suit local conditions (Abo 1994; Botti 1995), we did not find significant differences between Japanese and other acquirers in the HRM changes they brought about, with the exception of a longer-term employment philosophy. The lack of a clear difference reflected the fact that most companies, across all the national groups, introduced some or all of the operational and work practices associated with the Japanese approach, and this is consistent with the findings of Oliver and Wilkinson (1992).

The managing director of a UK pharmaceutical company J10, acquired along with its US parent by the Japanese licenser of the US parent, said, 'I think we have benefited from the takeover from being able to address issues which prior to the takeover would have been difficult to address, through lack of funding or lack of strategic direction.' In another acquired manufacturing company, J6, which was bought by a major Japanese firm, the CEO observed that: 'The main benefit has to be the investment that was made. Our subsequent success has stemmed from the fact that it gave us the breathing space to move forward in the market.'

Some Japanese parent companies were noted for their slow decision-making. One UK manufacturer (J6) which manufactured a specialist consumer product and received design help from its Japanese parent was producing both a Japanese and UK line of goods. A respondent there reported that: 'In a couple of instances we actually brought products to the market place based on their tooling and their designs before they got into the market place.'

On the other hand, where trust over a particular issue or a general range of management issues had been established, considerable independence was granted by Japanese parents. But the trust and respect had to be earned. Japanese 'advisers' were often managers sent abroad for two to four years in order to gain international exposure prior to promotion to senior management posts. In the case of one subsidiary this was described as: 'There are no formal links, there have been some placements of Japanese personnel, but they've been in new posts in staff roles not direct involvement in the day-to-day business. It's more for training.' However, in some cases these advisers had substantial expertise in some specialist area. J8's managing director said that:

I think that the most beneficial thing that happened is that we had a Japanese gentleman on this site who was dealing with general matters but who had a production background. Once I noticed that he was very strong on production-related matters, I changed his responsibilities to production and he has really done some nice things in production. Because he was an expert . . . he really took it on board and did some really good work.

In all acquisitions there is a balance between independence and intervention along the spectrum of integration. In the case of Japanese acquisitions the balance is often one where supportive independence outweighs any suggestion of a stifling form of intervention.

German acquirers

The survey indicates that the differences between German acquisitions and those of other countries in post-acquisition management practice all centre on one feature, namely less emphasis on formalization. German subsidiaries made much less use of formal meetings, had less formal planning, made less use of financial control systems, had a less planned approach to career development, used formal communication mechanisms less, and placed less emphasis on a cost control strategy.

German acquisitions were less likely to have parent company managers imposed on them as CEOs, or as marketing and technical directors. This is a quite distinctive profile and to some degree reflects the perception of subsidiary managers that their German parent companies exercised relatively less influence over their acquisitions.

The remarkable aspect of these findings is that they directly contradict one of the assumptions about German management practice found in the literature. Generally commentators tend to stress a high level of formality, rule-orientation, orderliness, and formal provisions for participation as defining characteristics of German management. These features did *not* distinguish the changes brought about by German investors in the UK in our sample; in fact it was quite the contrary. This may reflect, to some extent, the observation made by Stewart and her colleagues (1994) that German 'order' is demonstrated in structure rather than in process. Nevertheless, our findings question the accepted German characterization, at least for acquisitions. It is perhaps the case that German acquirers accord more with their conventional characterization in domestic acquisitions, where they are on surer cultural ground, than in international acquisitions where their experience is less, and they are more uncertain of what will work well.

Various explanations for this unexpected finding emerged in conversations with subsidiary managers. One UK managing director of an acquired company (G2) held that it was a generational issue: 'The Germans are quasi-formal, and the first management team was very traditional and formal. The new management, however, is much younger and much less formal. We have "casual days", "funny tie days" and "sandals days" and this sort of thing!' Other managers saw increased informality as a reaction to the problems of the recession in the early 1990s in that a more hands-off informal approach would preserve some of the small company characteristics that large German company might learn from in the recession. This approach was contrasted with an earlier approach which involved management quite literally 'by the book' with the rigid use of set procedures.

German managers were perceived to be closer to UK culture than many other nationalities, as the manager of a financial services company (G3) observed: 'The culture is not that different. A bit more formal, but they are in my opinion far closer to us than any other European lot. You wouldn't have any trouble having dinner with them.' German acquisitions illustrate the effect of management methods in the home country influencing but also adapting to practices abroad. As one managing director (G6) put it : 'We found that consensual board decision-making (as in Germany) might seem like a very cosy way to run a company but at the end of the day you need a focus for someone to say "Let's do this, chaps". Even if you disagree with him about it; then you can have an argument about it.'

Another managing director in a very similar position with another company acquired by a German company said that, having completed the acquisition, the German parent company actually fired the managing director of the UK company, not for any failing on his part, but because he was not seen to have any functional responsibility. This was despite the insistence of the other managers that the role of managing director was vital. The interviewee speculated that German companies, which until 1991 had experienced very little recession in the post-war period, had not until recently needed the unifying and directing influence of a managing director. Notably, with the coming of the recession in the early 1990s, both the German company and its UK subsidiary appointed managing directors.

German acquirers also took a long-term view of investment decisions and provided financial support. However, the managing director of a UK manufacturing company (G10) said: 'I think our financial director . . . would almost have welcomed being pressed more to be self-sufficient. It was almost a failing of the Germans to be as supportive as they were.' It seems that for such support to lead to success, the subsidiary must have some idea about the long-term direction of the company—whether that direction is self-generated or dictated by the parent. Support or direction by themselves are insufficient. This was reflected by the above managing director's sense that the UK company under its German owners suffered from a lack of strategic direction. German management seems to be influenced by the less demanding nature of the home financial markets, compared to those in the USA. The manager of a German subsidiary (G3) said something that would be very difficult for anyone in a US company to say: 'They are long-termist. They do not have making a profit itself as a prime matter. They are not profit driven. They want to know about quarterly results but they are not dominated by them.'

French acquirers

One of the distinctive post-acquisition changes characterizing French takeovers was the tendency to simplify the management structures of their subsidiaries, with fewer hierarchical levels and a smaller managerial component within their total employment. French parent companies also introduced a stronger emphasis on formal qualifications as criteria for selection and advancement, and planned career development within the subsidiaries.

Companies acquired by French parents less often had parent company appointees as CEOs, or as directors especially in the R&D and HRM areas. However, key decision powers tended to be reserved for the parent more than in the other companies sampled. It was not uncommon for a French managing director to be appointed in the first instance, and then to train a UK manager to take over from him after a year or so.

French parent company influence was also greater than in Japanese, German, and UK acquisitions. At the strategic level, the only issue which distinguished French acquisitions was that they emphasized the development of new products more strongly than did companies from the other countries. The distinctly French changes did not accord with the picture of French management portrayed in the literature. There was no compelling evidence that French companies are more specialized, use more written media, or prefer individual decision-making. The expectation that French companies tolerate tall hierarchies is in fact directly challenged by what has happened in the French takeovers in our sample. The only major feature attributed to French management practice which has survived present scrutiny is the tendency for subsidiary autonomy to be relatively restricted.

Certainly, the criteria for promotion at the top levels of French companies are similar to those described in the literature. According to one manager: 'What happens in Paris as regards appointments is all French and depends on which year you were at the Polytechnique.' Such comments may spring from denied opportunities, since another UK manager observed that 'Brits can only make it to a glass ceiling level'. So the idea that the French have a 'colonial' attitude to foreign acquisitions finds some support. The operational decisions may be made in the UK, but strategic ones belong in Paris.

French parent company influence was also high compared with all national groups except the Americans. This may be linked to the fact, noted by some interviewees, that it was fairly common for French managers to be installed, and then to hand over later to a UK manager. As one managing director commented, 'The form is to put a Frenchman in to run a new company, then after a few years replace him with a local.'

Where interviewees did refer to a French parent company taking a strategic view, it was usually by force of circumstances, such as having to persevere in the face of financial losses. Regarding this financial/strategic axis, the managing director of a UK financial services provider acquired by a Parisian bank (F3) commented: 'To us relationship management is important, but to them if something doesn't show profits in six months they lose interest. They are very short term. This is unsettling as you can't motivate people on this basis.'

One managing director observed on decision-making that: 'They veer towards collective decision-making. The main problem has been the bureaucratic nature of the French decision-making process, and the style of management.' Another interviewee said, 'Decision-making is collective, but the French are very autocratic, but on big strategic issues only.' This suggests that the issue may depend on the size of the decision being made. A French financial services company, for example, was said to reserve larger decisions for itself, but to allow its British subsidiary a lot of local autonomy over operational matters.

In some French acquisitions it was clear that to a certain extent it is up to a subsidiary to manage its owners as much as be managed by them. The possibility of being fairly autonomous in some respects though can have disadvantages, as pointed out earlier. The expectation that French companies tolerate tall hierarchies was not confirmed in the survey. One UK managing director commented, 'The levels of hierarchy are much fewer. Our UK parent had eight grades. Now there are far fewer.' More generally this is part of the view that French companies have tried to absorb their acquired companies to fit in with their existing French management structure. The overall view of French acquisitions provided by the interviews and survey results thus tends to belie the conventional views of what constitutes 'French' management style with hierarchical structures and centralized decision-making.

UK acquirers

A fifth national group is the set of UK acquirers, who were included in the survey primarily as a control group. Insofar as there may have been general trends within UK management practice during the ten-year period of the study, one would expect these to be reflected among the UK companies taken over by other companies of the same nationality. If this is the case, then there would probably be relatively few areas in which the UK acquirers introduced changes in their new subsidiaries which differed markedly from those within the rest of the sample. This turned out to be the case, with one major exception. UK acquisitions introduced a stronger financial orientation, and a higher increase in the use of financial control systems, than characterized the rest of the sample. This financial emphasis was even stronger than among the companies acquired by US parents. It accords with a supposedly key aspect of the UK approach to management. The supposed conservatism of UK companies may be reflected in the findings that UK acquisitions moved towards 'Japanese' operational practices less than did the other companies, particularly in respect of continuous improvement and outsourcing. Although the UK acquirers more often appointed their own CEO than did acquirers of other nationalities, their level of influence over changes in subsidiary management practice tended to be lower.

Conclusions

It is clear from the survey and interviews that the very process of being acquired and subsequently controlled by foreign investing companies led to significant changes in the acquired companies' management practices. Some changes were common among all the cases studied, such as a shift towards performance-related rewards and a stronger quality emphasis in operations. These probably reflected general trends among companies in response to competitive pressures and to the evolution of management thinking. Such changes may well have been accelerated by acquisition, but cannot necessarily be ascribed to it. Many other changes, however, demonstrated both acquisition and transfer of practice effects because they evidenced preferences that varied among different national categories of acquiring company. That a transfer of foreign practice took place is further indicated by the finding that foreign-acquired subsidiaries tended to introduce a wider range of changes than did their counterparts acquired by UK companies during the same period. These foreign acquirers were, with the exception of the Japanese, also perceived to have a more effective impact on change in their subsidiaries than were the UK acquirers.

The acquisition effect is in this way a complement to the transfer of practice effect; the former is a significant lever for the latter. Equally interesting, however, are the ways in which the type of management practice transferred from, or encouraged by, the foreign acquirers of UK companies varies in certain important respects. These were quite distinct for the US and the Japanese groups and close to their perceived characterization in the literature. For example, Japanese acquirers are much more likely to adopt a long-term view than their equivalents from the USA. The interviews clearly indicated that many UK companies acquired by Japanese parents owe their survival through the recession of the early 1990s to the willingness of their new owners to afford them financial support without an expectation of a short-term return. Others have noted this long-term attitude on the part of Japanese parent companies in the UK compared with US and UK parents and have ascribed it to the higher cost of capital faced by the latter (Garnsey et al. 1992). The US acquirers were on the other hand much more likely than other nationalities to absorb their acquisitions into their group in a very integrationist way, and to demand immediate short-term profits.

This and some other contrasts between American and Japanese acquirers accord with the conventional portraits of their respective approaches to management. The major exceptions concern the basis of payment, where subsidiaries across all the national acquirer groups reported a move towards performance-related payment systems (which has been associated with the

American approach), and the adoption of team-based work organization and continuous improvement systems (which has been associated with the Japanese approach). Such management practices are therefore no longer limited national practices, and are evidence of 'convergence' of best practice in multinational companies.

Little support, however, was found for the characteristics which have previously been associated with French and German management. Even though French and German acquirers were found to introduce some management practices of a kind which contrasted with the rest of the sample, these did not on the whole conform to what have previously been claimed as identifiable national approaches. There was a pronounced tendency for German companies to make long-term financial investments in a similar way to Japanese parent companies, but to be rather uncertain in their strategic approach to their acquisitions. In addition, two of the distinctive post-acquisition changes French and German companies tended to introduce fly in the face of existing assumptions about their national approaches to management. These are, respectively, the relatively strong tendency of French acquirers to reduce hierarchical levels and simplify management structures, and the marked tendency among German acquirers to reduce formalization among their new UK subsidiaries.

The reasons for these apparent deviations from existing assumptions about French and German management practice are not readily apparent. Contrary to our expectations, the trend among French acquirers was not accentuated by the peculiarity that seven of the thirty-two acquisitions were of UK water companies which probably offered particular opportunities for cutting down previously public-sector management. The moves towards informality encouraged by German acquirers may, as Lane (1989) has argued, reflect a newer German style rather than the older approach informing some characterizations. There could also be some special dynamics in the German interaction with existing UK practice insofar as their newly acquired subsidiaries may have been already more formalized than the German norm in respect of meetings and financial controls. Whatever the case, these findings suggest that accepted views of French and German management practice deserve further investigation, at least regarding their application to foreign direct investments. French and German management practice has, in fact, received less attention than Japanese and US approaches, and further research might well refine our existing conceptions.

Summary

- The management practices introduced by American and Japanese acquirers accorded quite closely with their common characterizations.
- The behaviour of French and German acquiring companies was less akin to their common characterizations. These characterizations deserve further investigation and may have to be revised.
- Practices like performance-related pay, formal planning systems, tighter cost control and overall financial management, and greater investment in training were common to all countries and therefore demonstrated some 'convergence' of management practices across nationalities.
- American companies tend to 'absorb' their new subsidiaries into the parent group.
- Japanese companies tend to acculturate their new subsidiaries to Japanese methods in a subtle and 'soft' fashion.
- French acquirers are frequently 'colonial' in their attitudes to their acquisitions.
- German acquirers are somewhat uncertain in their international integration methods and vary considerably amongst themselves.

8

Integration and Control

Acquisitions offer a purchasing company a strong position from which to introduce changes in management practice. However, the manner and extent of such changes may depend critically on not just the intentions of the new parent company but the degree of integration and control that is exercised over the new subsidiary in implementing such changes. These in turn may be determined by a wide range of factors affecting the degree of integration and control that a new subsidiary is subject to.

The literature on post-acquisition integration either tends to avoid national differences altogether or looks more at national differences between the acquired and acquiring company rather than between different nationalities of acquiring company. Thus, whilst differences in national management are much studied, the differences in national approaches to acquisition integration which this chapter addresses have been little studied.

Dunning's (1958) pioneering work on American investment in British manufacturing closely examines the degree of control exercised by parent companies and the extent to which their operating methods were introduced into UK subsidiaries. He concluded that most subsidiaries adopted substantially the same 'principles of management' as their US parent companies.

However, both control and integration involve specific management methods and practices and, as has been pointed out earlier, until the 1980s many students of management assumed that there were general principles of management that might be applied to situations, irrespective of the cultural heritage of the companies being studied. A critical factor in determining the impact of foreign management practices is the extent to which the new parent company integrates the new subsidiary into its organization and the degree of control it exerts over the new subsidiary. A distinction needs to be drawn, however, between integration of subsidiaries into a parent company and intervention by a parent company. Control of a subsidiary through intervention need not be accompanied by its integration into the parent, even if integration does imply the exertion of some control.

There is a considerable amount of work on the role of control in the management of MNCs. Most recently, Harzing (1999) analyses the control mechanisms used by multinationals and looks at among other things the role of expatriates and transfer of managers. Brooke and Remmers (1972) for example talk not so much of control and integration, but of the degree of centralization and how it is linked with the place 'where the most significant decisions are taken' which is of course related to the issue of strategic control and decision-making. Hennart (1993) views profit centres, hierarchy or centralization, and socialization as the three main means of control, with hierarchy being the extent to which HQs make decisions. Bower (1986) views management of the resource allocation process involved in managing a firm as comprising three stages, with corporate, integrating, and initiating phases such that a key issue is the information required for each of the phases. None of these studies, however, makes a clear distinction between strategic and operational control or between the different approaches to control and integration that might be adopted by parent companies of different nationality.

The importance of integration and control of subsidiaries goes beyond their possible effect on performance and might be seen to be associated with the possibility that different factors and in particular different origins of acquiring companies may be associated with differing approaches to these critical issues.

The research reported in this chapter therefore focuses on the control and integration of UK subsidiary companies, and addresses the possibility that distinct approaches to the control and integration of acquired subsidiaries may be associated with particular characteristics of acquiring companies and particularly their nationality. The additional group of companies acquired by UK parents during the same period is included as a control.

Major issues

The two major areas this chapter focuses on are: first, the level of integration of the subsidiary into the parent, and, secondly, the control methods and systems, both strategic and operational, adopted by the parent to control its new acquisition.

Integration

The importance of the extent to which an acquired company is integrated into its parent organization rapidly becomes apparent when talking to acquired companies. A number of writers have touched on the issue of integration. Norburn and Schoenberg (1994) identify the need for 'relatively specialized integration skills different from those required within an intra-UK context' (p. 33). They identify three needs; integration by facilitating a transfer from owner-management to professional management, integration by proactive transfer of skills to overcome a lack of integration, and, finally, the need to overcome potentially conflicting national cultures. Morosini and Singh (1994), whilst concentrating on implementing a 'national culture-compatible strategy' as a means to improving the performance of acquisitions, also draw attention to the difficulties of integrating resources across both acquiring and acquired companies, something seen as detrimental to the performance of the acquisition. Datta (1991) also highlights the importance of integration and the finding that procedural integration problems are less detrimental to performance of the acquisition than cultural integration problems associated with some but not all differing management styles. Shrivastava (1986) identifies three types of integration, procedural, physical, and managerial/sociocultural, the last of which is found by Datta to encompass the potentially important cultural differences in management style. Gall (1991) regards integration as a key organizational issue faced by management of a new acquisition and emphasizes the role of employee communication in building a positive post-acquisition climate.

Many factors may be said to exemplify integration of the subsidiary into the new parent company, ranging from replacement of company logos to total physical and administrative integration of the subsidiary into the parent company, so that the original subsidiary company can no longer be distinguished. However, one possible measure of the degree of integration is the extent to which parent company directors are appointed to the subsidiary company. Few examples of total and absolute integration are likely to be studied, however, since a subsidiary company must still be identifiable to the extent that its personnel can be interviewed. In the case where a subsidiary company's resources are dispersed widely throughout the parent company it may be no easy task to identify former subsidiary staff. The majority of the companies studied in this chapter thus still retained at least some vestige of independence, even if this only comprised a site or factory physically separate from the parent company and a legally separate subsidiary company registration. The degree to which the directors of such companies were drawn from the new parent company formed a key indicator of their organizational integration into the parent company, even if their locations precluded physical integration.

The overall degree of integration achieved following an acquisition and the degree of control involved in that integration process are thus issues of great interest, not necessarily because more or less integration might be of itself detrimental to performance, but because an inappropriate level of integration might be detrimental. Thus a tendency to over- or under-integrate as a result of cultural factors may result in sub-optimal solutions.

Whatever the perspective on acquisitions, however, there appears to be a continuum in the degree of integration, or what might be called a spectrum of integration (illustrated in Fig. 8.1). This spectrum of integration ranges from acquisitions with little integration (1–2 on the scale), through partially integrated situations (3–5), to those where integration is almost total (6–7). In the figure, A is the acquiring parent company and B is the acquired subsidiary.

Fig. 8.1 also suggests the way in which integration of the new subsidiary may vary. With a low level of integration (1–2), merely regular financial and other operating figures will be required for the parent to monitor the performance of the subsidiary. All main functions are retained by the subsidiary and reporting occurs primarily via the subsidiary CEO. Some top-level personnel changes may be initiated and restrictions are likely to be imposed on capital spending. The subsidiary will, however, continue to operate and present itself to the market much as before acquisition.

With higher levels of integration (3–5), the new parent is likely to take over and run centrally certain areas of activity. These are likely to include strategy, with finance, personnel policy and systems, procurement, product development, IT systems, and possibly the whole area of branding and management of the company image. Reporting occurs partly via the subsidiary CEO and partly by function. Depending on how the new parent regards the reputation of the subsidiary's name and trademarks, it may or may not decide to continue with them. At these partial levels of integration, the parent is likely to have recognized that it has something to learn from the acquisition. However, it will only centralize functions if it believe this to be to the advantage of the corporation as a whole.

The highest integration levels (6–7) correspond to total absorption of subsidiary functions into the parent's organization. Fully distributed reporting by function occurs. Brand names may be retained if they are strong but,

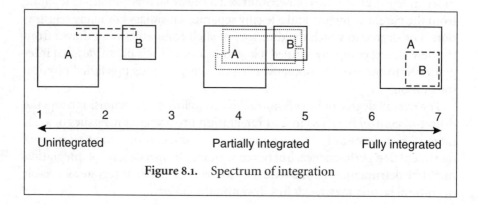

Figure 8.1.   Spectrum of integration

particularly in service organizations, may be discontinued after a transitional period.

Control

When one company acquires another it needs to exercise some control over the acquisition that is now acting in its name and using its resources. Whilst trust can itself be founded on factors that deliver control, external control is in part its antithesis since the greater the level of trust between the companies, the less the perceived need for tight external control systems (Faulkner 1999). Control can, however, take many forms.

Control systems may be limited to budgets and capital expenditure. They may involve imposing 'need for approval' requirements on identified decisions (Geringer and Hébert 1989). The control system selected illustrates the degree to which the parent is willing to grant a level of autonomy to the newly acquired subsidiary, and may be crucial in terms of influencing the level of motivation of the acquired company personnel. While not discussing national culture, Goold and Campbell (1988) draw attention to three main approaches (strategic control, strategic planning, and financial control) to managing subsidiaries depending on the degree of control and planning by the centre that is involved. There is of course the possibility that there is an overlap between integration and control, for example, appointing staff to key positions in the subsidiary company and thus exemplifying how integration might also result in greater control.

Control of new acquisitions is seen as a key issue by Calori et al. (1994) who consider the effect of culture on the process of integration and differences in control mechanisms in acquisitions by US, French, or UK companies of French or British firms. Calori et al. rely in their analysis on the control strategy dimensions of centralization and formalization identified by Child (1972, 1973). Their research suggests that French firms exercise higher formal control of strategy and operations and lower informal control through teamwork than American companies when they buy firms in the UK. American firms, however, are found to exercise higher formal control through procedures than the British when they buy firms in France. In fact Dunning (1958: 112), writing about an earlier wave of FDI, notes that: 'we may perhaps say with some certainty that US managerial and financial control is more likely than not to be fairly rigid for the first five years or so [after investing in a UK firm]'. Other research has shown that French decision-making is concentrated towards the top of hierarchies (Horowitz 1978; Hickson and Pugh 1995). Research by Maurice et al. (1980), comparing French with West German and UK manufacturing firms, finds that in France there are usually more levels in the hierarchy. French hierarchies tend to be more top heavy, with up to twice as many supervisors and managers as in German firms. Calori and De Woot (1994) add to this hierarchical characterization by noting that French companies have a far higher number of organizational levels and a lower level of participation than German companies or those from other northern European countries.

The issue of control is, of course, closely linked to that of autonomy. Research by Datta and Grant (1990) suggests that autonomy should be proportional to the unrelatedness of the acquisition's business. Abo (1994) describes the Japanese management system as very flexible, with few rigid job demarcations. Workers, supervisors, and managers collectively take part in the discussion of managerial and operational functions. Assembly-line workers are responsible for on-line inspection and quality. There is a use of 'implicit control' based on shared corporate norms and understanding.

One particularly useful distinction is between 'strategic' and 'operational' control. The former relates to larger long-term issues of concern to senior management, such as final approval for the subsidiary's budget, capital expenditure, appointment/termination of senior personnel, acquisition/divestment, formation of alliances, decisions about major contractual agreements, changes in the scope/direction of the company, and the introduction of major new products. Operational control relates more to day-to-day issues of greater immediate concern to management in the subsidiary. These might include issues such as operational decision-making, the formality or informality of planning, the degree of cost control exercised, the prevalence of formal meetings, and the use of financial control systems.

There are several examples in the literature of such a distinction being made between these different aspects of control. Child (1984) defines them and discusses the multidimensionality of management control. He also notes in connection with the centralization of control that in one study (Child and Kieser 1979) strategic decisions were found to be taken at board level whilst operational decisions were delegated to supervisory or superintendent-level manager in British firms and production-level manager in German firms. Macintosh (1994) makes a distinction between goals and ends of differing means of control, identifying bureaucratic, charismatic, market, collegial, and traditional control methods. The distinction between strategic and operational control also raises the question as to the relationship between them. To what extent are they substitutes or complements? This reflects the distinction made by Grinyer and Spender (1979) between 'participative' and non-participative conglomerates. The participative approach combines integration and control through more involved corporate-level managers. The opposite of such an approach is to reserve decision rights to the corporate level whilst using arm's-length controls. The importance of control of acquisitions and the variety of approaches to it are thus widely acknowledged in the literature.

Research questions

Bearing all these factors in mind, the national spread of acquiring companies researched permits us to examine the possibility that there may be differing attitudes towards integration and control of subsidiaries. The following questions therefore arise:

1. What are the profiles of subsidiary control and integration post-acquisition and are these related? What combinations emerge?
2. Are contextual factors, including acquirer nationality, associated with post-acquisition integration and control?
3. Do changes in or influence on particular management practices associated with post-acquisition integration and control differ by acquiring company nationality?
4. Are levels of integration and control of subsidiaries in any way correlated with measures of their post-acquisition performance?

We first examine the overall profiles of combinations of control and integration. We next consider the possible impact of various non-managerial (contextual) parameters on post-acquisition integration and control, before focusing on the possible association that integration and control may have with various post-acquisition changes in management practice. The degree of correlation between integration, control, and nationality, and also performance, is then described.

A particular focus is on the survey data gathered during the research. One of the problems of research involving concepts such as integration and control of subsidiaries is how to define or characterize them in terms that can be used in a postal questionnaire in a readily understandable and acceptable way. In the survey, control was assessed using two measures. The first, in respect of strategic control, was measured by the degree of centralization or decentralization of strategic decision-making. The second, in respect of operational control, was linked to measures of change following acquisition in the centralization or decentralization of operational decision-making. In both cases greater centralization implies greater control by the parent company. The degree of integration was assessed using a composite measure linked to the occupancy of key positions by parent company appointees including those of CEO, financial director, operations director, sales and marketing director, R&D director, HRM, and/or other equivalent staff.

Obviously no measure of integration is likely to reflect all conceivable aspects of the concept. However, there was no significant correlation between the measure of integration used and the two measures of control used in the questionnaire, indicating that the two concepts of integration and control are independent.

Profiles of subsidiary control and integration post-acquisition

The overall patterns of control and integration found are shown in Fig. 8.2, using data from Table 8.1.

In absolute terms, all acquisitions are more or less subject to increased centralization of strategic control, some degree of integration, and some degree of increased centralization or decentralization of operational control. If we examine the relative degree of the mean scores for these measures, however, we can see that the various nationalities of acquirer possess these characteristics in particular combinations. Taking the extreme opposites, US acquisitions seem to be associated with increased centralization of operational and strategic control as well as higher degree of integration whilst German acquisitions show much lower degrees of integration and strategic control and even decentralization of operational control.

Looking at the values in Fig. 8.2 one can characterize the US style as *interventionist*, the UK style as more *integrationist*, and the Japanese, German, and French acquisitions as various sub-styles of acquisitions depending on the combination of operational and strategic control exercised by the parent company. French acquisitions show high strategic but low operational control, or *directive* control, Japanese acquisitions high operational but low

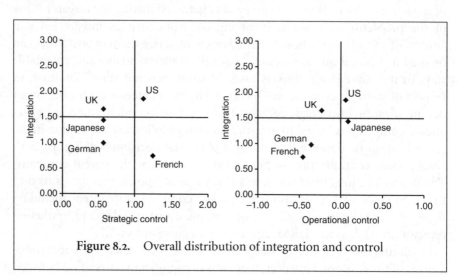

Figure 8.2. Overall distribution of integration and control

strategic control, or *advisory* control, and German acquisitions show both low operational and low strategic control, or *arm's-length* control, relative to the other nationalities. These, however, are very broad generalizations and the data must be more closely inspected to arrive at firm conclusions.

Post-acquisition control and integration: contextual factors

Table 8.1 presents correlations between indicators of post-acquisition integration and measures of strategic and operational control. The measures of integration show no significant correlation with the measures of control used, suggesting that the two features are independent. The overall lack of correlation between the measures of integration and control and the nature of the measures used, with strategic and operational control linked to centralization of decisions by the parent company and integration linked to installation of parent company appointees, suggests that control can be exercised by the parent company either through the appointees or through centralization of controls.

Table 8.1. Correlations between indicators of post-acquisition control and integration

	Correlations		
	Strategic control	Operational control	Integration
1. Strategic control[a] (N=198)	—	0.55[b]	−0.00
2. Operational control[c] (N=198)	0.55[b]	—	0.03
3. Integration[d] (N=140)	−0.00	−0.03	—

[a] This measure of strategic control was by the degree of centralization or decentralization of strategic decision-making.

[b] = p < 0.001 (one-tailed test).

[c] The measure of operational control used was linked to measures of changes following acquisition in the centralization or decentralization of operational decision-making.

[d] This measure is based on the extent to which the following positions or their equivalent are held by people from the parent company (i.e. appointed by the parent company from among parent company staff or from new staff appointed by the parent company): CEO, finance director, operations director, sales and marketing director, R&D director, HRM director, others reporting directly to the CEO.

When viewed by country, the measures of strategic control and integration are only positively and significantly correlated in the case of replies by German-owned companies (Table 8.2). This might support a view of German companies as being unduly concerned with control to the extent that installing their own staff is not sufficient; headquarter control still has to be exercised over them. In the case of acquisition by German companies, integration and strategic control are thus closer to synonymity than is the case for acquisitions by companies from other countries.

One illustration of this interpretation of Table 8.2 is provided by an engineering company acquired by a German parent (G2). According to the CEO of the German holding company within the UK, a new MD was imposed on the company by the German parent. He added, 'We imposed some German project management expertise by sending people on secondment to the UK company . . . [and] we imposed German financial controls.' As such the parent was both integrating the subsidiary by imposing staff in senior positions, and also exerting control.

The measures of operational control and integration are positively and significantly correlated for US-owned companies (Table 8.2) since US companies tend to absorb their new subsidiaries. As the MD of a UK chemicals company (US8) said of his new US parent company: 'It cannot cope with a stand-alone subsidiary. They have to integrate everything.'

So far as the measure of integration is concerned, only 19 per cent of companies had no key positions occupied by parent company personnel. The most common posts to be appointed by the parent company following acquisition were those of CEO and finance director. It is interesting to note that overall there was a significant negative correlation between operational control and the appointment of a new CEO by the parent company. Though there was no significant correlation in the case of strategic control, there was in contrast a significant positive correlation between both operational and

Table 8.2. Correlations between indicators of post-acquisition control and integration by country

	Strategic control		Operational control	
	Correlation	p (one tail)	Correlation	p (one tail)
US acquirers	r = 0.18	p = 0.112	r = 0.60	p = 0.000
Japanese acquirers	r = −0.27	p = 0.135	r = −0.02	p = 0.470
UK acquirers	r = −0.11	p = 0.257	r = −0.16	p = 0.179
French acquirers	r = −0.18	p = 0.201	r = −0.23	p = 0.136
German acquirers	r = 0.72	p = 0.004	r = 0.14	p = 0.329

strategic control and the appointment of a new finance director by the parent company. The same was true for strategic control, which became more centralized when parent companies appointed finance directors.

Strategic control, as measured by centralization of strategic decision-making, became more centralized after acquisition in 69 per cent of cases and more decentralized in only 19 per cent. Operational control, as measured by centralization of operational decision-making, was more centralized in 36 per cent of cases, as compared with 35 per cent reporting greater decentralization. All companies reported having at least one key decision retained by the parent company and about 25 per cent of companies had all the key decisions investigated taken by their parent company. Overall, there appears to have been a noticeable trend towards post-acquisition increased strategic control, more so than towards operational control, and also towards the integration of subsidiaries, even if these trends do not necessarily run in parallel for all countries.

A number of contextual factors were examined for their possible direct impact on strategic and operational control, and integration. These factors were acquirer nationality, sector (high-tech manufacturing, low-tech manufacturing, and service), size of acquired company, size of acquiring company, date of acquisition, and profitability of the subsidiary at the time of its acquisition. The results are shown in Table 8.3.

Table 8.3. Nationality and differences in post-acquisition integration and strategic and operational control[a]

Parent co.	Strategic control		Operational control		Integration	
	Mean	N	Mean	N	Mean	N
Japanese	0.57	28	0.07	28	1.45	20
US	1.12	69	0.04	69	1.87	45
French	1.25	32	−0.47	32	0.76	25
German	0.58	19	−0.37	19	1.00	14
UK	0.58	50	−0.24	50	1.67	36
Total cases	198		198		140	
Missing cases	3		3		61	
ANOVA p value	p = 0.112		p = 0.465		p = 0.002	

[a] Strategic or operational control means are mean measures of centralization (+ve) or decentralization of (−ve) ranging from +3 to −3. Integration is the mean number of key positions (range 0 to 7) held by parent company appointees.

There was no significant difference in strategic or operational control, or integration by industry sector. There was, however, a significant national difference in the degrees of post-acquisition integration. US and UK subsidiaries were significantly more integrated than companies with Japanese or German parents. French companies were the least integrated of all.

The differences between the levels of strategic and operational control by nationality were far less pronounced. There was a tendency for French, German, and UK companies to exercise less operational control than the others, while US and French companies exercised more strategic control than the other nationalities.

There was no systematic association between sector and integration or strategic control, nor between profitability at time of acquisition and strategic or operational control. There was a small but significant difference in integration according to the profitability of subsidiaries when they were acquired. Companies that were barely profitable on acquisition showed somewhat more integration following acquisition than those that were either profitable or unprofitable. Date of acquisition and size of acquiring company had no consistent implications for either control or integration.

Thus, the response to the second research question raised as to whether contextual factors are associated with post-acquisition integration and control is generally speaking negative.

Post-acquisition control and integration: changes in management practice

Another possibility is related to the second question above: whether the association between changes in management practice and integration or control differs according to acquiring company nationality. Other chapters examine the strength and direction of changes in management practice introduced into the acquired companies, the extent to which these varied according to the nationality of the acquiring company, and the influence that the parent company was reported to have had on the introduction of the changes examined. National differences between the acquiring firms are evident for some changes in management practice, but not for all. These findings suggest that some management changes may be more sensitive to nationality than others.

The relationship between post-acquisition strategic and operational control and integration and changes in management practice does indeed differ according to the nationality of the acquiring company. Tables 8.4, 8.5, and 8.6 list the national profiles of post-acquisition changes in management practice that are significantly associated with post-acquisition strategic control, operational control, and integration respectively. The tables show only those changes in management practice that we can be confident are associated with post-acquisition integration or control, with no more than a 5 per cent probability of this occurring by chance.

Strategic control

In companies acquired by American parents, an increased level of strategic control was significantly associated with a greater number of levels in the hierarchy, a higher percentage of managers and technically qualified staff, more formal meetings and formalized planning, less lifelong employment, a shorter financial time horizon, and a more financial and less strategic orientation to the company.

In the case of French acquisitions, strategic control was also significantly associated with a wide range of changes in management practice including a lower percentage of technically qualified staff, more of a need-to-know communication philosophy, greater use of financial control systems, shorter financial time horizons, and lower profitability.

There were few changes in management practice associated with strategic control by Japanese parent companies. There were also few changes in management practice which were associated with strategic control by UK parent companies, except that increased control was associated with more group working and outsourcing of distribution, and a lower percentage of technically qualified staff and decreased sales.

There were also few significant links between post-acquisition changes in management practice and strategic control among German-acquired subsidiaries. Greater strategic control was significantly associated with a functionally based organizational structure, greater job rotation, more formal communication, fewer offerings or development of unique products and services, but also with greater sales. This is not incompatible with the finding from case studies among some of the same firms that those taken over by German parents did not on the whole experience a determined or systematic post-acquisition reform of their management. Indeed, the German cases were not very consistent in their approaches to post-acquisition management (Faulkner et al. 1998).

Operational control

In contrast to strategic control, post-acquisition changes in operational control were associated with a different range of changes in management practice (see Table 8.5). In the case of US acquisitions greater operational

Table 8.4. National profiles: changes in management practice correlating with post-acquisition strategic control, categorized by nationality of acquiring company

Management practice: change towards	American (N=69)	Japanese (N=26)	UK (N=47)	French (N=28)	German (N=20)
Functionally based structure	✓				✓
More levels in hierarchy					✓
More job rotation of managers	✓				
Higher per cent of managers					
Lower per cent of technically qualified staff	✓		✓	✓	
Higher per cent of technically qualified staff	✓				
More formal meetings	✓				
More formalized planning	✓				
CEO not appointed by parent company				✓	
HRM director not appointed by parent company	✓	✓		✓	
Retention of decision to form JVs/alliances	✓			✓	
Retention of decisions about major contracts	✓			✓	
Retention of decisions about company scope/direction				✓	
Retention of decisions about new products	✓		✓	✓	
More use of financial control systems	✓				
Less lifelong employment					
Methods of distribution done less internally				✓	
Methods of distribution done more internally				✓	
More need-to-know philosophy					✓
Less formal communication					

Less use of automation/IT		✓	
Less implementation of JIT operation		✓	
Implementation of group working/workteams	✓		
Less emphasis on managing total supply chain		✓	
More single source procurement		✓	
Shorter financial time horizon	✓		
More financial less strategic primary orientation	✓		
Less offering of unique products/services			✓
Less development of new products/services			✓
Lower profitability		✓	
Greater profitability	✓		
Lower sales	✓		
Greater sales			✓

Note: ✓ = Correlation between the change in management practice and post-acquisition control at $p < 0.05$ (two-tailed test).

Table 8.5. National profiles: changes in management practice correlating with post-acquisition operational control, categorized by nationality of acquiring company

Management practice: change towards	American acquirers (N=69)	Japanese acquirers (N=26)	UK acquirers (N=47)	French acquirers (N=28)	German acquirers (N=20)
More levels in the hierarchy	✓		✓		✓
More job rotation of managers	✓				✓
No. of managers as per cent of total staff	✓				
Centralized strategic decision-making	✓	✓	✓		✓
Greater prevalence of formal meetings	✓		✓	✓	
CEO not appointed by parent company				✓	
Retention of decisions about major contracts	✓				
Retention of decisions about new products	✓			✓	
Less lifelong employment	✓				✓
Slower approach to promotion			✓	✓	✓
Lower amount of training				✓	
More annual increment reward systems				✓	
More use of personal marketing contacts				✓	✓
Methods of distribution subcontracted more			✓		
More need-to-know communication philosophy			✓		✓
Less implementation of TQM					
Implementation of statistical process control	✓				
Implementation of quality circles				✓	
Less operator responsibility for quality	✓				

Short-term planning horizon			✓
Top-down style and culture	✓		✓
More financial less strategic primary orientation			✓
More competing on price	✓	✓	
Less offering of unique products/services		✓	✓
Less development of new products/services			✓
Higher profitability		✓	
Lower profitability	✓		
Lower sales			✓
Greater sales	✓		✓

Note. ✓ = Correlation between the change in management practice and post-acquisition control at $p < 0.05$ (two-tailed test).

control was, *inter alia*, associated with more levels in the hierarchy, more managers, more formal meetings, less lifelong employment, and a top-down and more financial primary orientation to the company.

In the case of Japanese acquisitions, there were no significant associations between operational control and management practice. Acquisitions by other UK companies show a significant positive correlation between operational control and the number of levels in the hierarchy, formal meetings, slower promotion, subcontracting of distribution, and implementation of TQM.

French companies, on the other hand, show much more association between greater operational control and a number of post-acquisition changes in management practice. The assumption of greater operational control by French acquirers was generally accompanied by reduced levels of training, less emphasis on performance-related pay, more of a need-to-know communication philosophy, implementation of quality circles, more price competition, and less offering of new unique services and products.

Finally, German companies had a different pattern of significant correlations between changes in operational control and management practice. Among the German acquisitions, moves towards greater operational control were significantly correlated with an increase in subsidiary hierarchical levels, more job rotation, shorter-term employment and a slower approach to promotion, greater use of personal marketing contacts, a more need-to-know communication philosophy, shorter-term planning horizons, a top-down style and culture, and less emphasis on offering of unique products and services or developing new ones.

Integration

US and UK acquirers show the greatest tendency to integrate their acquisitions. Their post-acquisition integration of newly acquired companies was also associated with a wide range of changed management practices among US and UK companies (Table 8.6).

Among US companies, greater integration was associated with a reduced number of levels in the subsidiary's managerial hierarchy, increased job rotation, a lower percentage of managers, more formal meetings, and less ad hoc career development. In the case of UK companies, however, different changes in management practices were associated with greater integration. They included more rapid promotion, increased training, increased use of IT, a higher degree of outsourcing and multiple source procurement, greater cost control, and more development of new products. In UK firms, greater integration was linked with generally positive changes (such as more training, more new product development). As noted later, it was also linked to

Table 8.6. National profiles: changes in management practice correlating with post-acquisition integration, categorized by nationality of acquiring company

Management practice: change towards	American acquirers (N=45)	Japanese acquirers (N=20)	UK acquirers (N=36)	French acquirers (N=25)	German acquirers (N=13)
Lower no. of levels in the hierarchy	✓				
Job rotation of managers	✓				
Lower no. of managers as per cent of total employees	✓		✓		
Centralized strategic decision-making	✓				✓
Less individual managerial decision-making	✓			✓	
Less formal meetings	✓				
More formal meetings	✓				
Less ad hoc career development	✓				
Rapid promotion			✓		
Training			✓		
Customer involvement in marketing decisions			✓	✓	
Less need-to-know communication philosophy			✓	✓	
Use of automation/IT			✓		
Multi-source procurement			✓		
Higher degree of outsourcing			✓	✓	
More cost control			✓		
Development of new products/services			✓		
Greater profitability			✓		
Lower profitability	✓				
Sales					

Note: ✓ = Correlation between the change in management practice and post-acquisition integration at $p < 0.05$ (two-tailed test).

increased sales and profitability. By contrast, in US firms greater integration was associated with reduced numbers of managers, more formal meetings, and a poor level of profitability. One might further speculate as to whether the positive effects among UK companies are due to the integration being with acquirers of the same nationality or whether they reflect specific US/UK differences in the mode of integration. With US subsidiaries, integration and strategic control do not necessarily work in parallel nor always result in increased performance, even though integration is associated with operational control.

Integration had less leverage for post-acquisition change among acquirers of other nationalities. In French companies there was a significant association only between greater integration and a decrease in formal meetings, less of a need-to-know communication philosophy, and a higher degree of outsourcing. Among German acquisitions, greater integration was linked only with a move towards more strategic control. In Japanese acquisitions, level of integration was not related to any post-acquisition changes.

Acquiring companies therefore had generally different approaches to the relationship between strategic and operational control and integration. This reinforces the point that control, strategic and operational, and integration are separate issues. All three may be correlated with different changes in management practice depending on the nationality of the acquiring company. Thus while there are national differences, the overall picture is too complex to permit a simple categorization.

Integration, strategic control, and operational control: links with performance

The final question posed earlier in this chapter concerned the relationship between integration and strategic and operational control, on the one hand, and post-acquisition performance on the other. Chapter 12 will show that, overall, sales performance was inversely correlated with operational and strategic control though no overall correlation between profitability and control was observed. We can also say that there is no significant overall correlation between integration and profitability or sales performance.

However, as the answer to the previous question suggests, these overall results hide significant variations by nationality of acquirer, and it is therefore essential to deal with this issue on a nation-by-nation basis. We shall first note how the forms of control and integration are related and then examine whether these are significantly correlated with profitability or sales performance.

Previously Table 8.2 showed that there is not a consistent relationship between the two forms of control and integration, even within a given national group. There is, however, a significant and positive correlation between strategic and operational control among each nationality of acquiring company. The strength of this correlation differed by country, however, being noticeably stronger in the case of US acquisitions and weaker in the case of French acquisitions (Table 8.7).

US acquisitions showed a negative and significant correlation between integration and profitability, and between operational control and sales performance. A similar but not quite so significant negative relationship is present between strategic control and sales performance. The interviews suggest that one reason for these negative associations is that the imposition of an American CEO often led to cultural problems and declining motivation.

In stark contrast to the American case, integration correlated positively with superior sales and profit performance among UK–UK acquisitions. The improved profitability appeared to be helped by the appointment of fellow UK nationals to top subsidiary positions and the consequent lack of cultural clash. However, both strategic and operational control were inversely correlated with sales performance and showed no significant correlation with profitability.

For Japanese acquisitions there was no significant correlation between sales performance and integration or strategic or operational control. Japanese acquisitions did, however, show a significant correlation between profitability and greater strategic and operational control. In acquisitions by French companies, both forms of control but not integration were negatively correlated with profitability. No significant links with sales performance were found. Among German acquisitions, operational and strategic control were both significantly correlated with sales performance, but not profitability. Integration was not significantly correlated with either sales or profit performance.

This analysis assumes that post-acquisition changes in management practice have been largely introduced at the behest of the acquiring parent company rather than at the subsidiary's own discretion or initiative. The discussion of nationality profiles is predicated upon this *acquisition effect*. The assumption is in fact vindicated by the observation that the impact of post-acquisition changes on performance is normally greater when parent companies are reported to have had more influence over them and that, using overall measures, 'change' is highly correlated with 'influence'. Acquiring companies make a more significant contribution to the performance of their new charges when they actively instigate and facilitate the introduction of new management practices.

Table 8.7. National profiles: integration, strategic and operational control, and performance

	Correlation between operational and strategic control	Correlation between strategic control and profitability	Correlation between strategic control and sales	Correlation between operational control and profitability	Correlation between operational control and sales	Correlation between integration and profitability	Correlation between integration and sales
France	(r = 0.39, p = 0.026)	(r = -0.52, p = 0.005)	—	(r = -0.49, p = 0.008)	—	—	—
USA	(r = 0.60, p = 0.000)	—	—	—	(r = -0.26, p = 0.038)	(r = -0.42, p = 0.008)	—
UK	(r = 0.56, p = 0.000)	—	(r = -0.31, p = 0.03)	—	(r = -0.38, p = 0.008)	(r = 0.46, p = 0.006)	(r = 0.40, p = 0.018)
Germany	(r = 0.47, p = 0.043)	—	(r = 0.64, p = 0.035)	—	(r = 0.64, p = 0.034)	—	—
Japan	(r = 0.82, p = 0.000)	(r = 0.455, p = 0.044)	—	(r = 0.47, p = 0.038)	—	—	—

A final question concerns the causal or time-ordered association between control, integration, and performance. The above discussion would suggest that effects on performance result from decisions about control and integration but that, once made, the relationship is mutually reinforcing. This is perhaps illustrated by the case of one engineering company acquired by a US company where the attitude of the US parent was said by the UK MD to be 'you give us the money, we leave you alone', firmly linking performance to independence.

Conclusion

The present analysis has demonstrated that there are also many different attitudes to and effects of greater integration and control of subsidiaries. Several conclusions can be drawn from the survey.

First, the lack of correlation between the indicators of control and integration suggests that the two concepts are generally speaking independent. Integration need not necessarily involve control, nor vice versa. At the same time, the fact that integration is positively correlated with strategic control for German acquisitions and with operational control for US acquisitions suggests differences in German and US acquiring companies' attitudes to the relationship, or lack of it.

Secondly, Table 8.3 suggests that there is an overall trend towards integration of subsidiaries. This is also reflected in the fact that all parent companies tended to exercise a large degree of control by reserving many key decisions for the acquiring company. Over the sample as a whole, an average of 5.8 of the 8 key decisions investigated were reserved for the parent company.[1]

Thirdly, there was a noticeable difference between the degrees of integration and strategic and operational control according to nationality. US and UK subsidiaries were significantly more integrated than companies with Japanese, German, or French parents. French, UK, and German companies were less subject to increases in operational control by the new parent than companies with US or Japanese parents. While all companies showed a tendency towards increased strategic control, this was greatest among US and French companies (see Fig. 8.3).

Fourthly, there was no overall correlation between integration and sales or profitability. This overall result masks some important national differences.

---

1 In particular the following eight decisions: final approval for the subsidiary's budget, capital expenditure, appointment/termination of senior personnel, acquisition/divestment, formation of alliances (e.g. joint venture), major contractual agreements, changes in the scope/direction of the company, and the introduction of major new products.

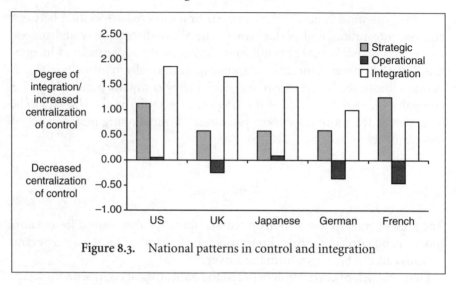

Figure 8.3. National patterns in control and integration

In US and UK companies, greater integration was linked to profitability and sales. However, the linkage was positive for UK companies and negative for US ones. This suggests either that cross-cultural integration is likely to be, if anything, counter-productive compared to integration of companies of similar nationality, or that the UK style of integration is more successful than that pursued by US companies.

Fifthly, changes in operational and strategic control appear to be closely linked, though not identical. However, as with integration there were significant national differences and, while increased strategic and operational control were associated with decreased profitability for French acquisitions, they were linked to greater profitability in the case of Japanese acquisitions. Increased strategic and operational control were also associated with lower sales for US and UK acquisitions, but higher sales for German acquisitions. In general, therefore, one can say that the effect of increased operational and strategic control over subsidiaries is negative in the case of US, UK, and French acquisitions but positive in the case of German and Japanese companies. The discriminating factor here may well lie in the generally 'softer', lower-profile approach towards control adopted in both German and Japanese UK subsidiaries.

Acquiring companies thus not only had generally differing approaches to the relationship between strategic and operational control and integration, but achieved differing results from their implementation.

Summary

There are many different paths to the achievement of good performance and there are many different attitudes to and effects of greater integration and control of subsidiaries. Overall the research shows that:

- Strategic and operational control are generally speaking independent concepts. Integration need not necessarily involve control, nor vice versa.
- There is an overall trend towards integration of subsidiaries.
- All acquisitions showed a tendency towards increased strategic control, but this was greatest in US and French companies.
- Parent companies exercised a large degree of control by reserving many key decisions for themselves.
- There was a noticeable difference between the degrees of integration and strategic and operational control, by nationality.
- US and UK subsidiaries were significantly more integrated than companies with Japanese, German, or French parents.
- French, UK, and German companies were less subject to increases in operational control by the new parent than companies with US or Japanese parents.
- There was no overall correlation between integration and sales or profitability.
- However, study of such correlations at a national level shows that the relationship between integration and performance can involve some important national differences.
- The data suggest that cross-cultural integration is likely to be, if anything, counter-productive compared to integration of companies of similar nationality, or at least that the UK style of integration is more successful than that pursued by US companies.
- Increased operational and strategic control are closely linked, though not identical.
- In general the effect of increased operational and strategic control over subsidiaries is negative in the case of US, UK, and French acquisitions, but positive in the case of German and Japanese companies.
- Acquiring companies thus not only had generally differing approaches to the relationship between strategic and operational control and integration, but achieved differing results from their implementation.

APPENDIX: ILLUSTRATIVE CASE STUDIES

A German acquisition: the 'preservation' approach to integration

The acquisition of G1-UK Pharmaceuticals by the German G1 Group falls squarely into Haspeslagh and Jemison's 'preservation' category of post-acquisition integration. The acquisition was of a successful company specializing in a market segment, generic pharmaceuticals, not served by the acquiring group. Acquisition of G1-UK provided an avenue for expansion into that segment and, in that event, to learn how to compete there. Even if this option were not taken up, the acquisition was in any event a sound portfolio investment. The acquired company was profitable and was achieving high levels of productivity from a relatively new plant. There was little benefit in integrating it organizationally into the parent group, but on the contrary much to be said for preserving its autonomy.

G1-UK specializes entirely in the production of generic pharmaceuticals. It was a private limited liability company when it was taken over in 1985. The owning family had 36 per cent of the equity and the venture capital company V1 held 30 per cent. The shareholders did well from the sale to G1 (the German acquirer). The price was about £16 a share, compared to a value of about £2.50 when it had moved in 1979 to a newly constructed facility. The acquirer, G1 Group, was at the time one of the world's largest chemical and pharmaceutical companies.

The managing director of G1-UK was our main informant for this case. He had been with the company since 1973.

Little post-acquisition change

After the acquisition, G1 kept its original name and separate legal identity, remained in its own location, and became a profit centre in its own right. The only managerial change was the appointment by G1 of an English finance director who came from its UK division. He was placed under G1-UK's previous finance director who became the new subsidiary's managing director. No other staff were introduced from the parent company. According to G1-UK's MD, the rationale was

to give me more time to take over marketing. The task they gave this man was to keep G1 at arm's length, not let the bureaucracy absorb us. Because we are in an industry sector where costs (generics are very price competitive) mustn't get out of line otherwise the bottom line can become red overnight . . . there was a recognition of how expensive central costs can be, so it was quite wise of the local G1 management. G1-UK has been here since the war and they had so many businesses in chemicals and paints. It had its own pharma division which was the research side retailing to doctors. And we are in the generic market, the own-branded prescription market, so we were complementary to the existing pharmaceutical business. They identified, and we knew it too, that the pharma market was going generic. Up to 60 per cent of prescriptions are generic, of which about 50 per cent are dispensed as generics. There were connections with the pharma price regulation scheme where the use of assets was very important. You get a better return if you are a UK-based company than if you are a foreign firm just importing. As it happened generics were excluded from that scheme about three months after they took us over. So that part of the calculation about the return on investment didn't come in, but our businesses boomed as a result of other things the government did.

The acquisition was a horizontal diversification for G1 into an area where G1-UK knew the sector and G1 did not. G1 left G1-UK alone because it was not in generics. It does not form part of the mainstream pharma division so the need for central control and coordination does not exist. A second reason for being granted a high level of autonomy is that G1-UK has been very successful. In 1985, it had sales of £7 million and profits of £400,000. By 1996, sales had risen to £45 million and profits to £3.5 million. The acquisition cost G1 just over £5.5 million and was estimated to be worth at least £60 million by 1997—or even up to £80–90 million for a purchaser who could realize synergies with its own operations. Indeed, a further reason for keeping the company separate is that this makes it easier to sell it again later on.

Shortly after the acquisition, G1 brought in a quarterly review of their strategic plan and more formalized planning. This was not seen to pose any problems by G1-UK's management. There were very few other changes.

Links between parent and subsidiary

G1-UK has retained its own legal identity and its own board of directors. The chairman of G1's UK holding company chairs the G1-UK board. At first, there were three G1 directors, who constituted a majority on the board. However, the number of these non-executive directors decreased over the years as people left the business and were not replaced. By 1997, there were just the financial director and the chairman from G1 and two others—the managing and technical directors—who were executives of G1-UK. G1's policy was to reduce the size of its subsidiaries' boards.

Neither the G1-UK managing director nor the technical director sits on any high-level G1 boards or committees. The policy link therefore functions through the G1-UK board and focuses on capital expenditure and finance. The managing director of G1-UK is its sole executive reporting channel to G1.

No G1 members sit on any G1-UK working groups or committees. There is, however, liaison within G1's International Production Group with all the plants around the world. This permits a cross-fertilization of ideas and sharing of information on equipment. For example, G1-UK had to move all its products from bulk dispensing packs into patient packs and provide a leaflet for patients. This required a large investment in packing machinery and it was able to use spare capacity at G1's Swindon factory. On the technical side, G1-UK has been working with Swindon on three slow-release products. It was said that, during the course of time following the acquisition, relations have become more open and people are willing to work more together.

Personal visits also play an integrative role. G1-UK senior managers travel periodically to group meetings. For example, at the time of our visiting G1-UK, its technical director was about to depart for an international meeting and exhibition at the group's headquarters in Germany. The chairman of the G1-UK board visits G1-UK every month from G1's UK holding company. There are also visitors on a fairly regular basis from all around the parent group, often to learn from its productivity which is the best for tablet production in the whole group.

Reporting relationships

All the functional areas in G1-UK report to the subsidiary's managing director, who is the sole reporting agent to G1. The finance director appointed from G1 also reports to the local MD. His main role is to align G1-UK to the G1 accounting system.

On the marketing side, G1-UK's sales channels are different from G1's. There was a big debate in G1 about whether to be in generics or not and the conclusion was to buy G1-UK but restrict its market to the UK. Over time that changed and during the 1990s G1-UK developed its export business. It uses G1 agents for exporting, but only at its own discretion where it thinks it will be good for the business. G1-UK has its own production and product development. It has very little fit with G1's businesses. G1 took over a couple of G1-UK's branded products where it had a product gap. Under this arrangement, however, G1-UK remained the producer and so shared the profit.

Quality of relationships with the parent company

G1-UK's managing director expressed satisfaction with the relationship between the parent group and subsidiary company primarily because 'they have left me to run the business'. This high degree of autonomy and preservation of a quasi-independent status does not, however, signify neglect by the parent company. The fact that the parent group concentrates on the production of bulk chemicals means that it cannot supply any relevant inputs except for paracetamol. It does not, on the other hand, place any constraints on G1-UK's purchasing. The parent group has also financed any necessary capital expenditure. While it does not allow G1-UK to raise capital on its own account, it has never refused any request for capital funding.

There have been a few conflicts with the parent group, but not of a serious nature. At one point G1-UK was restricted in its development of new products. The policy was to respect the group's intellectual property and G1-UK held back from challenging it. An independent generic company would normally have adopted a more proactive view. G1-UK was inhibited because it was expected to be friendly to the rest of the research industry, particularly German companies, which have the *Freundeskreis* understanding between themselves. There have also been a few cases where G1-UK was obliged by the group to do deals with branded companies which meant it had to take the product from them at a higher cost price than if it had developed the product itself or obtained it from the open market.

Resources from the parent company

Acquisition made it considerably easier to raise finance, both investment and working capital. Before being taken over, G1-UK had to secure finance from banks which was a time-consuming and uncertain process. Now the company can call down funds when these are required. The parent company controls capital expenditure but does not impose any limit on G1-UK's inventory. The parent group has also provided some plant and equipment particularly in furtherance of automation.

G1-UK has not taken up any products from G1. Rather the parent company has adopted two G1-UK products. Some G1 sales outlets are being used, but that is at G1-UK's discretion. Ten per cent of G1-UK's sales are exported. Hong Kong, Malaysia, South Africa, Thailand, Saudi Arabia, Jordan, and the Middle East are important export markets. It is in emerging economies, apart from China, that G1-UK chiefly benefits from G1 outlets. The acquisition has also given rise to economies in some areas of supply resulting from coordination between purchasing managers.

There have been only fairly small benefits to G1-UK in terms of management services. Shortly after it was acquired, a training manager in G1-UK set up training programmes for G1-UK managers. On the technical side, G1-UK's training is quite advanced and did not gain any benefit from the acquisition. There are now joint health and safety meetings with the G1 group of companies in the UK, which pool experience from different sites. There have also been economies in travel arrangements and in dealing with utilities: gas and electricity. G1-UK has a Treasury function which brings G1-UK cheaper loans. There is joint purchasing of insurance, which is particularly important in terms of product liability insurance. G1-UK is now covered by the worldwide policy of the group.

Impact of the acquisition on performance

Overall, the main benefit of the acquisition for G1-UK was that it brought it into membership of a group. Finance became easier and G1-UK no longer had the restraining concern of an independent company's board about cash flow and whether to take investment initiatives or not. 'We actually got on and did things and invested without worrying about the total balance sheet. We have probably grown faster. We were able to make decisions much more quickly and take advantage of the potential growth' (MD, G1-UK). On the negative side, the main limitation was the group's insistence that G1-UK surrender its few branded products to G1's pharma division. This did not change the pattern of G1-UK's research because it was copying brands and then branding them when they were off patent. G1-UK's focus is in fact on generics, which provides for large production volumes.

The acquisition contributed to G1-UK's profitability through helping it to increase its overall utilization of assets. At the time of the acquisition G1-UK was producing a billion tablets a year and working basically one shift. By 1997, it was producing 4 billion with frequent double-shift working. It was able to produce 4 billion because it was able to replace some of the equipment, with the investment capital being provided very speedily by the parent company.

Postscript

Not long before the time of our visit, the G1 Group merged with another pharmaceutical company. The new parent group intends to concentrate on branded research products and does not regard generics as part of its core strategy. As a result, it has downgraded the role of generics in its strategic portfolio and started to divest, particularly in the USA where it has loss-making businesses. It is no longer willing to invest in European expansion in generics, a development that G1-UK had begun to spearhead. The expectation was that G1-UK would continue to enjoy a highly autonomous status, unless and until it was sold off. As its managing director emphasized, the way of operating a generics company contrasts substantially with that suited to an ethical branded products company. 'You see in generics you have got to be fast moving, make quick decisions, have a lean management structure, and ethical companies aren't that sort of animal! Generics move very quickly, [whereas] the research for ethical products takes ten years.' Its days with the new G1 group seemed numbered.

A US acquisition: integration by absorption

US8-UK is a small chemicals company which was acquired by the MNC US8 in the mid-1990s as part of the acquisition of US8-UK's parent company UK01. The previous MD of US8-UK had set up the company in the 1960s and retired shortly after the acquisition whereupon the present MD, who was the main informant for this case study, had been appointed. The acquisition is a useful example of an attempt at integrating a small company into a large one while trying to retain the benefits of both. A measure of US8-UK's small size is shown by the fact that at the time of the acquisition US8-UK had a sales turnover of approximately £12 million and about ninety employees.

The process of acquisition

US8-UK's former parent company UK01 as a major UK company had a specific acquisitions and divestments group in its group headquarters in London. It was the experienced staff of this group which had dealt with the divestment of US8-UK and the associated negotiations. In contrast, while US8 was a multinational chemical company, the acquisition of US8-UK was handled by managers who did not primarily manage acquisitions and divestments and who were thus less experienced in such matters. In the opinion of US8-UK's MD 'it showed'. One critical factor though was that the acquisition of US8-UK by US8 was not a deliberate act but came about as a result of US8's wish to purchase US8-UK's former parent company UK01. US8-UK's business was in a slightly different sector from its parent's main field of business and as a result the first decision US8 was faced with following the acquisition of US8-UK's parent company was whether or not to sell or retain US8-UK itself.

Though US8 had naturally examined US8-UK as part of the due diligence process of the acquisition, at first they were not impressed by the company. However, they decided to keep it on after realizing the essential profitability of the operation. Having decided to retain US8-UK one might say that, unlike some other case studies, this was more a case of a decision not to divest than a decision to acquire so far as US8 and US8-UK were concerned.

Once this decision had been made, it became apparent to US8 that, first, there were a number of issues that the due diligence process had not uncovered that needed action and particularly investment by US8. Secondly, the two companies had very different working practices which would need addressing if the UK subsidiary was to be integrated into US8's family of companies. Two features thus dominated the post-acquisition process of change, first, investment by US8 which though small by US8's standards was huge by US8-UK standards, and, secondly, the operational changes needed to bring US8-UK into line with US8's working practices on issues like safety and environmental issues which, as a major US corporation, were standardized to a very high level across the entire group.

Post-acquisition changes

The most obvious changes other than the above-mentioned investment related to three main areas; financial controls, new product development, and management style. These were also linked with the overall issues of communication and integration.

Financial controls

US8 has a global financial management system into which information has to be fed in a certain form at a certain time. US8-UK on the other hand has had a conventional UK-based monthly reporting system. As a result, US8-UK has had to install the US system as well and run two parallel systems, one which is used by US8-UK to manage the business and one which is used to report to US8. The resultant tension between the methods of a large multinational and a small subsidiary that this illustrates were described by the MD as follows :

The key issue has been a healthy tension between a major US multinational which wishes all its sites to be US8 sites and behave in a certain way and which also recognizes that in buying small companies one can destroy value by insisting on large multinational company culture on a small site like this.

One other related area in which US8-UK resolutely resisted interference from US8 has been that of IT. Though the company's IT resources have been modernized the MD commented that the company has tried, with the exception of e-mail, to maintain a wall between US8 and US8-UK in terms of IT systems in order to avoid adding further costs which might be inappropriate to a company the size of US8-UK.

New product development

In at least one respect, US8-UK had an advantage in being acquired by US8 in that US8 was not only involved in the separate field which concerned US8-UK's former parent company but was also involved in the industry in which US8-UK itself operated. As a result, the synthetics division of US8 was able to give US8-UK a considerable amount of help in developing new products. In this it acted as a catalyst for creativity within US8-UK.

Management style and communication

Another key change that occurred following the acquisition related to the difference in management styles between US8-UK and US8. The first element in this was paradoxically that of language. Winston Churchill is quoted as saying that the USA and the UK were two countries divided by a common language and, in the words of the MD of US8-UK:

I think there's a major problem for British companies taken over by American companies. Because we speak the same language we think we understand each other. It would have been a lot easier if they spoke German or Chinese because that would have told us mentally, 'Ah there is a cultural difference,' and there is an enormous cultural difference between American companies and British companies.

Part of the differences related to the formality or lack of it in the management style of the two companies :

On the one hand there's a high degree of informality but on the other hand there's a very high degree of toughness and an insistence on conformity. You've got to conform or you're dead. Now with UK01 it went to the other extreme. A signal from on high was a signal for a wide ranging debate. Was this meaningful or useful? Were we going to obey it!

One also has to remember that this acquisition involved differences not only due to nationality but also to size, with US8 having about 1,000 times more staff and 4,000 times the turnover.

Integration

The above comments on management style are related to the way in which the two companies communicated and how this compared to US8-UK's relations with UK01, its former parent company. US8-UK had been kept at arm's length by UK01 but in contrast the aim of US8 was very much to integrate US8-UK into US8 wherever possible. According to the MD of US8-UK this involved several levels:

First of all the MD was part of a European site managers' group led by the manufacturing vice-president. He calls all his site managers together twice a year. Secondly, US8 synthetics division operates a similar sort of network. So the integrated operations director for US8 synthetics division calls his site managers together about every two to three months. About twice a year the US8 synthetics division business in Europe has what it calls an extended leadership meeting where it pulls together from Europe all the middle senior managers running its business for 2–3 days, so those are some of the ways I network into US8.

At the same time others reporting to the MD of US8-UK were also networking into US8. The MD, however, noted that it was important to filter such requests from US8 or one would spend all one's time networking into US8 and doing nothing else. As a result, the US8-UK site was not only a lot smaller than a typical US8 site but also a lot less integrated, simply because the MD rejected many potential links as having no real value to US8-UK. The problem as the MD put it was that, so far as activities involving links with US8 are concerned: 'It's pretty difficult if you aren't a long-time US8 employee to learn where you can get away with it and where in fact you don't have a choice.' Obviously with some areas such as safety there was no choice at all and integration was mandatory, but with others the position might be more flexible. A further feature of trying to integrate as small a company as US8-UK into as large a one as US8 was that staff in US8-UK generally had more than one area of responsibility, something relatively unheard of in their much larger parent. This could prove a difficulty with US8 which, as the MD of US8-UK put it:

could not cope with this organization as it was. For example they have great difficulty with having someone who has both manufacturing and business responsibility. No one else in US8 Europe has that joint responsibility other than the V-P for Europe. All the other bigger sites are split. They tried to separate them here and it didn't work but to be fair to them they recognized that and put it back.

There was thus a realization on the part of US8 that some attempts at integration went too far and had to be reversed.

Conclusions

Asked to assess the future relationship between US8-UK and US8 the MD of the former said that it depended entirely on whether US8-UK remains profitable. If it did not, it would very likely be rapidly divested.

Another key aspect of the acquisition has been the impact on company results. A significant effect of the investment from US8 has been an increase in US8-UK's ability to weather downturns in business. This is a not uncommon experience with acquisitions by companies with greater resources, though the time horizon for investment could vary considerably with the nationality of the parent company, with US companies tending to take a shorter-term view of investment. Overall, though, the MD of US8-UK thought that the acquisition had been a positive experience professionally. The key had been to try to integrate the smaller company in a way which did not destroy its flexibility, culture, and entrepreneurial attitude but gave it what was necessary in terms of embracing US8's core values.

There were redundancies following the acquisition but in general the MD of US8-UK said that these had been achieved slowly and with the minimum of disruption, mainly through voluntary redundancy and retirement. This was possible because US8-UK had control of the timescale involved. There are thus benefits to allowing subsidiaries some autonomy in management. At the same time, the key balance to be struck in managing an acquisition such as that of US8-UK by US8 is between integrating the new subsidiary totally, thus gaining all the benefits of a large company but at the same time losing the autonomy of the small firm, and having the benefits of being a small more flexible organization but sacrificing the benefits of the larger company in order to preserve them. Neither extreme was found to work and a balance, though difficult, had to be negotiated between the two companies.

9

Integration: A Closer Look

This chapter goes further into aspects of post-acquisition management that are conceptually linked to the general issue of integration. Drawing upon detailed information available from the forty case studies, the chapter first considers the methods of communication used, and the strategy and philosophy adopted by the new parent in relation to the subsidiary. It then takes a closer look at the level of integration of the subsidiary into the parent and the methods and systems adopted by the parent to control its new acquisition.

Communication is partly a matter of systems and style, but also a question of the communicator's skill at getting a message across. This is an area where nationality is very important, since different cultures have different attitudes towards communication and language barriers inevitably complicate the issue. What is undeniable is that differing nationalities have differing communication styles, ranging from the indirect, often unspoken style and 'implicit understanding' of Japanese culture, through the distant understatement and explicit comprehension of British culture, to the close but highly direct communication style of US culture. Relative to this continuum, Chapter 5 suggested that French and German communication styles might perhaps be tangential, differing on issues of logical necessity and formality respectively. The differences that exist between the parent and subsidiary's natural communication style are bound to play a critical role in the integration of any foreign subsidiary into its parent company's organization.

The parent company's strategy refers to whether it introduces a primarily strategic or financial orientation into its acquired subsidiary and its expectation or otherwise of immediate results and short-term profits. The parent's philosophy refers to the management style and culture it encourages in the subsidiary, and the extent to which it grants autonomy to the latter. Together, strategy and philosophy present a framework within which the new subsidiary will have to operate.

Chapter 5 also noted the frequent association of UK company strategy with a short-term orientation, both by academics (e.g. Lane 1995) and by those working in industry (e.g. Marsh 1995). Acquisitions by French companies on the other hand are expected to be strategic rather than based on short-term financial considerations. French strategy is often phrased in a quasi-military language in which the contestants adopt, by analogy, the stance of the great generals and marshals (Barsoux and Lawrence 1990). In contrast, US management culture places a stronger emphasis on achieving short-term financial results (Jacobs 1991) and many US companies tend to be managed for the short-term maximization of profits and the satisfaction of shareholders (Calori and De Woot 1994; Lawrence 1996*a*).

The strategic approach or philosophy adopted by a new parent company in relation to a new foreign subsidiary is therefore a further important component involved in the integration of a subsidiary into the parent's organization.

General findings

Each of the managers interviewed in the forty case study companies was asked to rate the degree of integration achieved by the acquisition on the scale of 1 to 7 described in the preceding chapter. On this scale 1 represents the least and 7 the greatest degree of integration. Taken as a whole the forty companies had an average integration level of 3.6. Within this overall figure there were, however, significant national differences in the level of integration. American companies were the most committed to a total integration of subsidiaries, with an integration level of 4.8, while Japanese and German companies tended to be the least inclined to integrate with average integration scores of only 3.1 and 3.0 respectively. French companies interviewed had an average integration level of 3.7. Analysis of variance indicated that the overall differences between the average integration scores for each country were significant at the 7 per cent level of confidence.

The most common form of control imposed was through financial means, namely approval and monitoring of subsidiary budgets, and control of capital expenditure. This form of control was generally allied to the provision of a strategic framework within which subsidiary decision-making was to be confined. Differences between national approaches in this area mirrored those found in levels of integration.

Parent companies were in most cases able to reassure their subsidiaries that their investment was part of a long-term strategy. However, communication between parents and subsidiaries clearly differed on a national basis. The American companies were professional communicators relishing the use of first names, holding regular meetings at all levels, establishing noticeboards to present mission and vision statements, and publishing company newspapers. Communication between Japanese companies and their UK subsidiaries did not seem as easy or open by comparison. German companies veered between the stiffly formal and the self-consciously informal. French companies seemed to suffer little self-doubt, communicating well amongst themselves but informing subsidiary staff only on a need-to-know basis and adopting what one interviewee referred to as a generally 'colonial attitude'. The four countries' attitudes to the four key areas of concern are summarized in Table 9.1 below.

These four areas of integration, control, strategic philosophy, and communication are now reviewed in more detail in respect of each of the four countries.

Comparisons by acquirer nationality

American companies

Integration

American post-acquisition management tended primarily towards total absorption even where this required some time for readjustment. In the case of a diversified US manufacturer's subsidiary US1[1] the new American manager noted: 'The people here seem to hate all things American, even the size of the notepads. Some of the personnel still have to adjust to the fact that they are now part of a very successful American-based multinational, not a little family company.' In this case the company was very much absorbed, and there were many other examples of total integration of UK companies by their US acquirers. US5 progressively absorbed a UK subsidiary, strengthening both control

Table 9.1.   National contrasts in parent–subsidiary relationships

	Integration	Control	Communication	Strategic philosophy
USA	Fully integrated	Targets/budgets strict financial control	Open but formal	Short-term financial
France	Partially integrated	Strategic and financial control	Need to know/ top down	Long-term 'imperial'
Japan	Not integrated	Budgets/systems 'advisers'	Need to know/ implicit	Long-term strategic
Germany	Not integrated	Varied: budgets/systems informal controls	Upward formality Downward informality	Long-term indistinct

[1] All companies for reasons of confidentiality are referred to by numbered codes denoting the parent company nationality : USn for US, Jn for Japanese, Gn for German, and Fn for French parent companies where n=1 to 10. Former UK parent companies are denoted by UKn.

systems and financial reporting. The MD said the new subsidiary 'has been totally integrated. There was about a year of separateness, but for full integration five years have been needed. We have a well-organized account management structure which doesn't tolerate weak performers.' In some cases the nature of the business made integration inevitable. For example, US3 (a US freight company) totally integrated a UK company into its worldwide organization, reorganizing its systems to match the global ones of its new parent.

Of the ten US acquisitions visited, five had an integration level of 5 or more, three were at the 3–4 level, and only two at the non-integrated 1–2 level. With an average score of 4.8, the preference of US parent companies was for a high level of integration, something that was also apparent from the results of the questionnaire survey.

Control

An emphasis on financial control and shorter financial time horizons was typical of the US subsidiaries. In many cases the change in financial controls was almost immediate due to an absence of the controls expected in a US financial environment, with quarterly reporting requirements that privately owned UK companies do not face. The MD of a small UK company (US9) acquired by a larger US parent observed:

The Americans had to justify their investment. They put in financial reporting systems much quicker and ones which were compatible with their own systems. What they have done has improved the business. It needed a financial controller rather than a part-time accountant.

The need for regular financial returns by US companies facing quarterly reporting constraints was common. According to the British MD of US10, this is also linked with a pragmatic style of management: 'He [the US CEO] said to me, "You know what style of management we have? It's the management of the Mafia—send us the money and we leave you alone!" . . . it worked very well.'

A requirement for consistency with the corporate profile often accompanied the financial controls. This could be tempered by a realization that there had to be a balance between integration through instilling big company values and preservation of the small company's entrepreneurial spirit and flexibility. However, all ten US acquired companies interviewed reported substantial tightening of control systems, especially the financial ones.

Communication

American companies also tended to pursue informal communications, albeit paradoxically in a relatively formal way. That is not to say that American parent companies are always formal but, as one MD of a US multinational manufacturing company's subsidiary (US1) commented:

US1 are a very open company with information, and make a philosophy of it. Before the acquisition it was generally the 'mushroom' principle that reigned and communication was I gather a bit random. . . . US1 set great store by full and open communication and the noticeboards are extensively used to keep all employees informed of what is going on, the level of the order book and so forth . . . [The management practices] are structured, professional, and informal.

Companies acquired by US parents reported moves towards shorter planning time horizons and a shorter-term employment philosophy. The toughness mentioned above also extended to employee relations as noted by the MD of US8:

I find American business culture pretty difficult. UK01 [the former parent] never talked about caring and valuing people but its actions showed that it did. US8 talks a huge amount about caring and valuing people but when the going gets tough . . . it doesn't care at all.

Strategic philosophy
The American philosophy of post-acquisition management appears to be very demanding with the threat of rapid intervention if results are not forthcoming. The MD of US10, who had also worked in a UK company which had been German owned, observed:

They expect instant returns . . . There's no well, we wait for three years, make sure there's synergies and then look for a return—they want it *now*. The shock is not just financial, . . . the speed at which change is to be introduced is quite extraordinary. So no doubt about it, a much more interventionist type of policy, much more dynamic, much more forcible, and much more demanding.

Despite a shortening of financial time horizons imposed by US acquirers, the larger size of many US parent companies relative to their UK subsidiaries meant that significant investments were still made in the subsidiaries. The MD of a small UK technology-based company (US8) said that the main benefit of the acquisition of his company was that: 'Our company was going down the tubes fast. US8 has been very successful in turning around the business and putting in huge sums of money. One must give them credit for that which our former owners probably could not have done.'
    Another MD of the UK service company US7 said:

Now we are preparing five-year plans . . . before we never went further forward than twelve months. But at the same time, there is pressure for quarterly results. . . . You

get all kinds of absurd requests to make more profit or collect more debt each quarter
. . . so we've noticed both a lengthening and a shortening of the time horizons.

While experiencing the financial demands of US ownership, the subsidiaries
of some US companies were given more autonomy over capital expenditure
and changes in strategy. One MD of US6's subsidiary said that it was possible
to push forward a strategy the parent company had not thought of. In the case
of his subsidiary, this was mainly apparent through marketing and liaison
initiatives which it, not its US parent, had initiated.

American acquirers tended to install formal multi-year planning systems,
adopt a global approach to business, but demand good short-term financial
results. The implication is that, if the company does not perform in a relatively short timescale, it will be divested or at the very least the MD will
be fired.

Japanese companies

Integration
The attitude of Japanese acquirers to integration contrasted strongly with that
of the Americans. Changes were achieved incrementally by a process of slow
adaptation to the parent company's norms.

For instance, a Japanese bank acquired a UK financial services company in
order to establish a presence in the City of London. Having done so, it introduced very few changes on the assumption that the British management
understood the business better. In another case, a UK pharmaceutical company was acquired inadvertently by a Japanese pharmaceutical firm when it
acquired a US-owned group in order to preserve a Japanese licensing arrangement. Although it had little involvement with management of the subsidiary,
it nevertheless provided the UK firm with substantial financial support and
technical assistance.

The new Japanese owners of a UK consumer products company (J3) also
gave it steady financial support and did not interfere in operational matters,
leaving the company essentially unintegrated. This hands-off attitude
surprised the director interviewed. In the case of a UK electronics company
(J4) acquired by a major Japanese company, which again remained unintegrated, the MD noted: 'Historically most of their sales organizations are
totally controlled from Japan . . . but not with us! We are quite an experiment
. . . the numbers are not crucial so long as we are going in the right direction.'

In all acquisitions there is a balance between allowing the subsidiary freedom from interference by the parent and seeking the benefits that closer integration could bring. In other words, there is a balance between independence

and intervention along the spectrum of integration. In Japanese acquisitions the balance is usually struck on the side of supportive independence.

Of the ten Japanese acquisitions visited, none had been integrated at a level of 5 or higher on our scale, six were at the 3–4 level, and four were left at the non-integrated level of 1–2, giving a low average of 3.1 overall.

Control

Japanese companies not only use budgets and financial control systems to monitor their acquisitions but also other methods of keeping informed. They usually encouraged their new subsidiaries to assume rather more decision-making autonomy, but at the same time uniquely introduced 'advisers' into them. These 'advisers' were often managers sent abroad for two to four years to gain international experience prior to promotion back in Japan. In one subsidiary it was said that:

There are no formal links, there have been some placements of Japanese personnel but they've been in new staff roles. . . . The few that have done it have been perceived by J10 to be up and coming managers and have come to learn about management internationally rather than take part in day-to-day management.

In many cases, however, these advisers had substantial expertise in a specialist area. J8's MD said that once he realized one Japanese manager was a highly skilled engineer he was able to make very good use of his expertise in production management. The advantages of specialist technical support were also available as the MD of J6 found: 'We ran into a problem on a product. It required technology on adhesives which we hadn't got experience of and they quite easily said, we'll send our adhesives man in. . . . But then they had all these experts, very, very, focused experts.'

In general where decisions were required from Japanese parent companies they could prove rather slow in arriving. The MD of a UK retailing company (J7) said that a problem with their Japanese parent was 'Getting a clear answer, a clear "Yes, go ahead". We keep battling away and sometimes they'll never say no. If they said "No, go away" we'd know where we stand but their culture doesn't permit them to say "No".' Another MD of a Japanese subsidiary (J6) noted: 'It was very frustrating, it would sometimes take weeks to get an answer. In reality you actually knew the answer to it. It was very annoying for the guys on the shop floor.'

On the other hand, where trust over a particular issue or range of issues had been established, considerable independence could be expected. But this trust and respect had to be earned. The MD of J8 commented:

I learned very quickly . . . that because of the communication problems, they are only interested in figures not written words. It makes my life very much easier. My first presentation in Tokyo was to the effect that we needed 3–4 years to get things going. Where we stand today is where we predicted we would be [four years ago] ... achieving what you promise is very, very important to a Japanese ... So it's a very happy relationship.

The ways in which Japanese acquirers stand out compared to the other national groups support some but not all of the normal characterizations of Japanese management practice. Their long-term and strategic and collective orientations were clearly apparent. As the MD of a pharmaceutical company's subsidiary (J10) said: 'There is a feeling that we should know what we need to do and that we don't need to go to [our parent] for counsel. But they know what is going on and have been very supportive.'

Overall the attitude of Japanese companies towards control was to have faith in budgets and forecasts, but expect them to be met in detail. It was also to give considerable operational latitude but to take the big decisions in Japan, often agonizingly slowly.

Communication

The area of communication can be a difficult one in a Japanese acquisition for both linguistic and cultural reasons. For example, in one interview with a previously family-owned engineering company (J1) the MD noted:

Because all the Japanese company's managers speak good English, language is not a problem on a day-to-day basis. It does, however, pose a barrier in terms of control and information. Virtually all written communication to and from Japan is in Japanese and I cannot understand it. Nor is it translated for me. I therefore don't know for certain exactly what they are saying.

Language problems can thus lead to communication barriers. In another Japanese acquisition (J10), the interviewee qualified the matter:

I think language is undoubtedly an issue at times but it's never a significant problem. I think it can be at the more junior level ... When it's just straightforward technical reports it's no problem, but when they are trying to get over areas of subtlety it can be difficult.

Communication barriers due to language could be overcome more easily where technical terminology was involved, partly due to the preponderance of *gairaigo* or imported foreign words in technical Japanese.

Strategic philosophy

The strategic philosophy of Japanese acquirers was consistently long term, even if the strategic details could often appear to be rather fuzzy and ad hoc. The MD of a UK pharmaceutical company (J10) said:

I think we have benefited from the takeover from being able to address issues which prior to the takeover would have been difficult . . . through lack of funding or lack of strategic direction. . . . Sometimes their patience for a return amazes even me. They seem quite laid back about it . . . the return on these things will stretch way out into the future.

In another UK company (J6) which manufactured a specialist consumer product and was bought by a major Japanese firm, it was said that: 'The main benefit has to be the investment that was made. Our subsequent success has stemmed from the fact that it gave us the breathing space to move forward.' The same company is also a good example of the 'slingshot effect' in that the subsidiary was eventually sold due to the parent's financial difficulties in Japan, and left having received substantial technical and financial support. This, when taken together with their own in-house development, arguably put them ahead of their former Japanese parents.

With the exception of a longer-term employment philosophy, no significant differences were found between Japanese and other acquirers in respect of personnel policy changes. Also virtually every company had introduced some or all of the operational practices associated with Japanese companies. It appears that Japanese acquiring companies adjust their HRM practices to suit the local UK context, while in the operations area most companies have gone a long way towards adopting a Japanese approach, as Oliver and Wilkinson (1992) concluded.

In each of the ten Japanese acquisitions visited, the major merit of their new owners was said to be their long-term philosophy and willingness to back their purchase with financial resources. The logical incremental approach commonly ascribed to Japanese companies meant that, while detailed plans were often not in place or apparent, it was possible to discern the general goals behind their acquisitions such as developing market potential through closer customer relations or becoming more international.

German companies

Integration
In a similar way to Japanese companies, German acquirers tended to avoid closely integrating their new acquisitions. Of the ten companies interviewed, none had an integration score above 6, five were in the 3–4 range, and the other five were at the 1–2 non-integrated level, the average German score being 3.0.

A high-tech instrument company (G4) acquired by a German competitor with a larger global presence was left alone by its new parent. The MD observed: 'They have never sought to change anything. They really have left us alone, I don't think we have learnt much from them, but they may have learnt something about the flexibility of a small company, and what they need to do to become more flexible.'

It is worth noting that where little change occurred it was often due to the subsidiary's management gaining the trust and acceptance of the new parent's management and convincing them that it knew its business better than they did.

Control
The German attitude to control revealed by the case studies is quite varied. It ranges from board representation and use of management accounts to putting in a MD who then controls directly. The subsidiary managers interviewed generally felt that their German parent companies exercised relatively little influence over their acquisitions. Compared with other nationalities, the German acquisitions were less likely to have parent company managers as CEOs, or as marketing and R&D directors. One successful subsidiary (G4) of a German acquirer commented that: 'We report with management accounts on a monthly basis which we send direct to Germany. . . . Since we have never been wildly off budget, there is no major response to these. Anyway financially we outperform our parent as a whole.'

Even less successful companies enjoyed a fair degree of freedom. One manager (G6) said: 'We are visited from Hamburg once a quarter. They get involved in the thinking as well as the numbers. But in general their aim is to keep a tight rein on the finances and not worry too much about how we achieve the results.'

But there were also more muddled companies. A (G8) director said: 'The German company is just owned by three people and has a combined board of five people, all of whom came over in the first few months to see their new acquisition . . . to be totally honest all of their views totally differed.'

Another German company (G9) started out very autocratically, but showed that personal relationships as well as success could influence the degree of freedom a subsidiary enjoyed. The MD of the subsidiary commented that:

We would use G [parent company] where we needed them but push them away where we didn't. . . . we were able to wave our results as justification for the UDI that we declared. It was a quirk of the changing times within G and our success that led them to that method of control. It was also personal. I very quickly developed a relationship of 100 per cent trust with the chairman in both directions and he left it to me.

Communication
The issue of personal relationships also concerns communication. On the issue of formality, two photographs belonging to the MD of a UK company

sold to a German parent (G10) who had also been part of a US-led MBO illustrate the point. One showed the US-led MBO team at an outdoor party celebrating the fact that they had just bought the company. The other showed a row of sober-suited people in a wood-panelled room the day the contract to sell the company to the German company was signed. This, the UK MD felt, graphically illustrated the difference in formality between the two cultures.

Strategic philosophy

German parent companies, like Japanese companies, took a long-term view of investment decisions. However, this could have an apparent downside by being almost too beneficent. The MD of a manufacturing subsidiary G10 said:

I think our financial director . . . would almost have welcomed being pressed more to be self-sufficient. It was almost a failing of the Germans to be as supportive as they were. Quite frankly I think it would have done us good if they had said, 'Look, there's no more money—you've got to sort yourself out'.

It is worth noting that G10 was subsequently sold. Looking at other acquisitions it seems that there are two requirements for long-term financial support to be a success. The acquired subsidiary not only has to have the support, but also some idea about how to use that support and about the long-term direction of the company—whether that direction is self-generated or dictated by the parent. Support or direction alone is insufficient. This was reflected by the sense of the MD just quoted that the UK company under its German owners suffered from a lack of strategic direction: 'It failed to have a long-term strategic objective. The business objectives were not known by the board, so how on earth could they be transmitted to the rest of the troops?'

German management is clearly influenced by the nature of its domestic financial markets, which differ from those in the USA. For example, an American company executive would be unlikely to echo this description of his parent company's attitude offered by the manager of its UK subsidiary (G3): 'They are long-termist. They do not have making a profit itself as a prime matter. They are not profit driven. They want to know about quarterly results but they are not dominated by them.'

It is worth remarking that although German companies may be long-termist in outlook, that does not alter the fact that some of the companies acquired by German parents, such as G10 above, were subsequently sold on despite considerable investment. One has to conclude that a German parent company with a long-term horizon may only offer a subsidiary temporary protection from subsequent events, something which might equally be said of Japanese acquisitions with long-term horizons.

French companies

Integration

French acquirers tended towards the middle of the integration spectrum, with an average level of 3.7. They appeared less determined to integrate acquired companies than American parents, but more so than Japanese and German parents. Four of the ten companies visited were at an integration level of 5 or above, a further four at 3–4, and two at a non-integrated 1–2 level. They varied from total integration of a previously British IT consultancy company to form a French-based transnational, to water companies that have been largely left alone to operate substantially as before. This latter result is due, at least in part, to regulatory restrictions. A manager in a French-owned UK public utility company explained: 'The general philosophy is "local management" . . . although they are interested in this high-up view they really leave the rest of it to local management. . . . Because we are a regulated business there's a limit to what they can do.'

Control

National characteristics reveal themselves much more in the French companies' manner of exercising control. In general, they operate very hierarchically with French managers determining major decisions. They look upon acquired company personnel with a 'colonial' attitude, much in keeping with the attitude to acquisitions noted by Empson (1998). An executive from a French-acquired aerospace company (F1) stated: 'Things are decided informally amongst Frenchmen to the exclusion of British middle management. If contacts were plotted, pretty well all the informal links would be between the French.'

The British part-time chairman of a French-acquired financial services company (F2) said: 'They have difficulty in understanding the British concept of a board. So far as they are concerned a board is a kind of registration. It is like a levee, not a discussion and decision-taking body.'

French companies place great emphasis on the distinction between strategic decisions (to be made by French managers at headquarters) and operational decisions (to be made by local managers on the spot), though financial controls remain important. As an executive from a French-acquired water company (F10) noted: 'They appointed a French financial controller . . . that is one post they try and keep for themselves. On the operational side it's all local.'

Communication

Communication tends to be very hierarchical and top down, with little involvement of British managers in the decision-making hierarchy. The head of a financial services company (F3) acquired by a French bank said: 'Communications are largely on a need-to-know basis. I don't get involved in the Paris business at all, although I try to network as much as I can. I don't ferret around with things that don't concern London.' An executive of an engineering company (F4) added: 'I don't think most of industry in the UK, certainly a TQM-inspired participative modern ethos, has the power element that the French have built in to everything.'

Strategic philosophy
French companies generally have a long-term strategic philosophy in relation to acquisitions. As a manager in a major French electronics company's subsidiary (F1) put it: 'A strategic rather than a financial orientation exists; it has to, since the company loses money. However, it is thought to be important to stay in the market.'

The MD of an acquired high-tech manufacturing firm (F9) said:

The way in which the business is being approached is interesting—'the centre and several self-sufficient satellites'—but in my opinion it was never going to be a workable philosophy because it weakens the whole thing rather than strengthens it . . . It's wonderful to manage a subsidiary where one is totally empowered but on the other hand how is one going to grow the business without the help of the group?

This indicates that the issue may depend on the size of the decision being made. A French financial services company, for example, was said to reserve larger decisions for itself but to allow its British subsidiary (F3) a lot of local autonomy. Indeed, in one French acquisition the parent management made it clear from the outset that it would run its acquisition on an operationally decentralized basis. An interview with the personnel director of the subsidiary revealed that when asked in a meeting 'What do you want us to do?', the president of the French parent replied, 'Monsieur, if we have to tell you what to do, we have the wrong people.' The parent company involved itself in setting broad strategic targets for its subsidiary, but then left it to the local management to decide how to achieve them operationally: it was a case of 'these are our broad targets; now what are you going to do?' It is characteristic of this operationally decentralized policy that nobody from the parent company sits on the subsidiary's board of directors or occupies a managerial position within it.

In other words, the French management considered that it was not for them to influence the UK management but rather for the UK management to run their business. This apparently surprised the particular UK manager who said he had always regarded French companies as bureaucratic and centralist. It also shows that it is up to a subsidiary to manage its owners as much as to be managed by them.

Conclusion

This chapter has concentrated on four main issues: the level of integration of the subsidiary; the control methods and systems adopted by the parent; methods of communication; and the strategy and philosophy of the new parent concerning the new subsidiary. Each of these factors depends on and reflects the attitude a parent takes to integrating a company into its overall corporate structure. Some previous research (e.g. Calori et al. 1994) has looked at differences in control mechanisms between nationalities, but the broader studies of post-acquisition integration (e.g. Haspeslagh and Jemison 1991) have tended to discuss differences between acquired and acquiring companies rather than national differences between them.

Haspeslagh and Jemison (1991) characterized acquisitions in terms of their needs for strategic interdependence and organizational autonomy. At first sight these two axes seem to be orthogonal. However, with needs for autonomy and interdependence being in some sense opposites, it would seem that replacing them with a single measure of the overall need for integration would distinguish types of acquisition more economically. This is reinforced by the fact that Haspeslagh and Jemison (1991) found no instances of their holding category of acquisitions (those with a low need for both autonomy and strategic interdependence). The present research confirms, however, that whatever their relationship, it is important to take into account needs both for organizational autonomy and for strategic interdependence. For example, there were several German acquisitions where the new parents wished to keep their subsidiary intact precisely in order to preserve and learn from their unique managerial character. There were also companies such as the US-acquired freight company where absorption was total, leaving almost no trace of the subsidiary's former independent existence.

There are also other factors that affect the degree of integration to be pursued. Haspeslagh and Jemison (1991) mention both acquired company quality and acquisition size. The present investigation has also identified as relevant the controls applied by the parent, its methods of communication, strategy, and philosophy, as well as our focal variable, nationality. Capabilities embedded in acquired companies, requiring organizational boundaries for their preservation, are not necessarily of lesser strategic value than others which require the boundaryless conditions of absorption to maximize their benefits. It seems therefore that the overall choice to be made comes down to the key dimension of integration.

Therefore, the complexity of the issues involved in acquisitions revealed by the present research has paradoxically suggested a simplified categorization of acquisitions using the degree of integration of subsidiaries. While Haspeslagh and Jemison (1991) characterized acquisitions in terms of their need for strategic interdependence and organizational autonomy, the scale we have employed simply ranges from not integrated, through partially integrated, to fully integrated where the subsidiary organization is no longer distinguishable within the parent company. This does not ignore the fact that many components contribute to deciding a company's position on this scale of post-acquisition integration, nor does it concentrate on particular components to the exclusion of others. In presenting such a scale, one must at the same time emphasize the multidimensional nature of post-acquisition integration.

The main findings of the research were summarized in Table 9.1. American subsidiaries tended to be significantly more integrated than other nationalities and German and Japanese subsidiaries significantly less integrated than others, with French subsidiaries somewhere in between. The case studies also indicated that, despite differences in the degree of integration, similar means of control were used, albeit not all applied to the same degree. A key example was financial controls related to investment, but more common cost controls were also involved as well. The use of advisers and/or informal controls in Japanese and German subsidiaries contrasted with the stricter financial controls of US companies. The way in which parents communicated with their subsidiaries also showed distinct differences between the four nationalities studied, with the main parameters being the degree of formality/informality, the degree of openness or more limited need-to-know communication, and the directness of communication. As expected, Japanese companies operated more on a need-to-know and implicit communication style, US companies were open but formal, while French companies tended to a more autocratic top-down style. German companies who might be expected to be unduly formal were found to be upwardly formal in dealing with their parent but downwardly very informal in communicating with their subsidiary.

One can also try to summarize the findings in terms of the overall strategic philosophy of the four acquirer nationalities. US companies tended to a short-term financial approach to the three key issues, while the other three countries were predominantly long term in their approach. However, they differed in that while Japanese companies had a strategic approach generally involving substantial financial support, French companies had a more 'imperial' approach, and German companies a range of indistinct approaches though generally informed by long-term horizons.

The research findings allow several points to be made. First, while there are many similarities between acquisitions in general, there are substantial differences in approach by acquiring companies of different nationalities. Secondly, communication is critical in building links between parents and subsidiaries but words must be backed by consistent actions if credibility is to be maintained. Linguistic and cultural problems with communication need more attention than they usually receive. Thirdly, several control styles are possible, ranging from the very strict financial controls favoured by many US parents to the much more *laissez-faire* attitude of Japanese parent companies and even some French companies. Fourthly, having a parent with long-term horizons may only insulate a subsidiary temporarily from subsequent short-term events.

One might compare these findings with those of Goold and Campbell (1988) who drew attention to three main approaches to managing subsidiaries (strategic planning, strategic control, and financial control), depending on the degree of control and planning by the centre that is involved. Our research shows that strategic and financial control and planning are important elements of managing an acquisition. However, it also demonstrates that many other elements are involved, which are likely to be equally important to the success of the acquisition. These include the differing cultures of the acquiring and acquired companies and communication between them. This again emphasizes the multidimensional nature of post-acquisition integration.

The research also suggests several areas for further investigation. Investigating potential links between integration and performance is one area. To anticipate Chapter 12, it is worth noting, however, that despite the distinct national approaches to managing the control and integration of subsidiaries, no one country's acquisitions were significantly more successful than any other. This all leads to the overall impression that it is not so much whether companies control, communicate with, or integrate new subsidiaries but the particular ways of so doing that they adopt in any given situation. Norburn and Schoenberg (1994) suggest that with an international acquisition there is a need for relatively specialized integration skills different from those required within an intra-UK context. Our work suggests that such skills and the approaches adopted will differ from nationality to nationality. The multi-dimensional nature of acquisition management and the issues of integration, control, and communication are therefore shown to be open to different national approaches, but none the less important for that. They remain of continuing interest as important factors in managing the acquisition process.

Summary

- There are several key dimensions to the relationship between acquiring and acquired companies concerning subsidiary integration and control, communication, and parent strategy and philosophy towards subsidiaries.

- Each of these dimensions differed according to acquirer nationality.
- US subsidiaries tended to be integrated with their parent company, subject to strict financial controls, with open but formal communication with their parent companies and a generally short-term financial strategic philosophy.
- French subsidiaries tend to be less integrated than US subsidiaries, subject to strategic and financial control, with a top-down, need-to-know communication style and a generally long-term and imperial control style.
- German subsidiaries showed little integration, a mixed set of informal controls, upwardly formal and downwardly informal communication style, and a long-term strategic philosophy.
- Japanese subsidiaries also showed little integration, used 'advisers' as well as financial controls, with communication which was in part need to know and part implicit, and a long-term strategic philosophy.

10

Processes of Post-acquisition Change

Changes processes

This chapter addresses the issue of how the foreign acquirers from each country tackled the problem of bringing about change in the management of their new acquisition, and the effectiveness of their different methods and styles. In each scenario, the acquirers buy a company in a particular state of health, and change is initiated by either the new parent or the subsidiary or both. Varying contributions by either or both parties in the form of methods, resources, and appointments are employed to effect this change, and various results are achieved in the form of company performance following the change process. This process is illustrated in Fig. 10.1.

Distinctly different approaches were adopted in the task of bringing about change and improving performance in newly acquired companies. It is appreciated that other factors than the national identity of the acquirer are likely to influence post-acquisition behaviour, such as the economic condition of the subsidiary at the time of acquisition, the prior international experience of

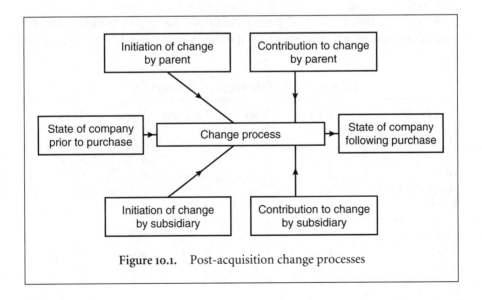

Figure 10.1.   Post-acquisition change processes

the acquirer, the relative size of the partners, and perhaps the industry involved. It is impossible to control formally for all possible factors in a study involving substantial qualitative research elements. However, a range of companies in a wide cross-section of industries was chosen for the survey and to interview, in order to seek to avoid bias in any particular direction, regarding these other possible influencing factors.

As shown in Table 10.1, of the forty companies visited twelve were acceptably profitable at the time of purchase, a further twelve were barely profitable, and sixteen were making losses. By the time the visits and interviews were carried out, the number of profitable companies had increased to twenty-two, the break-even ones reduced to nine, and the remaining loss-makers were only nine. So with 78 per cent of companies in profit after acquisition compared with 60 per cent prior to acquisition, a qualified approval could be given to the takeover process.

An important issue is which of two parties initiates any post-acquisition change. In the companies interviewed the initiator was by no means always the acquirer, as shown in Table 10.2. In fourteen cases the acquirer led and in a further four acted as catalyst, but in thirteen cases the subsidiary claimed to have initiated the changes. In three companies, changes were attributed to the joint efforts of the parent and subsidiary, and in the remaining six acquisitions, little change was said to have taken place. It is thus as likely that change will be initiated by the subsidiary as by the parent company following an acquisition, though, as can be seen in Table 10.2, initia-tion by the parent is more frequent where US parent companies are involved.

As regards the method of post-acquisition change, in twelve cases the subsidiary was absorbed into the parent or had a managing director appointed

Table 10.1. Profitability of companies visited

Companies	USA	Japan	Germany	France	Total
Acceptably profitable					
Before	4	0	4	4	12
After	8	4	4	6	22
Just profitable					
Before	3	4	3	2	12
After	0	3	3	3	9
Loss-making					
Before	3	6	3	4	16
After	2	3	3	1	9

Table 10.2. Initiators of change

Change initiator	USA	Japan	Germany	France	Total
Acquirer	6	2	3	3	14
Acquirer as catalyst	1	2	0	1	4
Subsidiary	2	5	3	3	13
Both	0	1	1	1	3
Little change	1	0	3	2	6

Table 10.3. Method of change

Change method	USA	Japan	Germany	France	Total
Absorption	5	0	0	0	5
MD appointed for turnaround	1	1	3	2	7
Joint action by parent and sub.	1	4	0	2	7
Hands-off approach	2	2	1	0	5
Action by subsidiary	0	3	2	3	8
Decisions from HQ of parent	0	0	1	1	2
Little change	1	0	3	2	6

by the parent imposed upon it, as shown in Table 10.3. However, in seven companies the change was effected by the parent and subsidiary companies working together. In the other companies, the parent company either adopted a hands-off management style (five companies) more or less leaving the subsidiary to manage itself, or (in eight companies) allowed the subsidiary to effect changes for which the subsidiary's management team had obtained prior approval. The degree of independence possessed by subsidiaries thus varied considerably, and subsidiaries were by no means confined in all cases to close management by their new parent companies.

All acquirers provided finance, even if only in the sense of making the purchase. However, there was a wide variety in their attitude to dividends, some leaving the money in and some taking it out. As shown in Table 10.4, some positively improved the credit rating of the subsidiary by providing credit support for local loans. Only eighteen, just under half of those interviewed, provided strong technical and other support activities to bring the

Table 10.4.   Resources introduced

Resources introduced	USA	Japan	Germany	France	Total
Finance	10	10	10	10	40
Technology	6	4	4	4	18
Systems and IT support	1	0	0	0	1
Mediocre products	1	1	0	0	2
Asset investments	0	0	2	0	2
Credit support	0	2	2	0	4

Table 10.5.   Parent company appointments

	MD and others	Senior appointments	Advisers	Junior appointments	None	Total
USA	4	0	0	0	6	4
Japan	1	4	2	4	1	10
Germany	3	2	0	2	4	7
France	3	0	0	1	6	4
Total	10	6	2	7	17	
% of cos.	27	15	5	17	42	

Note: Some rows and columns add up to more then the total of 40 cases or 10 per country as some cases involved appointments in more than one area.

subsidiary up to the standard of the parent. The numbers in the table exceed forty, since some parents contributed resources under more than one heading.

In terms of monitoring progress in bringing about change, 27 per cent of the companies appointed a new managing director to the subsidiary and sometimes other senior executives, a further 15 per cent made senior appointments but left the existing managing director in place, and 17 per cent made junior appointments, often ostensibly just for training purposes, but presumably also to monitor events in the subsidiary. An astonishingly high 42 per cent made no appointments to the subsidiary at all, but merely tied it into a parent company-appointed board resident in the parent company's country, and only Japanese parent companies appointed advisers (see Table 10.5). It is interesting that although the Japanese only appointed a new managing director in one case, they made the highest number of appointments to their subsidiaries overall.

National approaches

US companies

The US acquirers were the most internationally experienced of the four nationalities surveyed as shown in Table 6.9. Although international experience is often important in achieving high cross-border performance, this is only the case where the experience has led to increased know-how, which does not always follow (Simonin 1997). In cases where experience is not learnt from, a somewhat fire-fighting style of management may be adopted. The US acquirers were also the most likely to buy an already profitable company, as this clearly seemed the best way to achieve their overriding objective, good short-term profits.

The change process in US acquisitions tends to be characterized by three main features. Change is initiated by the new parent company, it is often effected by absorption into the parent company, and strong support is usually given to new subsidiaries, not just in the form of finance, but also in support activities and technology. As the managing director of a UK firm acquired by a major US MNC (US5) said: 'After the takeover in 1990 they progressively absorbed us, and we are now totally integrated into US5 (UK). There were huge negatives at first. "The Yanks are coming; they have no sense of irony." This took three years to settle down.' However, companies usually experienced an increase in performance following acquisition by a US company.

Five out of ten US companies absorbed their new subsidiary into the American parent's organization and systems in such a way that the subsidiary could no longer be clearly distinguished from the parent. This involved adoption of the parent's logo, brands, and company culture and left little trace of the original company's former independent identity. This was very much acquisition by absorption in the form identified by Haspeslagh and Jemison (1991). An example of such an absorption is that described by the general manager of US1:

We are now a professionally organized part of the Health Care division of US1 and fully integrated into its organization structure. I formally report to the EBC [European Business Centre] for manufacturing and to North America for business applications and R&D. There is no one person, but an integrated multi-point approach. When stand-alone businesses are acquired for example their R&D is not closed down but linked in to the worldwide network.

In this approach to absorption of acquired companies, the USA was unique. No other nationality used the total absorption approach to its acquisitions in any of the situations researched, with one French exception. US companies appear to adopt either an absorption approach or one which leaves the subsidiary nominally independent, but subject to substantial intervention by the parent. Thus US parents are the main source of change in acquisitions by US companies (cf. Table 10.2).

One interesting aspect of the integrationist approach favoured by several US companies was that it did not necessarily involve imposing US-appointed managing directors onto the new subsidiaries. In four cases the US parent did appoint a new managing director, and took over the running of the new subsidiary. However, in six cases the parent company made no new appointments, and worked through the existing management team. There was also no use of advisers, senior sub-managing director appointments, or junior trainee appointments. In other words, they had slim and direct management lines from subsidiary to parent.

The integrationist approach could, however, lead to problems, as the general manager of the acquired subsidiary of US3 noted:

National cultures are different but the systems are the same. The US expats have had to adjust here. They expected to put in an exact blueprint of US3 in the new country and were surprised when it didn't work. They have then had to go back and for instance Anglicize it in the UK particularly for the softer personnel issues.

One positive aspect of the American integrationist approach was that such companies were also the most likely to supplement the finance provided with whatever other managerial and technological support services were needed to bring the new subsidiary up to the required standard. As the managing director of the new subsidiary of US4 put it: 'Quality was improved dramatically. US4 provided people for product design, training and management services . . . They brought money, armies of bureaucrats, and international professionalism.'

However traumatic an acquisition by an American company might be to a small new subsidiary frightened of losing its identity and autonomy as it disappears into the maw of the corporate monster, the result was in most cases a substantial improvement in its economic performance. Of the ten companies acquired, only two were not acceptably profitable when they were visited, whereas six had been so at the time of acquisition.

The difference of US company attitudes to acquisition was summed up by the MD of a UK company acquired by a German company G10 who had also experienced US management: 'So if I was to say what is the lesser of the two evils—is it the benign neglect of the Germans and their avuncular style of management, or the helter-skelter dynamics of the Americans?—I would go for the American style quite frankly.'

Even if individual preferences for particular styles of management must also be allowed for in the comment, this does illustrate the difference in approach of companies from the two countries. However, the Americans are not always teachers rather than learners. As the manager of a UK subsidiary (US8) put it:

The strategic planning group came to talk over the takeover. They're not daft and they recognize that there's been some learning on both sides which will help them in future to integrate smaller companies in a way which will not destroy the flexibility and culture and entrepreneurial attitude but gives them what they need in terms of embracing core US8 values, so they look at this as some form of role model for the future.

This suggests that, while US companies can and do add value to their acquisitions, they may, at least sometimes, take care not to stifle the advantages which are part of being a smaller company.

Japanese companies

The Japanese acquirers were the least internationally experienced of the countries researched (see Table 6.10). Most were large domestic companies seeking to become more international. In their selections of acquisitions, they also bought more loss-makers than the other nationalities (see Table 10.1). Despite this, their track record at improving performance was good. However, their company attitudes towards acquisitions, and to the implementation of change following them, differed quite markedly from those of the other nationalities investigated. This is characterized by several distinctive features. The manner in which change was effected was much more by cooperative or indirect means than other countries. Consistent with this low-key approach to managing subsidiaries, most of the initiatives for change among the companies interviewed came from the subsidiaries themselves, rather than their Japanese parent companies. Finally, the support provided by the Japanese parent companies, particularly financial support, played a large role in making implementation of such subsidiary initiatives possible.

The economic condition of the companies acquired seems to have been of far less concern to Japanese companies than it was to companies of the other nationalities. Six out of the ten Japanese-owned companies visited were making losses at the time of purchase, and the other four were only close to break-even. This suggests that Japanese companies made their purchases more for strategic reasons than short-term financial ones. A further factor may stem from differences between the UK and continental European accounting practice and Japanese accounting practice. There is less pressure on Japanese parent companies to consolidate the accounts of their poorly performing foreign subsidiaries with their home accounts than on UK or continental European companies. As a result, Japanese companies have another reason to take a more relaxed and longer-term view of making their subsidiaries' operations profitable (S. Tomohide, personal communication, 1998).

Despite these differences Japanese companies do not seem to have been less successful in making previously unprofitable businesses profitable. Of the ten companies interviewed, four had been raised to an acceptable level of profit, three were just profitable, and only three remained as loss-makers following acquisition (see Table 10.1).

The critical difference was how that change was effected. Japanese companies intervened less and imposed their culture and systems on their subsidiaries far less than other nationalities. The managing director of a UK company acquired by a Japanese firm (J10) said of his firm's acquisition:

When the acquisition took place, J10 said, 'Well, we know nothing about trading in the international market so therefore we're not going to tamper with the organization. You carry on with what you've been doing over the past 100 years.' . . . It might have been better if there had been more integration, at least at an earlier stage. To this day there has been no integration. It's almost as if the companies are associates.

So far as initiation of change was concerned, the subsidiary was frequently the main source of change (see Table 10.2). In only one case was a 'change-maker' executive from Japan (J1) installed with the remit to shake up the new subsidiary in the manner of a troubleshooting US executive, and this seems to have been a noticeably unsuccessful experiment. Generally, the method of bringing about change was either by leaving it to the local team, with the Japanese parent company merely encouraging or setting an example, or by the Japanese parent and subsidiary working closely in a joint team (see Table 10.3).

The Japanese acquisitions also illustrated a point noted earlier and seen in the American cases. In any acquisition there is a balance to be struck between allowing a company the freedom to pursue its aims without interference from the parent, while also allowing it to benefit from the parent's resources, such as finance, technology, and R&D, so that it can take advantage of being an integrated part of a larger group. In the case of the Japanese companies, this balance sometimes erred on the side of a lack of integration. In the case of one UK company acquired by a Japanese company (J2) the UK managing director commented:

The Japanese financial director tells me what I need to know and I tell him what he needs to know and there is tremendous trust between us. If we had not been part of J2 we would not be here today, but they had absolutely no international experience and so said when they arrived, 'We're not going to change anything. Everything will remain the same.'

Of all the resources put into their subsidiaries by Japanese parents, financial assistance was the most significant. There were several examples of this, with the help taking a variety of forms, usually as guarantees or finance for investment. For example, one managing director of the UK subsidiary of a large Japanese company (J8) said:

the activities, when they were taken over by the Japanese were loss making and we needed secure guarantees. We needed time and our credit rating wasn't very good and we got letters of comfort from our parent company which were accepted by the banks here, and because of our parent company's massive involvement with Japanese banks we also got funding through these banks in London.

Japanese parent companies used their domestic financial muscle to improve the subsidiary's credit rating. As the chief executive of a Japanese-owned UK merchant bank (J5) explained:

The only resource they put in was money. Two major defensive injections. To give you an idea how bad it was the bank had capital of £30 million. Loan losses were £120 million. It lost all its capital four times over! But our Japanese parent bank have a comfort letter to the Bank of England as do all foreign-owned financial institutions, which is a huge advantage to us, as we as a small bank have a higher credit rating than Rothschilds, Hambros, and so forth, because we have a big brother shareholder. But the Japanese produce no actual business for us.

In many cases the amount of financial support and relaxed attitude to short-term performance surprised the UK managers as the managing director of J6 noted: 'I've had a lot of dealings with companies like TI who measure cash flow sometimes daily; yearly would be an innovation for J9, but that's from one extreme to the other. Over the years they have had a very, very long-term view.'

Japanese companies had a varied approach to monitoring or change-making appointments. They were the only nationality to make use of monitoring 'advisers' located in the subsidiary (see Table 10.5). Although they only appointed a managing director outright in one case, they frequently made senior appointments while leaving the UK Managing Director in position. They also often made junior training-type appointments, which allowed for some monitoring. However, the only overall trend discernible in the appointments made was a reluctance to take direct responsibility for the performance of the new subsidiary. The concept of a team approach was much more in the ascendant, and although it might take longer, was no less successful than more direct methods of intervention.

French companies

Most of the French acquirers in the sample were pretty experienced internationally (see Table 6.11) and had therefore developed a distinct style of international management. They tended to buy already profitable companies, or strategically important ones (see Table 10.1), which they were generally successful at bringing into profit. From the interviews, it appeared that French companies were very self-confident in their approach to their new acquisitions. Indeed they were liable to display a very 'colonial' attitude in a number of cases, discussing proposed courses of action only with fellow Frenchmen. As the managing director of the subsidiary of F4 put it: 'The French hierarchy is a "power" hierarchy, and it is the power that we find the most difficult to live with . . . They do have an arrogance and a dominance characteristic that one finds very difficult.'

There was little consistency in how the French acquirers handled their new subsidiaries (see Table 10.2). Sometimes they initiated change unilaterally, and in one case they acted as the catalyst for change. However, in other cases the subsidiary initiated the change process itself. In one company, the process was initiated by both sides, and in two cases there was little change to report at all. French initiators often tended to discuss strategic matters with other Frenchmen, and then issue orders. But more often there was either a joint task force working on change, or one composed of only local management. Perhaps the best way of characterizing the French companies' attitude towards their subsidiaries is to say that they were more adamant that either the subsidiary was there to represent the parent's business and had to deliver the performance required, or else that the direction was a matter which required close involvement of French managers, seconded or appointed from the parent company.

Despite the view of French managers as centralist bureaucrats looking down on local managers, the overall picture that emerged of French companies' approach to integrating their acquisitions is somewhat variable, and depends strongly on individual company culture and specific circumstances. The attitude of French companies to monitoring or bringing about change was also mixed. In three cases, they moved in by appointing a new managing director and senior staff, but in six cases they made no new appointments and in one appointed only juniors (see Table 10.5). While there is a noticeable tendency towards a rather elevated centralist approach, this may not be incompatible with allowing subsidiaries a fair degree of independence. As the managing director of the UK subsidiary of F5 put it: 'The French are very autocratic. My boss feels he is the boss and he decides, yet at the same time he doesn't interfere with me.'

A French pharmaceutical company (F9) was also accorded a fair degree of independence. As the UK managing director said: 'The philosophy of my boss was to see the company as a stand-alone company, the wording is an affiliate, rather than a subsidiary. That was a good initial aim but, to be a bit critical, it didn't give us the leverage of being part of a bigger group.' This again brings us back to the independence–integration dilemma facing parent companies in dealing with their subsidiaries. The UK manager recognized that there could be a problem inherent in being accorded some independence. Nevertheless, as with the other nationalities, French acquirers provided the stability of finance, credit support, and sometimes some actual managerial and technical support activities (see Table 10.4).

French attitudes towards longer-term strategic investments contrast with American short-term profit expectations. As the UK chairman of the subsidiary of F2 commented: 'The French are strategic to a fault. They were too tolerant of loss, much more than the British would have been. With this went a tendency to centralization and bureaucracy and to fitting things into strategy.'

German companies

The German acquirers were very mixed in international experience, including major German-based MNCs and other large German companies with little such experience, but seeking to increase their international reach (see Table 6.12). They were equally mixed in the economic condition of their acquisitions at the time of purchase (see Table 10.1). However, the ten companies visited consistently failed to turn around their loss-makers. At the time of interview the profitable companies were still profitable, the break-even one still breaking even, and the loss-makers still making losses.

German acquirers sometimes lacked the confidence that their proven domestic management methods would translate effectively onto an international stage. Their actions tended therefore to be far from clear-cut and purposeful. The UK chief executive of the German engineering parent (G2) of a Tyneside company commented:

G2 are very long-term oriented, and that has been reflected in the culture. It is almost an adverse reflection, as there is a casualness in attitude to losses. They don't seem to view this as seriously as we do in the UK where a loss is a serious matter. They are very traditional, and isolated in terms of the world market place. The German market is different from the world market. They are willing to let people find their feet. But they don't bring a flow of benefits. They haven't really tried to impose any particular industrial concepts or ways of working on us.

There was little consistency in the areas in which changes were initiated. In the ten German cases visited, the parent rarely took the lead (see Table 10.2).

Some of this apparent indecisiveness among German parent companies might be due to the structures of their senior management and boards, with the two-tier governance system and collegial philosophy (Lane 1989). Some support for this view comes from one managing director of a UK subsidiary of a German company (G10) on whose board he sat:

I think the overriding influence I found was that there was a rather strange non-hierarchical way of running the company. There was a board of directors formed from G10 which was the immediate parent, and there were four members, myself and three Germans. We were all called *Geschäftsführer*. All MDs which was slightly strange. None of us had seniority over the others except that one was known as *Der Sprecher*—the spokesman for the board.

However, the benign neglect suffered by G10's subsidiary also provided an opportunity for it to develop with the German company's support. But this situation could lead to complacency about the availability of support to bail the company out of any mistakes. As the same MD noted: 'It's like if you get into difficulty, ring up Dad and he writes a cheque out. Quite frankly I think it would have done us good if they had said, "Look, there's no more money—you've got to sort yourself out."' Similarly, as the managing director of the company bought by G1 put it: 'We have been left alone because we are not part of the mainstream pharma division so the central control isn't there. There is nobody in the centre interested in our operation really.'

If the UK subsidiary looked up to such a German board for guidance it could sometimes receive mixed advice as one subsidiary managing director (G8) stated:

To be totally honest all of their views totally differed. So we produced a five-year business plan and rang them up and they said, 'Oh, that's good, get on with it,' and that's exactly what we did. We did look to them for guidance in the early days, but their ability to make decisions was somewhat strange to say the least.

Whichever factors led to this indecisiveness, there was a distinction between the companies which reacted to such confusion by treating it as a disadvantage to be endured and those who treated it as an opportunity. For example, the same UK managing director of G8, having encountered a hydra-like German management style, decided to propose and pursue his own plans.

Just as in the case of Japanese companies, German companies found independence and integration both to have benefits and this required a balance to be struck. One example (G9) was in the area of career planning. As the UK managing director put it:

The downside is that by pushing away corporate G9, you don't actually do yourself any favours in terms of development of yourself and your people. And after five years of it you begin to feel a bit lonely . . . I don't think we've suffered yet from that but eventually we will.

The UK manager of an engineering subsidiary (G6) observed that:

The number of changes have been pretty minimal and have happened through their decisions but after consultation. Numbers employed have actually gone down slightly. The company's position hasn't changed much since the acquisition in either profits or sales.

An acquired firm often needs direction, and if this is not provided by the parent company, it has to be provided by the subsidiary's own management.

In common with most other nationalities and especially Japanese parent companies, German parents could be a particularly useful and generous sources of funds for their subsidiaries, often supporting them to such an extent that without them the company would have ceased to exist (see Table 10.4).

Apart from the provision of finance to the acquired company, it is notable that acquiring companies (except the Americans) take a long-term strategic view of their investment. It appears that for any subsidiary to be a success, it not only has to have financial support from the parent company, but also some idea about how that long-term support is going to be used, and about the longer-term direction of the company. Just one or the other is insufficient. While the ideas about how to direct the long-term future of the company can come from either the parent or the subsidiary, if they come from neither, the acquisition will merely drift. This seems to be precisely what happened in the case of several of the German acquisitions studied. The acquisitions by German companies can therefore perhaps be characterized by their generous financial but indecisive strategic support, and this is shown by the methods used to implement change.

In three of the companies interviewed, a 'change-maker' was appointed in the form of a German managing director for the new subsidiary. In one case, change came from Germany, where it was decided behind closed doors, but only after consultation with the local management team. In the remaining cases, the subsidiaries took advantage of the new stability that came from being part of a financially powerful group to carry out the necessary changes themselves, often under the watchful eye of monitoring parent company executives. However, in three companies very little change had occurred at all (see Table 10.3).

German companies were very varied in their response to new acquisitions in terms of new staff appointments. In three cases they appointed a new managing director, in two cases they satisfied themselves merely with some senior appointments, and in two cases with some junior appointments. In four cases they made no appointments at all to the new subsidiary (see Table 10.5). As the G3 UK managing director mentioned: 'The acquirers put one or two key appointments into us and some reporting systems but otherwise left us alone.'

This of course left the success of the new subsidiary very much at the mercy of the incumbent management, who could either use the opportunity to move on to greater things or drift in the state they were acquired in, kept afloat by the German parent's financial support.

Conclusion

As Hampden-Turner and Trompenaars (1993) argue, the forms of capitalism and hence management practice vary substantially by nationality of acquirer, and recognizable national paradigms are clearly evident in many cases. There is therefore likely to be a variety of different methods of integrating new acquisitions, which are at least partially influenced by nationality. It is even possible, as we suggest elsewhere, that there is no single best-practice way of treating a newly acquired company, and getting good performance from it.

Haspeslagh and Jemison's (1991) taxonomy of acquisition methods fits to a considerable extent with various national styles as well as other contingent situations. USA acquirers seemed to prefer the absorption approach. The Japanese preference, however, tended towards preservation or, where advantage could be clearly seen, symbiosis. The French, however, had their own distinctive style which we have dubbed colonial, whereas the German acquirers in our sample vacillated between all identified styles, without a clear preference, save that of avoiding absorption.

The way in which individual acquirers behaved also depended in part not just on nationality, but also on the condition of the acquisition company at the time of purchase, and the acquirer's company culture and hence preferred management methods. Thus, where an acquired company was in crisis, a more interventionist approach was adopted than in a company making acceptable profits. Furthermore acquirers with little international experience tended, as might be expected, to be more tentative in their actions than acquirers who were major MNCs and who therefore had extensive prior experience of integrating acquisitions into their group, and dealing with employees from different countries.

Methods of integration varied widely, however, and Hunt's (1988) claim that most acquisitions are hands on in the first year was certainly not confirmed. Many were distinctly hands off. However, there were discernible differences between approaches by companies of different nationalities, irrespective of the international experience of the acquirer or the economic condition of the subsidiary.

The American acquirers made the most effort to ensure that their acquisitions were profitable at the time of purchase. They then tended to absorb them into the parent company systems and to demand rapid high financial performance. One way or the other the US absorptive management style usually achieved high performance in their subsidiaries, as at the time of interview only two US acquisitions were still making losses, and these were believed to be destined for imminent drastic action by their parent.

Japanese companies were less concerned to buy existing profitable companies, as their aims were more long term than those of American companies. They tended to be gentler in their treatment of their acquisitions, often acting primarily as a catalyst, rather than as an owner. They were the only nationality to appoint 'advisers' to monitor events in the new subsidiary. Their results were no worse than those of American companies, however, which was remarkable given their relative inexperience internationally. Considering the better initial condition of the US acquisitions, this cooperative and catalytic post-acquisition change style was generally very successful.

The French style tended to be 'centralist'. They either appointed a new French managing director and took decisions after discussions in France, or they left the local team in day-to-day charge of operations, but decided high-level strategy at headquarters in France. This contrasts somewhat with Calori et al.'s (1994) experience that the French tended to exercise high formal control of both strategy and operations. The French approach was also generally effective.

German companies were less successful or certain in their methods. There was no discernible German method of change-making, as their actions varied from appointing a new managing director to give orders, to leaving well alone and hoping for the best. This eclectic, perhaps unfocused, and largely non-interventionist approach achieved no turnarounds in their troubled acquisitions, but maintained profit in their profitable ones. The institutional factors identified by Whitley (1992a, 1992b) and Lane (1995), particularly the two-level board structure, may have played a role in inhibiting leadership, but this does not provide an adequate explanation for the relatively poor performance of those German acquisitions visited.

A number of hypotheses arise from our findings on the processes of post-acquisition change that warrant confirmation through further research:

1. No one method of treating a new subsidiary is consistently more effective than another in achieving superior performance, but the confidence of the acquirer in adopting a particular method consistently is an important success factor.

2. American acquirers are typically 'absorbers', the Japanese 'preservers' or believers in symbiosis, the French 'colonialists', while the Germans lack a clear integration style.
3. American acquirers seek short-term profits and hence tend to buy already profitable companies.
4. Japanese, French, and German acquirers adopt a longer-term strategic outlook, and are thus less concerned with their acquisition's current profitability.

Further research of a quantitative nature is needed to establish the importance of national management paradigms in the determination of the integration process as against factors such as the international experience of the acquirer, the relative size of the partners, and the economic condition of the acquiree at the time of purchase. However, the sharp contrast between US and Japanese change processes suggests that there is more than one way to realize value from an acquisition and therefore no necessary clear best practice.

Summary

- US acquirers were the most internationally experienced and most likely to buy companies already in profit and then integrate them very positively.
- Japanese acquirers were the least internationally experienced and often bought loss-making companies for strategic reasons, turning them around through a low-key cooperative approach.
- The French were confident internationally and tended to exhibit a distinct style in which they exercised strategic control but delegated considerable operational control to the subsidiary.
- German companies were mixed in their international experience and were relatively unsuccessful in turning around loss-making acquisitions.
- All except the Americans tended to take a long-term strategic view of their acquisitions.
- There was no clear 'best practice' in achieving post-acquisition change.

APPENDIX: CASE STUDIES

J3: a case of preservation

J3-UK, the subsidiary

J3-UK is a household name in vacuum flasks. In fact it is so well known as to be a virtual generic. It makes glass flasks, however, which are cheap and breakable. Its image is a rather tired and old-fashioned one, and although it has diversified somewhat in recent years into Euro-coolers, coffee jugs, children's lunch boxes, and barbecues, it still had a rather old portfolio in 1989 at the time of the acquisition. At the time of the research it made approximately 170,000 flasks a week and about 250,000 fillers. In 1989 there had been little investment for some time in production facilities, people, or systems at J3-UK. It was basically an English company turning over £30 million annually with 500 employees, based in Thetford, Norfolk (where the fillers were made), and Brentwood, Essex (where the completed flasks were assembled). It had been expanding in recent years into Germany and France, organically and into Belgium, France and Italy through distributors. At the time of the acquisition by J3 the company was already part of an American group. The American group treated it as a cash cow, invested very little in it, and siphoned off its profits for investment elsewhere, presumably believing that the vacuum flask market was mature to ageing and presented little opportunity for growth. (The Japanese have left virtually all the profit in the company, except for a small annual royalty.) The American group made losses overall, but J3-UK made about £1–3 million profit per annum in most years, although the recession of the late 1980s did push it into losses.

J3, the acquiring company

J3 is a large Japanese industrial company strong in industrial gases, with a wide range of products, one of which is stainless steel vacuum flasks. These are unbreakable, and far more expensive than J3-UK's traditional range. J3 encourages J3-UK to sell them, but J3-UK believes them to be too expensive for volume sales in the UK. J3 has been concerned to broaden its range into household products and is bent on global expansion, but at the time of its purchase of J3-UK was relatively inexperienced internationally, operating outside Japan only in the Far East. Its aim, however, was to expand, so as to achieve two-thirds of its sales in industrial goods and one-third in consumer products. The UK acquisition was a move in this direction. J3 is not a strongly market-oriented company and advertises little. It is strong on industrial products, and in new product development rather than brand marketing.

Post acquisition integration, Japanese style

The Japanese company has managed its new UK subsidiary largely from afar, and made no attempt to change it is any radical way. There is a formal review of performance twice a year, once in Tokyo and once in Brentwood, and monthly accounts are sent to Japan. Although Japanese executives from J3 visit from time to time, there are no 'advisers' from Japan sent to keep an eye on J3-UK.

All communication is supposed to be through one person in the J3 Tokyo office, but this leads to a considerable communications block. There are no day-to-day informal contacts, as there might be with an American owner. As the Japanese bought the American company as well, much of the UK's regular communication is still through the US office, and as such the US short-term attitude still survives to some degree; for example attitudes within J3-UK remain more individual than team-based ones. Communication within the company is more informal internally than it was, assisted by newsletters and periodic general gatherings for ceremonies and celebrations as well as the usual grapevine.

The Japanese have not been very decisive in tackling the poor performance in the US vacuum flask business, and this has slowed the growth of the UK operation due to constraints on funds. They have also made no real contribution in the area of staff training and development. Their nature is described by UK executives as being controlled, hands off, and helpful. But this has both an upside and a downside for the development of J3-UK in that the hands-off behaviour means that contributions that perhaps could be made to the UK company's development are not made, and progress is therefore slower than it might be with a more interventionist new owner. However, there has been considerable investment by the Japanese in new computer systems, product development, and new plant and machinery for J3-UK.

J3 have established a workable three-year planning system, and expect the numbers to be achieved. New initiatives generally originate in the UK, are sent to Japan for consideration, amended, and then generally approved. They then become a set of agreed objectives for J3-UK to achieve. The three-year plan is then cast in stone and deviations from the plan have to be explained. The Japanese absorb and like detail, which slows up decision-making.

The Japanese are quite formal in their attitude to planning, while still allowing a certain amount of flexibility for the company to work within. They like to know what is going on.

Despite this, they are careful not to get too involved in operational decision-making, and confine their input to overall control of strategy. They keep out of the areas of operations and personnel as far as possible, but control investment strategy closely, and give strong direction in terms of banking. Japanese banks are used rather than the traditional UK clearing banks. J3-UK has a limit of only $50,000 discretionary expenditure, and any change in the scope of the business also needs approval.

There has been quite a lot of product development since the acquisition, but it has not been stimulated or directed by the Japanese. Modernization of the product development process (e.g. computer-aided design) and of the production plant has been initiated internally, and only then approved first by the USA and then by J3. However, J3-UK has seen substantial efficiency improvements, largely stimulated by the need to cut costs to survive the recession of the late 1980s. Tiers of management have been removed and staff jobs thinned down a lot in order to reduce costs. This has not been a Japanese initiative, but one made necessary by the difficult trading conditions in the UK during that period.

The Japanese culture still puzzles executives at J3-UK, and they feel that their relationship with their parent is one of visitors. They do not feel that they are part of 'the family' at all. The degree to which the new owners have been hands off, yet supportive in their behaviour and responsive to rational argument when backed by figures, has also surprised them. The J3-UK R&D director claims to be a bit disappointed that the Japanese have not got more involved on the technical side, as this is supposed to be their strong suit.

J3-UK had been a very traditional company and reluctant to change, as the marketing and sales director explains:

J3-UK launched a new vacuum flask in 1993, which took eighteen months and £2 million to develop. However, in the week preceding the launch a number of long-term employees (25–30 years with the company) approached me with the concern that the new flask was far too revolutionary, and really the old one we had been marketing for the last twenty-seven years still served its purpose. So why were we going to all this risk of launching the new one? Subsequently we launched it and it has been extremely successful. But the attitude was a reluctance to change which was very typical of the company.

The arrival of the Japanese and their rather non-interventionist style is not changing this culture very dramatically or fast, although there is some change. There are no Japanese on the J3-UK payroll.

Performance

The feeling of financial security generated by the Japanese has improved attitudes and hence long-term performance. The company is far more profitable than it was before the acquisition largely due to the time allowed by J3 for the company to reinvest and modernize its operations. The long-term philosophy of J3 has been crucial to the improvement of performance. J3-UK is now a company with strong financial backing, producing a range of products for which there is a stable if unexciting demand, and run in an efficient cost-effective way. The conversion of the company through new product development into a high-growth company with a more fashionable and modern range of goods is, however, still far away.

Conclusions

The process of post-acquisition integration by the Japanese J3 company has followed the style typically associated with Japanese companies of cautious incremental action, with concern to retain the good aspects of the acquired company's culture and activities. J3's international inexperience, and its role as a Japanese industrial product development company rather than a global brand marketing company, have accentuated this. It has, however, retained tight strategic and financial control of its new subsidiary, and has given the UK company the confidence to spread its wings into new activities in the knowledge that the financial resources are behind it to ensure that its initiatives will not get aborted for lack of funds. Thus by means of this cautious approach, J3 has been able to facilitate the necessary improvement in sales and profitability in J3-UK that was hampered by the previous owners' treatment of it as a cash cow with few if any profit opportunities.

US1: a case of absorption

US1-UK, the subsidiary

US1-UK was a small medical implants company in the north of England founded in 1984 by six local entrepreneurs, three of whom continued to work for the company after the acquisition. At the time of its acquisition by US1 it was a bit run down and lacked the capital for expansion. US1 was its largest customer at the time. However, US1-UK won the Queen's Award for exports in 1990. It specialized in metal implants for hip joints. The raw materials and the labour force were all available locally. US1-UK had seventy employees and sales of about $6 million at the time of acquisition. It had a very local north of England culture.

US1, the parent

US1 is one of the largest corporations in the USA. Its turnover at the time was in the region of $15 billion. It had 60,000 product lines, many of which were not famous brands. Scotch tape and Post-it pads were perhaps the best known of them. Abrasives and adhesives formed the backbone of the company's technologies and competences. However, expansion meant venturing far from the company's origins. It owned a multitude of small companies and when on the acquisition trail always tried to find a link between the products and technologies of the new company and those of its current portfolio. The medical goods area—implants, cardiovascular pumps, and other surgical tools—was vaguely related to the US1 business of producing woven stocking material. US1 has a major technical centre in St Paul, Minnesota, including a health care centre for R&D in addition to other R&D facilities in Japan, the UK, and Germany which link in closely to St Paul. Acquisitions with existing R&D facilities are linked in to the worldwide network. Our informant was the Scots-born but US-trained manager of the Rotherham plant, flown in from the USA by US1 to carry out the post-acquisition integration.

The process of change

US1 normally adopts the most common form of US integration of subsidiaries, namely that of absorption, and so it was the case with US1-UK. The little Rotherham family company was absorbed into the US giant, and became part of its Health Care division with only production amongst its business functions remaining distinct and dedicated at Rotherham near Sheffield. US1 moved the company into a new factory in 1991, but in the same Rotherham area. It invested about $5 million in expansion of the company, brought about a sales increase from $6 million to $30 million, and expanded employment from 70 to over 100. It improved the level of technical skills by recruiting from the competition, and it expanded the product range from metal implants for hips to include knee and shoulder implants too.

With regards to new product development, USi has introduced a very market-driven approach. It has set up a surgeons' panel which strongly influences new product development. It is struggling hard to reduce the time to market which is currently about three years for a new product and five months for a 'me-too' product.

USi has a target that at least 30 per cent of sales should come from products that are less than four years old. Our informant claimed proudly that this target should be achieved this year: 'Next year it should be 60 per cent. In 1993 when I arrived it was no more than 10 per cent.'

Organizationally within USi the Rotherham plant was regarded as a 'site' and our informant was termed a site manager. Sales and marketing were carried out in Loughborough, and the board was effectively a European Business Centre (EBC) executive committee. Company accounts were absorbed into those of USi-UK, so the profit performance of USi-UK was no longer separately identifiable. USi skills and facilities worldwide were available to USi-UK as a matter of normal procedure with R&D driven from the USA. The Rotherham site has, however, retained its R&D function and had it strengthened, but it has been tied in to the US R&D network. Our informant told us that until his arrival in 1993 the level of absorption of the USi-UK into USi was fairly limited; however, now that had all changed. Committees, task forces, and project teams are all used to develop the identity of USi-UK as part of USi, and encourage the development of team spirit, which is a very important integral part of the USi company culture.

Once a year there is a senior USi management visit. In addition our informant's US superior comes over every two months to have a strategic planning meeting, and the UK site manager goes to the USA about three times a year for business updates and more strategy discussions. Informal communication between the USA and the UK by phone, fax, and e-mail is daily.

USi takes a very formal approach to communication as a way of spreading the company culture. The USi mission statement hangs in every office, and notice-boards are extensively used to keep all employees informed of what is going on, and the level of the order book and other key indicators of the company's health are reported regularly on them. Previously information was communicated only on a need-to-know basis, the 'mushroom principle' as our informant described it. USi is very concerned to make USi-UK a real part of its identity both within the company and externally with customers. In pursuit of this aim it has converted all packaging to USi standards.

It has also introduced the USi principle of Human Resource Management. This involves a basic award system called the Outstanding Contributor Award, which can range from a 'thank you' gift of a little clock to a team, or £50 per team member, to a £350 weekend away award. Bonuses can be up to 10 per cent of salary, but USi is trying to move away from individual bonuses, since they encourage individual competitiveness and the company prefers to emphasize teamworking. Generally it is USi's company policy to rotate site managers on a four-year basis. This will eventually take place at USi-UK but is not doing so yet although the IT manager has moved to Loughborough.

Training, particularly on-course training, has been substantially increased to improve the level of skills. Planning has been put on a more structured and long-term basis with a sophisticated planning system extending six years into the future replacing the old annual budgets, which were the only form of planning in the company.

As is normal in a US company, the employment philosophy is very short term and a fairly high turnover of staff is expected. However, this does not differ much from the pre-acquisition situation, when it was possible to get fired on the spot if anything out of place was said to any of the owners.

US1 has found considerable resistance locally to what is perceived as the Americanization of the company and some difficulty in inculcating the American style of professional informality in the company. 'The American style is very informal. However, this doesn't always seem to go down very well in Yorkshire. The locals seem happier with class distinctions and clear hierarchies, but that is just not our way, we are structured, professional, and informal.'

Many of the major decisions are taken by US1 off site, and as for the others, it must be remembered that the US1-UK site is now run by a US1 manager. He has responsibility for quality control, production planning, product pricing and purchasing decisions, and limited technological innovation. However, US1 takes decisions at a level above him on management moves, strategic priorities, financial control, sales and distribution, and capital expenditure.

Performance

Despite the anti-American attitudes of staff in the company, US1-UK has made great strides in terms of sales, profit, and the development of the profit range since US1 bought the company. It is now part of a major global corporation and has all the financial and staff support advantages that this brings with it. Although still an SME in size, at $30 million annual sales it is the worldwide centre for medical implants in US1 and is run in a very professional fashion, having been subjected to the characteristic American absorption approach for acquisitions, which has involved transforming its culture from that of a small family-owned north of England private company into a subsidiary of one of the world's great corporations.

Conclusions

The characteristic American style of integrating new subsidiaries by absorbing them is seen in almost paradigmatic form in the case of US1 and US1-UK. The US company set about changing virtually everything about the UK company, except its basic products, making it virtually unrecognizable as the small north of England rather unprofessional company that it had been. Organizational reporting relationships, structures, and systems were installed to tie the UK company closely into the parent. Action was taken to change behaviour in the areas of communications and human resource management, particularly in the areas of training and reward systems. The

US company culture was made to pervade the subsidiary and a US-trained manager was installed to run the Rotherham site and increase the level of Americanization of the company. Much of this was successful, and the company grew, widened its product range, and became the US1 world centre for medical products. However, some of the site manager's comments suggested that all was not well, and that such a blueprint for integration could not be followed quite painlessly. The 'hearts and minds' of the employees did not appear to have been won over, and as such key qualities for a successful company of commitment and identification with the company mission have to be regarded as suspect. This suggests that even in the most rigorous 'absorption' endeavours, US companies bent on post-acquisition integration of foreign subsidiaries might be wise to take some note of the existing culture of the subsidiary, and amend their plans, if only marginally, to preserve some of this culture if they are to win the long-term loyalty of their new employees.

11

Human Resource Management

Introduction

Human resource management (HRM) is frequently a neglected area of functional strategy. HRM policies can provide significant control mechanisms for companies wishing to integrate acquisitions, yet are seldom used explicitly and in a focused way for this purpose. An acquirer's HRM policies can have a strong effect on its ability to get the best results from its new subsidiary. The way it treats its employees will affect their motivation, and the attitude that employees bring to their work. This was one of the foundations for Cisco's successful acquisition history, noted in Chapter 1. HRM policies are as important as those concerned with strategy, structure, market selection, and product development, which are frequently regarded as more salient in corporate boardrooms.

HRM may therefore be defined as the range of policies and practices used to facilitate integration, commitment, flexibility, and the quality of working life, as well as meeting broader business goals such as changing organizational values, structure, productivity, and delivery mechanisms (Brewster and Tyson 1991). The principal HRM policies considered in this chapter are those concerned with recruitment and staffing including termination, training and career development, personnel appraisal, and compensation and reward policies including promotion. The chapter visits the somewhat contentious issue of whether there are such things as best HRM practices consistent across nationalities or whether, by contrast, companies of different nationalities generally adopt HRM strategies that reflect their national cultures.

Frayne and Geringer (1990) claim that HRM policies and practices can offer three specific control benefits, which apply to acquisitions as well as other situations:

1. Through training programmes, they can improve the employees' ability to perform more effectively and hence realize more value from an acquisition.
2. They can subtly spread the parent company's culture, objectives, and mission to an acquired company.
3. They can help to develop a unique culture in that company.

Performance appraisals in particular help the parent company to understand better the strengths and weaknesses of the personnel in its new subsidiary. They provide another mechanism through which a parent company can develop a positive dialogue with its new employees, and thereby foster the development of a new identity with the parent group.

Compensation and reward systems are important in attracting the right quality of recruits and in subsequently retaining them. Bonuses tied to performance and clear career development paths help to convince employees that they are valued and their contribution is being noticed and appreciated.

Pucik (1988) points out how HRM activities can support and complement line management in providing a supportive climate and appropriate systems for organizational learning, both by the subsidiary and by the parent. Pucik conducted his research into Anglo-Japanese joint ventures, but the conclusions apply equally well to acquisitions. From looking at twenty-three such ventures, he concluded that a primary reason for poor performance lay in poorly designed and executed HRM strategies. As a result, parent companies could fail to communicate their strategic intent adequately to staff; learning may be given a low priority, and selection may have a low HRM input resulting in low-quality staff, or staff of widely varying abilities. A further commonly neglected area is language and cross-cultural training, which can greatly assist efforts to integrate cross-border acquisitions.

The convergence issue

There is currently a lively debate on the degree to which there is a convergence of human resource policies across diverse national cultures, as a result of increasing globalization of markets and hence companies. Some studies have reported strong convergence between national practices such that there is, for instance, only limited difference between Japanese and Western HRM strategies (Shadur et al. 1995). Both strategies adopt team-based work, extensive training, single status facilities, and long working hours.

Further evidence of convergence is found in the reported globalizing of French industry (Huault 1996), leading it to adopt more American-style HRM practices. Japan is also under pressure to change for the same reasons, with its traditional long-term approach to employment under threat in an increasingly competitive world. Both France and Japan are becoming less nationalistic in their HRM policies, and are moving towards more individual empowerment, greater flexibility, performance-related pay, more concern to retain specialist skills in the workforce, and the seeking of greater commitment from employees. In this regard, Morton and Beaumont (1998) suggest that internal benchmarking can effectively transfer global best practice in HRM, so long as account is taken of the local context and the need for a degree of adaptation to local management practices.

There is, therefore, some evidence of convergence of HRM strategies across nations, but cultural differences are still seen to be important (Sparrow et al. 1994). For example American, British, and German companies tend to emphasize openness and equality in work relationships. They tend to have flexible work practices, a low perceived need for centralization, and a strong vertical hierarchy. Japan on the other hand does emphasize the importance of the vertical hierarchy. Japanese companies tend to have a culture with high respect for authority and a homogeneous work ethic. Empowerment, diversity, and equality are little emphasized in Japanese companies.

Difficulties of convergence suggest that national cultures may continue to influence the ways in which companies are run; for example the Americans emphasize standardization of output, the Germans standardization of skills, the French standardization of processes, and the Japanese standardization of values (McGaughey and de Cieri 1999). French managers have a high need to exercise power; they seek to avoid ambiguity, and to eliminate uncertainty in their tasks. They have difficulty in adopting US performance management concepts, as they are very protective of their autonomy and status within the organization, and do not want it threatened. Continental European companies have stronger legal barriers to hiring and firing than the USA, lower employee mobility, and stronger links between educational achievement and career progression. They also have greater government intervention in the area. This influences their attitudes to HRM policies.

While some commentators emphasize international convergence in HRM practices, others emphasize the need to adapt to local conditions and cultures. Ngo et al. (1998) suggest that there is global integration and local adaptation. Easterby Smith et al. (1995) emphasize that cultural factors are very important in HRM policy development, and that ease of transfer from one culture to another can be very difficult. The more similar the culture, the easier the transfer. Hodgetts and Luthans (1990) confirm that the greater the cultural diversity between one country and another, the more likely it is that most HRM practices cannot be literally transferred, the 'hard' factors being easier to transfer than the 'soft'. Adler and her colleagues (1986) suggest that, while organizations are becoming more similar in their macro-variables, they may be maintaining their dissimilarity at the micro level. By macro-variables they mean organization structure or technology; by micro-variables they refer to people's behaviour within organizations.

Caligieri and Stroh (1995) claim it is not national culture that is key to the establishment of HRM strategies so much as the organizational philosophy of the company. The 'centricity' of the corporation is seen as more important than its country of origin. Thus ethnocentric companies tend to maximize control from the centre in order to integrate subsidiaries. Polycentric companies have host nationals managing their subsidiaries, and therefore have high local responsiveness and little common corporate culture. Geocentric companies balance the two factors of central policy control with local responsiveness. Corporate values are their instrument of socialization. They have many inter-company transfers in order to develop this quality.

Tayeb (1998) notes that most companies have corporation-wide HRM policies, but that they find it more difficult to apply these policies in the form of country-specific HRM practices. The policies emerge from high-level decision-making, whereas their application requires actual changes in behaviour. Companies generally have to be responsive to local conditions. The major factors influencing a subsidiary's HRM practices are, she claims, the organization culture of the subsidiary, in terms of its history and its leadership, business and technology imperatives, the parent's HRM policies, location, and institutional factors.

Edwards et al. (1996) note that HRM policies in international companies vary greatly, from those involving high local autonomy to those with a strong role for the centre in making policies uniform, and with a well-developed system of management development planning. The more mature the MNC, the more likely it is to have a corporation-wide attitude to HRM, but there are a wide variety of other contextual factors that also influence HRM activities.

Sparrow (1995) notes that there are some distinctive national patterns of HRM shaped, he believes, by certain structural factors such as level of state ownership in the economy, average size of organizations, extent of family stakeholders, national business systems, employer–employee bias, attitudes to authority, values, management styles, level of contracting out, and the overall perceived importance of HRM in organizations. These differing national factors impede or facilitate convergence in HRM policies and practices.

The differences between national HRM policies and practices is noted by many commentators, despite some evidence for convergence within MNCs. At the policy level, the USA is strong in its support of training and career development, whereas Germany tends to have low support for career development (Adsit et al. 1997). France is high on understanding customer requirements and on respect for employees, whereas Japan is less strong in these areas. France is not rated highly at helping subordinates learn from their mistakes.

Poole and Jenkins (1997) characterize UK company policies as emphasizing flexibility in production, using significant levels of outsourcing, and having a considerable residue of Taylorism. The nature of rewards shows considerable government influence through tax incentives and laws on option provision for senior executives, and management development is fairly well addressed. Performance appraisal, and training towards the achievement of NVQs (National Vocational Qualifications), is also becoming increasingly common.

Wever (1995) describes the German approach to HRM as very 'negotiated'. Business and labour are seen as social partners, with co-determination as the watchword. Expertise is the route to promotion, not performance. The US approach is more unilateral. It relies on market-led processes and seeks proven performance and individual achievement. Where local and central cultures clash, US companies make changes that help to blend the cultures. Table 11.1 summarizes the conclusions of some important research contributions to the analysis of national HRM practices. There is a presumption that acquiring companies are likely to apply such practices to their new subsidiaries.

Findings

The findings from the survey and the case studies showed substantial convergence in certain post-acquisition HRM practices, such as moves towards performance-related pay, increases in training, and team-based product development. At the same time, considerable national differences remained, as shown in Table 11.2.

American HRM practices

According to the survey, US companies showed a preference for performance-related pay and for an increase in largely on-course training. They were the most short term in their recruitment and termination policies, and were not strong on installing job rotation in their companies or on planned career development. They emerged as having the least open communications, preferring a 'need-to-know' formal approach that contrasts with the more open approach espoused by Japan, Germany, and France. American companies showed themselves more team based in new product development than their new subsidiaries had previously been, and they adopted a very top-down cultural style. The interviews confirmed that US companies place a high emphasis on formal training, and this is carried forward into their new acquisitions. As the retiring ex-owner of an insurance-related company (US9) noted:

The area of greatest change was perhaps training. We used to do as much technical training as was necessary to use the technical systems, and when we had reached the stage where my analysts were managing other analysts without any management skills then I thought, where can I send them to learn at least supervision skills? They weren't

Table 11.1. HRM policies characteristic of different countries

	USA	Japan	Germany	France	UK
Pay and performance (Huault 1996)	Performance related	PRP growing but less than USA	PRP growing	PRP growing but less then USA	PRP growing
Recruitment (McGaughey and de Cieri 1999)	Short term	Less lifetime than earlier	Longer term than USA; legal constraints	French long; local less so; legal constraints	Less short term than USA
Training (Shadur et al. 1995)	Large resources (Adsit et al. 1997)	Increasing	Increasing	Increasing	Increasing
Career planning (Wever 1995)	Strong in this area (Adsit et al. 1997)		Expertise based but low priority (Adsit et al. 1997)		
Product development (Shadur et al. 1995)	Team based	Team based	Team based	Team based	Team based
Culture (Sparrow et al. 1994)	Open; market led (Wever 1995)	Hierarchical; respect for authority	Open; negotiated, technical	High power, status important (McGaughey and Cieri 1999)	Open
Appraisal					Increasing (Poole and Jenkins 1997)
Promotion			Expertise is route (Wever 1995)	Emphasis on formal qualifications	Variable

keen because they were true analysts and not keen to manage others. But from the moment I retired everybody was trained. . . . After I had gone many more people went on many more courses . . . everyone has gone on courses. The training was given a further push by the introduction of formal performance appraisal by the new owners.

American firms are particularly keen on payment for performance, believing strongly in the power of monetary reward to motivate. As a manager in a US-based global facilities management company (US7) said: 'Our reward systems

Table 11.2.   Post-acquisition trends in HRM practice

	USA	Japan	Germany	France	UK
Pay	Performance related	PRP growing	PRP growing	PRP growing	PRP growing
Recruitment	Short term	Lifetime	Long term	French long; local less so	Less short term than USA
Training	High; on-course	On the job	Technical bias	To a ceiling	Increased; courses
Career planning	Little	Steady and slow	Ad hoc	Highly structured	Very variable
Product development	Team based	Team based	Team based		Not very team based
Culture	Top down	Bottom up; consensual	Top down	Top down	Top down
Appraisal	Regular and formal	Subtle; not transparent	Growing	Growing	Regular annual
Promotion	Fast and performance based	Slow and seniority based	Based on technical expertise	Emphasis on formal qualification; fast	Variable
Communications	Formal; need to know	Open when asked	Open and informal	Open and formal	Need-to-know approach

are very performance oriented. Performance-based bonuses can be up to 100 per cent of salary. There is also commission for sales which is not capped. So the reward-for-performance culture is very real.'

US companies are strong on formal appraisal systems, with consecutive poor appraisal reports leading to 'separation'. They also understand the need for an ambitious executive to see promotion opportunities if he or she is to stay long term with the company. As an executive with a US-based global freight carrier company (US3) put it:

The acquisition has meant that the company has been turned into a much more professional one with much wider job promotion opportunities. I have been with US3 for eight years and have a lot of responsibility and have 750 people reporting to me; much more than I could expect elsewhere for my age (29). To be a shareowner, you need to be at least Supervisor level which is normally for mature people, generally graduates, 30–5 years old.

However, the formality and rulebook orientation of US companies do not generally inhibit their entrepreneurial spirit and turn them into bureaucracies. As an executive of the facilities management company said:

Career development is very ad hoc, rather than planned. US5 is a very entrepreneurial company and reacts to events. It doesn't plan five years ahead. It retained its entrepreneurial spirit by remaining pretty autonomous within its major industrial holding group.

There was little in the evidence from American acquirers to contradict the most common characterizations of their national approach towards HRM, except that our sample saw little evidence of the career planning observed by other commentators (Adsit et al. 1997).

Japanese HRM practices

Most Japanese HRM practices are reported to be very different from American ones, reflecting the distinct Japanese culture. The four pillars of Japanese practice are generally recorded as lifetime employment, seniority-based promotion, house unions, and consensual decision-making; a fifth might be quality circles (Gill and Wong 1998). Tayeb, however, found (1994) that Japanese companies entering the UK tend to adapt their HRM style to fit British socio-economic conditions and culture.

It became clear from our survey that companies acquired by Japanese parents had adopted the originally American practices of performance-related pay and formal training, although not to the extent of the US companies. For example, in a Japanese-acquired industrial goods company (J1):

On the payment side, the most significant thing the MD has been pursuing has been the concept that individual shop-floor machine operators should have their rates of pay assessed each year and basically even the same grade operators end up on different rates of pay according to our view of their contribution to the company. And he calls this 'evaluation'. The concept would be that it should be carried out by their own managers . . . The union side have agreed to this, but with the utmost reluctance and a good deal of reluctance from me as well. This is one area in which we are not really in step with each other, myself and the chairman, but I have to go along that line and he says he has to go along that line as well because Japan wants it. (British general manager)

Such a practice would normally be more closely associated with American management thinking. However, more conventional Japanese attitudes were manifest in other of the same company's HRM practices. As the same manager observed:

One of the first things that happened after the acquisition was that the senior Japanese manager, then deputy chairman, posted a notice saying there would be no redundancies—'an open-ended guarantee'. In fact, employment has risen 50 per cent since the acquisition.

Japanese companies did in fact introduce many of their more expected HRM policies to their acquisitions. They took the most long-term approach of the four nationalities in their recruitment and termination policies. They exhibited the slowest promotion record of all nationalities. The management style introduced by Japanese acquirers was also the most bottom up, being based on the achievement of consensus through the hierarchy before major action was taken. As might be expected, they installed team-based product development, a characteristic that is normally found in their domestic operations. Although they appeared to be very open in their communications style, they tended not to provide information unless it was requested. They had a strong belief in training but, in contrast to American companies, the on-the-job method was just as popular as sending employees on courses.

The interviews confirmed that collectivism, long-term attitudes, consensual decision-making, and a concern to develop skills tend to be reflected in Japanese HRM policies. Within another Japanese acquisition (J9) the importance of a company appreciating and showing that it appreciated the value of its people was noted:

I think the major benefit is having a longer-term view of the future, the fact that there is a future, the willingness and ready availability of technology skills that (J9) have and probably making people here realize the value of people. What they have brought to this organization is to show people here how much you can really get out of individuals by allowing them to really fulfil their own potential. It's about giving people the opportunity to go out and learn more. It's a learning culture. We've got many more people here who go to night school in their own time. We allow them to take subjects from O-level maths, even O-level Japanese, through to some engineering skill and these are people who haven't been in any form of education for 15–20 years. It's stimulating the mind and when it comes to solving problems and improving their own workplace, their mind is more prepared to do that, whereas before they stagnated. They weren't paid to think; they were paid to do what they were told, so I think it's the Japanese culture. The philosophy of investment in people is the additional benefit, so there's the technology and the long-term view but also the benefits of investment in people.

The interviews confirmed that Japanese companies place great emphasis on the value of training, but are more likely to emphasize 'on-the-job' training, secondment within the company and training to instil aspects of the company culture in new employees who may not have been exposed to it previously. For example in one Japanese-acquired UK industrial company (J1): 'A Japanese technical manager was seconded to us for almost three years; three Japanese operators arrived to assist in the training of UK operators, as soon as newer equipment arrived about nine months after the takeover.'

In another industrial company (J2):

There was a personnel exchange in engineering and manufacturing. Two Japanese executives (one director, one manager) came to the UK. Then there was an exchange of foremen and key workers (including shop stewards) to learn each other's working practices, and which continued for the first ten years after acquisition. It started with the quality area but then extended into other areas.

Japanese companies are less likely than American ones to employ a formal and transparent personnel appraisal system. This does not 'mean, however, that such appraisals are not made, of Japanese as well as local staff. As the managing director of a UK polymers company (J8) said of the Japanese personnel seconded to him: 'When somebody here goes back to Japan, my report on his achievements here will have an effect on his progress back in Japan.'

Thus, while globalization and the perceived need to adjust to local practices encourage some contemporary Japanese HRM practices to move towards what might be called the Western approach, as with payment systems, they continue to retain a distinct Japanese flavour in other respects. The need to value people is seen as paramount, and also to reify the 'team'. Long-term employment is pursued wherever possible, teamwork is emphasized, and promotion tends to be slow.

An able, ambitious, and temperamentally tough international manager would be strongly advised to join an American MNC rather than a Japanese one if he or she wants to be in a position of real authority, and to be a high earner by the age of, say, 35 years. However, if their career falters for any reason, political or otherwise, the American company is likely to be far less forgiving, and such executives are likely to find themselves a victim to the firm's ruthless 'separation' policy with no route back to favour within that company.

French HRM practices

Huault (1996) reports that in acquisitions French executives are frequently seconded to the UK to spread their knowledge through the English management, and to attempt to develop a common way of thinking, that is, the French way. Exchange of UK managers to France may help here too. It is an informal and subtle HRM control mechanism.

We have already noted that French acquirers seem to be dominated by a very nationalistic and indeed 'colonial' attitude to their new subsidiaries. The picture that emerged from the survey confirmed this, and painted a consistent picture of the French management and indeed HRM style. The French appear the most concerned with formal qualifications for promotion, and the most likely to adopt HRM practices that involve planning career development in a systematic structured fashion.

Like other nationalities, French acquirers adopted performance-related pay and to that extent they showed some convergence with the practices of the other nationalities observed. They were notable in having the fastest promotion record of the countries surveyed. They were very top down in management style, but open in their communication style.

It emerged in most of the case studies that there was a tendency for the French, in typical 'colonial' fashion, to train their new foreign employees only up to a certain level. There were a few exceptions, however. One example is where the British chief executive of a French-acquired consultancy ended up running the newly developed transnational, and operating from Paris. However, it was not uncommon for host country executives to have limited promotion prospects. As the UK manager of a French-owned defence equipment company (F1) said:

Brits can make it to a glass ceiling level. This has changed a bit in the last three months as a Brit has been promoted to run the military simulator business globally. Generally the attitude has been a colonial one . . . internationalization has for years been part of the French company's rhetoric, but there has not been much action in this direction. Executive X was sacked as CEO last year apparently because he was always pushing in the internationalization of personnel and appointments direction; too much so it seems for the government shareholder.

He continued: 'Personnel links have been all one way, with French people coming to the UK, and there has been quite a bit of that. I know of only one Brit who has responsibilities for a French part of the company.'

As the managing director of the UK services subsidary of a French group (F5) stated:

The group's HRM philosophy is lifelong employment, and planned career development, and I agree with this. There are attempts to internationalize postings but you need to speak French fluently to be fully mobile. We are a French group working internationally rather than an international group.

However, the French too are influenced by international practices that are regarded as 'best practice'. As a recently retired director of a newly globalizing IT consultancy (F6) put it:

Career development has improved as a result of our recent systems restructuring as the organization is less fragmented and people feel they are part of a real organization. We have even recruited a human resources director from IBM. He is a young, dynamic guy doing a really good job. We used to think HRM was just about paying salaries. Again the changes have not been driven by our parent company.

The importance and benefit of lateral networking within the company is one aspect of HRM practice that was particularly emphasized by the French companies. As a French adhesives company (F7) executive observed: 'From an HR point of view we do "network" and try to see a situation where we have cross-company management development and where we look for exceptional people with business experience in different areas, rather than moving them around.' And in a newly French-owned water company (F10): 'There is strong provision of HR policies and training in the group. For example in pipe-laying and pipe-manufacturing we are expected to link up with other companies in the group and to share expertise with them.'

As in all the nationalities researched, performance-based pay has become a feature of HRM practices in French acquisitions. In the services company (F5) mentioned above, the UK managing director stated:

Reward systems are more performance based than we are used to. We were on a system in which pay was based on straight salary. With the new French owner there is salary plus a bonus related to the bottom line. They believe in the old saying 'turnover is vanity, profit is sanity'. Also, if you are starting up a new country there are share options as well. For example I own 3 per cent of the company that handles my new products. I link my team's bonuses to their objectives, not to profits.

Thus French HRM practices remain distinct, but French companies are not blind to the development of common international HRM practices. They have moved steadily towards their adoption in their acquisitions, but in their own time and their own way. The previous comment, to the effect that 'we are a French group working internationally rather than an international group', perhaps offers the most insightful summary of the situation.

German HRM practices

The survey reveals German companies as aware of international HRM practices and striving to adopt them, even when they conflicted with traditional German domestic practices. They were shown to be very open and informal in the communication style they introduced into their acquisitions. Like companies of other nationality, they moved towards the adoption of performance-related pay. They espoused team-based product development, and they increased the resources devoted to training, but to the least extent of the nationalities studied, and without a strong preference for on-the-job or training courses. On the other hand, the German acquisitions were relatively top down in management style (perhaps more in keeping with German tradition), were the most ad hoc in career development, and did not employ job rotation to any major extent.

We have noted how the approach of the German companies to cross-border acquisition lacks clarity of purpose or approach and is difficult to relate to the practices of the other nationalities with any confidence. A few things can be said, however. The German companies seemed to have some difficulty in accepting 'management' as a function in itself, as Lawrence and Edwards (2000) also note. Indeed, in one company the managing director was fired because the new owners could not understand what his function was. The consensual and somewhat formalistic nature of German top management procedures, and the dual board structure, mean that the concept of the CEO as an independent leader figure is somewhat foreign.

Therefore, although German acquirers are in favour of training, their emphasis is likely to be more on technical training than on management training. The comment of a manager in a UK newly German-owned pharmaceutical company (G1) represented the more usual case: 'In the early days there was a training manager in G1-UK who was helpful in setting up training programmes for managers. As a result our technical training is pretty well advanced.' In some other companies, however, the German attitude was less than positive in this area. As an engineering company executive from G2 noted: 'The owners did not place a high priority on training. We've taken some young Turks and given them access to company-sponsored training schemes, such as part-time MBAs and professional qualifications. Nothing much from Germany.'

Without placing much emphasis specifically on HRM policies, the business attitudes expected of German companies were evident in the way in which the acquirers treated their new employees. They took a long-term view and did not favour a hire and fire approach. They listened and adjusted to UK conditions. Promotion was generally restricted to the UK company, and there was little evidence of any planned career development. Heavy emphasis was placed upon technical proficiency as the key criterion for promotion.

UK HRM practices

The survey revealed the UK control companies as most closely related to the US ones in HRM and indeed many other styles and policies. This is not to say that they were carbon copies of the US companies. For example, their recruitment and termination policies tended to be far less short-termist than those of US companies. They were similar to the other nationalities in the adoption of performance-related pay and in increasing training in their new subsidiaries, and like the Americans showed a preference for the courses method. Like American companies again, they tended to adopt a need-to-know approach to communications. They were not very team based in new product development and they were generally top down in their management style.

Conclusions

HRM is a critical but often neglected area of management, providing subtle but potentially effective control mechanisms by which a parent company can influence its acquired subsidiary. HRM can also assist organizational learning by both parent and subsidiary, and facilitate smooth integration of the new subsidiary in the parent group by creating an appropriate identity for it, as well as spreading the parent's culture and an understanding of the parent's strategic intent.

Our research confirmed that firms of different nationality differ in the HRM practices they tend to apply to their acquisitions. There were, at the same time, signs of convergent practice in certain areas. There are also a few aspects in which our findings vary from those found in the recent HRM literature.

National differences are still apparent in policy and practice towards recruitment and termination within acquisitions. Japanese companies were more long term, and had less managerial job rotation, than did companies of other nationality. The Japanese tend to adjust their HRM policies to suit the local context so their attitudes were more akin to British ones than they would be if they were operating in Japan. The HRM policies that American companies applied to their acquisitions were short term on recruitment and results oriented, and they remain the most likely to 'hire and fire'. French acquirers attached importance to formal qualifications as criteria for promotion, while German acquirers looked for technical expertise. The Japanese still favoured seniority. Career development was often planned in the French companies, but not by other nationalities. The French were also noticeable for their 'colonial' attitudes regarding the 'glass ceiling' for non-French personnel. The Americans, and the British to some extent, used HRM as a very conscious integration tool, and one in which the new subsidiary was taught the 'way we do things around here'. The Japanese were more subtle in their approach in some ways, but used HRM to convey their business philosophy, which tended to include a long-term approach to business, concern for people, and a relatively slow and considered approach to promotion and to decision-making in general. The French used HRM in a 'modern' way with regard to performance-related pay, and career development paths, but did so without losing their distinctly French national character. Finally the Germans approached HRM policies in a less clear and purposive way and arguably failed to be so effective in their integration efforts partly for this reason.

There were a number of minor ways in which our findings differed from those of previous investigations. We found little evidence that American companies did much career forward planning, at least within their acquisitions, contrary to Adsit et al. (1997) who found that they did. We did not find much team-based product development in UK acquisitions made by other UK companies, in contrast to Shadur et al. (1995). Sparrow et al. (1994) found Japanese companies to be very hierarchical with a high respect for authority. Our findings, while not directly contradicting this, found that Japanese companies introduced a bottom-up culture and consensual decision-making style. In most other respects, our findings on HRM practice confirmed previous work.

There were significant signs of convergence towards accepted 'best practice'. They were manifest in compensation policies where the American system of individual performance-related pay was becoming increasingly adopted even in acquisitions made by the Japanese, the most collectivist of the nationalities covered. Increased training was also a general post-acquisition development, although the Japanese differed from the other nationalities in favouring on-the-job training rather than training by means of courses. Team-based new product development was also adopted by all nationalities, although UK companies were the least forward in this respect. Finally, companies of each nationality increased their use of appraisal systems, albeit in a very 'up-or-out' way by American companies and in more subtle ways by the others, particularly the Japanese. All in all, the 'convergence' thesis gains some support from evidence on post-acquisition change in the HRM area. Moreover, there is anecdotal evidence from the case studies to suggest, along with Ngo et al. (1998), Easterby Smith et al. (1995), and Hodgetts and Luthans (1990), that some adaptation of the practices adopted in the parent's home country is invariably necessary to take account of the local context.

Summary

- Convergence across nationalities in HRM policies was evident in post-acquisition moves towards performance-related pay, training, and team-based product development.
- Most acquirers also made adjustments to suit local culture.
- American HRM reflected a short-term individualistic national business culture.
- Japanese HRM, although adopting some American methods, generally reflected long-term, consensual, team-based, collectivist national philosophies.
- French companies have also been influenced by international HRM best practice but still tend to display a singularly ethnocentric approach that gives precedence to managers of French origin.
- German companies were the most anxious to adopt international practices in their acquisitions, even when these conflicted with their national tendencies. For example, they force themselves to be informal.

Performance after Acquisition

Introduction

Chapter 3 noted that acquisitions provide the purchasers with a strong position from which to introduce changes in the search for improved performance. The social justification for acquisitions is, indeed, that they bring about improvements in the performance of the firms that are taken over. There are several ways in which acquiring companies are expected to have a positive impact on the performance of their new subsidiaries. They can provide additional resources, especially working and fixed capital. They may be in a position to benefit from economies of scale or scope through integrating the acquired firms with their own operations. Horizontal acquisitions enhance the acquirers' market positions. Acquiring firms may also be able to introduce performance-enhancing improvements to the strategy and management of their new subsidiaries.

Most studies have focused on the performance of acquiring firms. There have been relatively few studies examining the post-acquisition performance of acquired companies (e.g. Datta 1991; Brush 1996; Very et al. 1996). The research that has been conducted points to resistance against the introduction of changes within the newly acquired subsidiaries as one reason for disappointing performance (David and Singh 1993; Gall 1991). Resistance and impaired motivation in acquired subsidiaries can result from obvious fears about job security, threats to status, blocked career prospects, and additional pressures for results (Marks and Mirvis 1992). It may also reflect less tangible, but nonetheless real, difficulties that people find in accepting changes that are seen to reflect an alien culture and social identity (Child and Rodrigues 1996; Very et al. 1996). Any acquisition involves a new social identity and is liable to introduce a new culture.

This is self-evidently the case with cross-border acquisitions. Datta and Puia (1995) found that acquisitions involving a high level of cultural distance tended to result in greater negative shareholder value. When acquisitions in the UK are made by foreign companies, the changes they introduce or encourage in their newly acquired subsidiaries may be quite substantial in cultural terms. The globalization of markets and the multiple management cultures now faced by UK management imply that inward FDI, through the control and influence it gives foreign management, will stimulate the adoption of management practice which contrasts with the past practice of the acquired UK firms. The balance between direct application of foreign management practice and its adaptation to local conditions leaves open the question of how far and in what manner FDI induces domestic changes and impacts on the performance of acquired affiliates.

The rationale for introducing new forms of management practice is that these are expected to contribute positively to levels of post-acquisition performance. There are, however, several qualifications to this expectation. The new management practice reflects the acquiring company's assumptions, and will be identified with its dominant position. As just noted, it may not therefore be wholeheartedly accepted and implemented. Secondly, changes in management practice may be a necessary rather than sufficient condition for performance enhancement among acquired subsidiaries, with financial investment and other resource provision being equally, if not more, crucial (Chakrabarti 1990; Brush 1996). Indeed, some changes in practice, such as a greater emphasis on new product development, will depend upon new investment. Third, as a Mercer Management Consulting study indicated (Smith 1997), the calibre of the management handling the process of introducing changes can be a critical factor for success. The impact on performance of changes in management practice *per se* may therefore only be modest and difficult to achieve, but nevertheless worthwhile.

It is, moreover, difficult to distinguish cause and effect between some changes in management practice and performance, except through very close observation of each case. Additional training, for example, may improve performance through the way it develops competencies within the acquired subsidiary but, equally, extra investment in training may only be sanctioned if performance is expected to be sufficiently good to permit additional funds to be released. If both processes occur simultaneously, it becomes virtually impossible to disentangle cause and effect. Only a positive association can be noted.

This chapter addresses the possibility that new forms of management practice introduced into acquired subsidiaries contribute towards improvements in their performance. It enquires whether changes in management practice introduced by the acquirers of the 201 UK firms were associated with their levels of post-acquisition performance. The national spread of acquiring company permits us to examine the possibility that there may be more than one effective management philosophy towards post-acquisition performance enhancement. The chapter raises the following questions:

1. Are contextual factors, including acquirer nationality, associated with post-acquisition performance?
2. Are changes in management practice associated with post-acquisition performance?
3. If so, how does their impact compare with that of contextual factors?
4. Do acquiring companies of different nationality pursue different paths towards the improvement of post-acquisition performance?

We will examine the possible impact of various non-managerial (contextual) parameters on post-acquisition performance, before focusing on the possible contribution made by changes in management practice.

Method of performance evaluation

This part of our investigation relies primarily on the postal questionnaire described in Chapter 6. Given the acceptance limits to postal questionnaires as instruments to secure detailed information requiring time and effort to prepare, the indicators of post-acquisition performance employed were of an evaluative kind, as shown in Fig. 12.1.

Respondents were asked to compare the acquired company's post-acquisition performance with that of their main competitors in order to standardize, as far as possible, evaluations across different sectors and time periods. Other questions were addressed to the post-acquisition growth of sales (for which data on sales turnover were collected) and the profitability of the company when it was taken over.

To the best of your knowledge, since its acquisition has your company's position vis-à-vis its main competitors with respect to Profitability and Sales improved or worsened?

1. Profitability   Worsened ←———— no change ————→ Improved

            −3   −2   −1   0   +1   +2   +3

2. Sales   Worsened ←———— no change ————→ Improved

            −3   −2   −1   0   +1   +2   +3

Figure 12.1. Indicators of post-acquisition performance

Post-acquisition performance and non-managerial parameters

Table 12.1 presents correlations between the indicators of post-acquisition performance. The two subjective measures, profitability and sales performance vis-à-vis main competitors, tend to vary together, sharing 41 per cent common variance. Evaluations of sales performance are more highly correlated with percentage sales growth following acquisition than are evaluations of profitability, indicating that the two subjective measures have discriminatory power of the kind intended.[1]

Almost half (47 per cent) of the acquired companies were reported to have been loss making, or failing to achieve satisfactory profits, at the time they were acquired. The majority of respondents said that the post-acquisition performance of their companies vis-à-vis their main competitors had improved. Two-thirds (68 per cent) reported that there had been an improvement in profitability since being acquired, and 72 per cent reported an improvement in their companies' sales position. Only 20 per cent reported a worsening in their profit position and 18 per cent in sales, compared to their main competitors. Overall, post-acquisition sales performance appears to have improved marginally more than profitability.

A number of non-managerial parameters (contextual factors) were examined for their possible direct impact on post-acquisition performance. These parameters were acquirer nationality, sector (high-tech manufacturing, low-tech manufacturing, and service), size of acquired company, size of acquiring

Table 12.1.   Means, standard deviations, and product–moment correlations between indicators of post-acquisition performance

	Mean	SD	Correlations	
			2	3
1. Profitability (N=169)	1.02	1.76	0.62[a]	0.21[b]
2. Sales (N=169)	1.67	1.59	—	0.35[a]
3. Percentage sales growth (N=158)	100.49	177.09	—	—

[a] $p \leq 0.001$ (one-tailed test).
[b] $p \leq 0.01$ (one-tailed test).

[1] The discriminatory power of the two measures is also indicated by the fact that the correlations between them varied across different national groups of acquiring companies. These were: US acquirers $r = 0.74$, $p \leq 0.000$; Japanese acquirers $r = 0.43$, $p \leq 0.05$; French acquirers $r = 0.35$, $p \leq 0.05$; German acquirers $r = 0.73$, $p \leq 0.01$; UK acquirers $r = 0.59$, $p \leq 0.000$.

company, date of acquisition, and profitability of the subsidiary at the time of its acquisition. There was no systematic association between any of these factors and post-acquisition performance. This means that the response to the first question, concerning the possible influence of contextual factors, is a negative one. Acquirers of different nationality do not on average achieve different post-acquisition performance results, and the other contextual factors taken into account are not predictors of such performance either. One should bear in mind, however, that the evaluation of performance 'vis-à-vis main competitors' is intended to deflate variations due to differences in sector economic conditions. This still leaves open the possibility that such differences would have a systematic impact on subsidiaries' performance, if this were assessed in absolute rather than relative terms.

A similar explanation may account for the surprising absence of any association between founding conditions and post-acquisition performance. The dates of acquisition spanned both the recession of the 1990s and the half-decade preceding it, and we had expected that firms acquired in the recession might have experienced a more marked performance turnaround. We similarly expected acquisition to have had a greater positive performance impact on acquired firms that were performing badly when acquired.[2] The assessment of post-acquisition performance vis-à-vis competitors means, however, that, while the recession of the early 1990s may have deflated performance, it is likely to have affected competitors in much the same way, so leaving the acquired firm's *relative* performance unaffected. Another possibility, which we now explore, is that *internal* changes in management practice have had a more significant performance impact than contextual factors.

Post-acquisition changes and performance

Chapter 7 examined the strength and direction of changes in management practice introduced into the acquired companies, the extent to which these varied according to the nationality of the acquiring company, and the influence that the parent company was reported to have had on the introduction of the changes. A varied picture emerged in that there were stronger across-the-board post-acquisition changes in some areas of management practice than in others. Moreover, national differences between the acquiring firms were evident for some changes in management practice, but not for all. For instance, higher levels of cost control were introduced into the majority

---

[2] Performance when acquired was not associated with date or period of acquisition.

of acquired firms, and this did not vary significantly between the national groups.

On the other hand, we noted in previous chapters how in some areas of management practice national categories of acquirer contrasted both in the changes they introduced and in the manner of their introduction. These contrasts accord closely with previous characterizations of the management philosophies of American and Japanese companies, though not for French and German companies. Given the absence of systematic differences in post-acquisition performance according to acquirer nationality, these findings suggest that some management changes may have a general impact on performance across the sample as a whole, while others may be more sensitive to nationality. With this in mind, we first look at the changes that had a relatively consistent impact on post-acquisition performance before turning to those where the performance-related profiles vary according to acquirer nationality.

General influences on performance

Table 12.2 lists the post-acquisition changes in management practice which were associated with post-acquisition profitability and sales performance. These results are taken from the sample as a whole without regard, at this stage, for the nationality of the acquiring company.

The introduction of a greater emphasis on developing and offering unique products or services, a differentiation strategy (Porter 1985), was associated with both superior profitability and sales among the acquired subsidiaries. A stronger projection of marketing image, a shift towards a bottom-up style and culture, and more open communication were also related to better performance along both dimensions. Greater emphasis on cost control and the slimming down of management were linked to superior profitability but not sales performance. The adoption of a strategic rather than financial orientation, decentralization of decision-making, an increase in teamwork, and more emphasis on formal qualifications were all associated with improvements in sales but not in profitability.

It is highly likely that these relationships are causal, that changes in management practice have an impact upon performance rather than the other way round. One cannot be so confident about the direction of causality in the case of some other changes, such as more rapid promotion, more training, and increases in employment, which could just have easily been a consequence of improving performance as its cause. There is causal ambiguity with a further factor which, although not assessed in terms of *change*, denotes an important aspect of the way that parent companies managed their

Table 12.2. Changes in management practice correlating with post-acquisition profitability and sales performance (N=169 acquisitions)

Management practice:	Profitability		Sales improvement	
change towards	Correlation	p (two-tail)	Correlation	p (two-tail)
Developing unique products/services	0.28	0.000	0.25	0.001
Offering unique products/services	0.27	0.000	0.24	0.002
Stronger projection of marketing image	0.28	0.000	0.41	0.000
Strategic (rather than financial) orientation	n.s.		0.24	0.002
Bottom-up style and culture	0.17	0.025	0.22	0.005
Greater job rotation of managers	n.s.		0.18	0.017
Higher employment in the company	n.s.		0.30	0.000
Longer-term employment philosophy	n.s.		0.20	0.011
Greater emphasis on formal qualifications	n.s.		0.18	0.023
Decentralized strategic decision-making	n.s.		0.15	0.048
Decentralized operational decision-making	n.s.		0.20	0.011
More open communication	0.21	0.006	0.21	0.006
More rapid promotion	0.17	0.029	0.20	0.011
More training	0.16	0.040	0.24	0.002
Greater group working/use of work teams	n.s.		0.21	0.014
Greater cost control	0.16	0.034	n.s.	
Lower percentage of managers	0.18	0.018	n.s.	

Note: n.s. = not significant.

acquisitions. This was the finding that profitability was better among subsidiaries that were granted greater autonomy.[3]

Factor analysis of the post-acquisition changes was conducted in order to simplify interpretation. The areas of management practice, such as R&D, which did not apply to all companies were omitted from this analysis in order to maximize the number of valid cases. The factor analysis pointed to three sets of post-acquisition changes that were often found together and hence formed a clearly identifiable approach. The third configuration was not related to performance across the sample as a whole. It focused on control,

[3] Autonomy was assessed by reference to eight decisions: final approval for the subsidiary's budget, capital expenditure, appointment/termination of senior personnel, acquisition/divestment, formation of alliances (e.g. joint venture), major contractual agreements, changes in the scope/direction of the company, and the introduction of major new products.

consisting of moves towards centralization of decisions and more use of financial control systems. The first two configurations did, however, predict acquisition performance.

The first configuration is a package of strategic, style, and HRM changes. Many of its components featured in Table 12.2. They consist of changes towards:

- developing and offering unique products and services;
- a longer-term planning time horizon;
- a bottom-up style;
- decentralized operational decision-making;
- open communications;
- more training;
- planned career development;
- rapid promotion.

This package of changes was significantly related to improvements in both profitability and sales on the part of acquired companies when judged vis-à-vis their main competitors.

The second set of changes was exclusively organizational in nature. It consisted of changes towards product-based organizational structures, with fewer specialized departments, less employment, a lower percentage of managers, and fewer formal meetings. These changes were clearly in the direction of slimmer, more focused organizational profiles. They led to improvements in sales performance. Rather surprisingly, they did not lead to significant improvements in profitability.

Nationally specific influences on performance

Further examination indicates that the performance-related profiles differ according to the nationality of the acquiring company, with the Japanese presenting a particularly singular case. Tables 12.3 and 12.4 list the national profiles of post-acquisition changes that are linked with post-acquisition profitability and sales performance respectively. The tables show only those changes in management practice that we can be confident are associated with performance, with no more than a 5 per cent probability of this occurring by chance.

In companies acquired by American parents, a good level of profitability was fostered by the development of new distinctive products or services (Table 12.3). This policy was supported by a stronger projection of the companies' marketing image. The same pattern tended to characterize those companies acquired by UK parents as well, though in their case the introduction of

Table 12.3. National profiles: changes in management practice correlating with post-acquisition profitability, categorized by nationality of acquiring company

Management practice: change towards	American acquirers (N=62)	Japanese acquirers (N=20)	UK acquirers (N=48)	French acquirers (N=28)	German acquirers (N=11)
Developing unique products or services	✓				
Offering unique products or services	✓				
Stronger projection of marketing image	✓				
Greater cost control			✓	✓	
Centralization of strategic decision-making		✓	✓	✓	
Centralization of operational decision-making		✓	✓		
Decentralization of strategic decision-making				✓	
Decentralization of operational decision-making				✓	
More open communication				✓	
More informal communication				✓	
More rapid promotion	✓				
Performance-oriented reward systems				✓	
Greater use of automation and IT				✓	

Note: ✓ = Correlation between the change in management practice and post-acquisition profitability at $p \leq 0.05$ (two-tailed test).

greater cost control also contributed towards good performance. Projection of a stronger marketing image and greater cost control were associated with achievement of superior profitability among the French-acquired firms. However, moves towards decentralization, more open and informal communication, performance-oriented reward systems, and the greater use of new technology also appear to have contributed to the post-acquisition profitability of the French-acquired firms.

The Japanese acquisitions did not achieve good profit performance through the introduction of any of these changes. By contrast, the Japanese subsidiaries that increased the centralization of strategic and operational decision-making in their acquisitions tended to report the best levels of profitability. There were no significant links between post-acquisition changes in management practice and profitability among German-acquired subsidiaries. While this could reflect the small size of the German sub-sample, it is also compatible with the finding from cases studies among some of the same firms that those taken over by German parents did not on the whole experience a determined or systematic post-acquisition reform of their management. Indeed, the German cases were not very consistent in their approaches to post-acquisition management, as previous chapters have noted.

As before, post-acquisition sales performance was associated with change over a wider range of management practices. The national profiles are set out in Table 12.4. Companies with American acquirers achieved a good level of sales performance through much the same approach as had given them superior profitability. They stressed the development of new distinctive products, backing this by a stronger projection of their marketing image than before and a stronger strategic orientation. The American subsidiaries with superior sales performance supported this approach through a number of organizational developments. They fostered a bottom-up style and culture, decentralized operational decision-making, introduced more training, and promoted teamwork. They also reported a change towards more rapid promotion though, as we have already noted, this could well be a concomitant of better sales performance rather than a cause. A further indication of the strong market orientation among the more successful American subsidiaries is the fact that they reported the strongest correlation between post-acquisition profitability and sales performance of any national group (see n. 1 above).

The UK-acquired firms came the closest to this US profile. UK subsidiaries with good sales performance had also strengthened their marketing image and development of unique products or services. They decentralized operational decision-making, opened up communications, and introduced more training. By contrast with the American-acquired firms, the UK subsidiaries with good sales performance reported that they had adopted a longer time horizon in their planning and had increased the formalization of their planning process. They also increased cost control, rotated managers more between functions, and increased the percentage of technically qualified personnel. Overall, the picture emerging for the UK-acquired group is that firms had secured good post-acquisition sales performance by improving new product development, adopting a more systematic and longer-term approach and improving the quality and use of key staff. The implication is that many of them had been deficient in these respects before being acquired. There was quite a high correlation between profitability and sales performance for the UK national group, though it was not as strong as that for the American subsidiaries (see n. 1 above).

The other national groups did not achieve superior post-acquisition sales performance through a product-innovating strategy, or at least to anywhere near the same extent as the Anglo-Saxons. The only points of similarity were that those Japanese and French subsidiaries strengthening their marketing image, and adopting a more strategic orientation, tended to achieve better sales performance like the US and UK companies. In the French group, other changes in management practice associated with good sales performance were an increase in cost control and more informal, open communication. Among the German acquired companies, a centralization of decision-making and reduction of outsourcing were linked to good sales performance.

The Japanese-acquired companies were again the most distinctive in the post-acquisition changes that had a positive impact on sales performance. The better-performing Japanese subsidiaries normally shifted towards competing on price and a reduction in the range of their suppliers. They not only strengthened their marketing image but, alone of all the national groups, cultivated closer customer relations. The Japanese subsidiaries achieving the best post-acquisition sales performance also strengthened their strategic orientation and centralized both strategic and operational decision-making. In the HRM area, these companies tended to move towards a long-term employment philosophy, a higher percentage of technically qualified personnel, and an increase in total employment.

Acquiring companies of different nationality therefore had their own ways of fostering performance improvements in new subsidiaries. Although there were certain similarities in the profiles of beneficial changes they introduced, none were predictors of improved performance across the board. Some, but not all, of the changes positively associated with subsidiary performance reflect the national approaches to management that were otherwise evident within this sample of acquisitions. Instances are the emphasis on strengthening operational decentralization and training among the high-performing American acquirers, and that on strengthening steady, close relationships

Table 12.4. National profiles: changes in management practice correlating with post-acquisition sales performance, categorized by nationality of acquiring company

Management practice: change towards	American acquirers (N=63)	Japanese acquirers (N=20)	UK acquirers (N=48)	French acquirers (N=26)	German acquirers (N=11)
Developing unique products or services	✓✓✓		✓		
Offering unique products or services	✓✓			✓	
Stronger projection of marketing image	✓	✓	✓	✓	
Greater customer involvement in marketing decisions		✓			
Strategic (rather than financial) orientation	✓	✓			
Greater emphasis on competing on price		✓			✓
Single sourcing					
Reduced outsourcing					
Longer planning time horizon			✓	✓	
Bottom-up style and culture	✓		✓		
Greater job rotation of managers between functions					
Higher employment in the company	✓	✓	✓		
Long-term employment philosophy			✓		
Higher percentage of technically qualified staff		✓	✓		
Greater emphasis on formal qualifications					
Greater cost control					
More formalized planning					
Centralization of strategic decision-making		✓	✓	✓	✓
Centralization of operational decision-making		✓	✓✓	✓	✓✓
Decentralization of strategic decision-making			✓✓✓	✓✓	
Decentralization of operational decision-making	✓				
More open communication					
More informal communication					
More rapid promotion	✓✓				
More training	✓✓			✓✓	
Greater group working/use of work teams	✓		✓		

Note. ✓ = Correlation between the change in management practice and post-acquisition sales performance at p < 0.05 (two-tailed test).

with customers, suppliers, and employees among high-performing Japanese companies. This suggests that some, *but only some*, national management practices have a significant performance impact.[4] Some examples can serve to illustrate the different national patterns.

An IT systems service company acquired by an American parent company (US5) in 1990 has since then achieved both high profitability and sales growth compared with the rest of its sector. It illustrates the kind of post-acquisition changes that characterize successful American acquisitions in the UK. First, the development of new unique services and strengthening of the market image. The managing director of one service division commented:

> The greater emphasis on unique services means we try hard to differentiate ourselves. We are not the cheapest in the market, so we have to work very hard to convince clients of the quality of what we do ... [The acquiring company] has always been successful over its thirty years of life. The reasons are probably because the basic concept underlying it is right, i.e. the delivery of a service of value to the customer ... Image projection is much stronger than it was in [the pre-acquisition firm]. We have ... got the attention of the media [and] we also pay some attention to PR.

Second, operational decentralization. The UK subsidiary had 'considerable autonomy from the USA'. It was said that its parent understood the importance of cultural differences and so 'does not impose in any way'.

An illustration of the Japanese profile of post-acquisition changes related to success, and the contrast it presents, is provided by a Midlands engineering company (J1) acquired in 1992. Its post-acquisition experience has been successful in what had become a very depressed sector. When acquired, the firm was on the verge of bankruptcy. Since then, its sales have expanded considerably and after four years it returned to profitability. Its parent company achieved this through introducing a longer-term strategic perspective (including a guarantee of no redundancies), and several major top-down initiatives. Two such initiatives are regarded as particularly important contributions to the company's turnaround. The first brought in technological improvements backed by heavy investment; the second was an emphasis on establishing personal relationships with customers. Two senior Japanese managers were largely responsible for these changes in practice which, at least while they were being introduced, reflected a marked increase in decision-making centralization. The subsidiary's general manager noted that:

> [The technical manager] was a very strong personality, a very influential personality at all levels in [the parent company] right the way to the top. He had the ear of the

---

[4] In considering this finding, it is important to bear in mind that the present analysis is reporting on those changes which gave better post-acquisition results, not on the degree and nature of change *per se* which might typify different nationalities of acquiring company.

company president . . . He drove us very hard in the technological improvements and also in a lot of attitude changes on the shop floor.

The Japanese MD, according to the same respondent, took an active role in promoting customer involvement:

He stressed the need to establish a personal relationship with individual customers. The [Japanese] very much react to individual problems with individual customers, and they expect us to react quickly to such problems. In a lot of cases, their concept of reacting to a customer is to go and see him.

A third example illustrates several aspects of the French success profile. This is the case of a castings company (F4) that went into receivership in 1991 and was acquired by a French group in the following year. At the time we visited it five years later, the acquisition had turned the company around to the point at which it was now holding its own against severe competition. Much of the post-acquisition change could be described as decentralization subject to systematic guidance from above. The parent company did not introduce any of its own appointees into the acquired company, which it also allowed to operate on an autonomous basis. At the same time, the French parent insisted on the introduction of more rigorous practices, notably Total Quality Management, a more systematic approach to marketing supported by the parent company's much larger sales force, greater cost control, and opera-tional flow-line improvements. It also brought in a stronger strategic orientation backed by an annual review process. These changes were not, however, introduced without some resentment among managers in the acquired company. While the British MD of the acquired company acknow-ledged the benefits of the more rigorous approach, he did not welcome the 'bureaucracy' that in his view accompanied it:

They have been incredibly mechanistic in setting up this network of reporting and statistical measuring controls. It is very difficult to get the 'feel' through these approaches. They are so strategically and procedurally minded that the science offends our feel for the business . . . we are scientists trying to become artists whereas they are trying to turn artists into scientists.

It is therefore apparent that acquiring companies of different nationality are able to secure favourable levels of post-acquisition performance through intro-ducing their own typical strategies and practices. Different national approaches do succeed, implying that the assets and competencies of acquired UK com-panies can be harnessed in different ways with the potential for equally good results. This degree of strategic choice (Child 1997) is only somewhat qualified by the sector-related contrasts which appeared in the correlations between changes in management practice and post-acquisition performance.

Some contingent conditions

Sector contrasts were most evident when comparing high-technology with low-technology manufacturing acquisitions. Among the high-tech acquisitions, changes towards a bottom-up style and culture, and less use of cost and financial control, were associated with superior profitability and sales performance. By contrast, among the low-tech acquisitions, changes towards a bottom-up style and culture were only associated with good sales performance, and even then not so strongly as among the high-tech firms. In the low-tech group, it was primarily a move towards greater cost and financial control that was associated with better performance. Greater emphasis on developing and offering unique products also improved profitability and sales performance, especially the latter. It appears that in high-technology firms, moves towards freeing people up from financial restrictions and encouraging their participation favour high performance, whereas the performance of low-technology acquisitions benefits when they move towards both greater product differentiation and financial control.

The above analysis has assumed that post-acquisition changes in management practice impacting on performance have been largely introduced at the behest of the acquiring parent company rather than at the subsidiary's own discretion or initiative. The discussion of nationality profiles is predicated upon this acquisition effect. The assumption is in fact vindicated by the observation that the impact of post-acquisition changes on performance is normally greater when parent companies had more influence over them. Acquiring companies make a more significant contribution to the performance of their new charges when they actively instigate and facilitate the introduction of new management practices.

The contrast is particularly marked in the case of strategic changes. In those acquired firms whose parent companies are reported to have exercised high overall influence over post-acquisition change, the correlations between strategic and market orientation and performance are consistently greater than among firms whose parent companies exercised low influence. Thus among the high-influence half of the sample, a greater emphasis on offering new products or services was positively related to profitability and to sales performance, whereas among the low-influence group there was no relationship at all. Among companies with high acquirer influence, a stronger projection of marketing image was related positively to profitability and sales performance, whereas there was again little relation among the group with low acquirer influence.[5]

---

[5] For acquisitions in which parent companies exercised high influence, a greater emphasis on offering new products or services was positively related to profitability ($r = 0.34$, $p = 0.006$) and to

It was almost invariably the case that acquiring companies supplied additional finance to their acquired subsidiaries, with many providing additional technological support as well. The provision of finance was often in response to instances where the acquired firm was making a loss, was unable to generate sufficient profit to reinvest, or faced a deteriorating situation. It would appear, nevertheless, both from the survey and from the case studies, that it was usually changes in management practice, backed by the active involvement of the acquiring company, that laid the ground for performance improvement, rather than just the provision of funding itself.

It is the nature of change introduced into acquired subsidiaries rather than the parent company's influence that impacts upon performance. For the sample of companies as a whole, there was no connection between parent company influence *per se* and acquisition performance.

A closer look in terms of parent company nationality did, however, highlight one very marked exception to this general picture. Among the Japanese acquisitions, parent company influence over post-acquisition management correlated negatively with the profitability of subsidiaries. Japanese subsidiaries experiencing poorer profit performance than their main competitors had parent companies exerting stronger pressures for change across quite a wide range of areas, namely strategy, company philosophy, organization, operations, procurement, and communications. Bearing in mind that, compared to other nationalities, Japanese companies generally exercise less influence over their acquisitions and do not integrate them tightly, these findings suggest that they intervene only when their acquisitions fail to attain satisfactory profitability. The ten case studies of Japanese acquisitions bear out this pattern of cause and effect. The Japanese parent companies were generally slow to exercise direct influence following acquisition, but eventually did so in cases where a subsidiary experienced considerable difficulty.

Although the profitability of the acquired firm at the time of its acquisition was not related to the post-acquisition performance reported on the questionnaires, it nevertheless plays a role. First, the changes made to management practice tend to have a somewhat stronger impact on performance among those firms whose profitability at the time of acquisition was not satisfactory. Second, while profitability at acquisition is not correlated with the *types* of change introduced (and hence the national success profiles), it is correlated with the *degree* of change that is brought in. The poorer the profitability of the subsidiary when acquired, the greater the amount of change that tends to be

sales performance ($r = 0.29$, $p = 0.018$). For the same companies, a stronger projection of marketing image was related positively to profitability ($r = 0.33$, $p = 0.008$) and to sales performance ($r = 0.53$, $p = 0.000$).

introduced into it. In other words, as expected, acquisition is frequently used as the lever for making changes aimed at company turnaround. It is clear, however, from our findings that not all post-acquisition change is equally beneficial for performance, whatever the vigour with which it is introduced. Indeed, as we note below, some changes were not correlated with the performance of acquired subsidiaries at all.

Changes in management practice unrelated to post-acquisition performance

So far, we have focused on changes in the management practice of acquired subsidiaries that impacted upon, or were at least correlated with, their competitive performance. The fact that some changes were not associated with performance is, however, also of interest. This may be because they were introduced more or less across the board, or that their relation to performance is highly contingent on other factors. We noted in Chapters 8 and 9, for instance, that over the sample as a whole the degree of post-acquisition integration was unrelated to performance, though closer examination of national sub-groups revealed certain connections between the two variables. It is also useful from a practical point of view to identify those changes it may not be worthwhile to prioritize.

There were two areas of quite widespread post-acquisition change that bore no direct relation either to profitability or sales performance. One concerned operations and R&D. The adoption of more automation and IT was not related to either criterion of performance. The same was true of most advanced operational techniques. The majority of firms within the sample had introduced employee responsibility for quality, and continuous improvement since their acquisition. Half of the firms had moved toward team-based research or development, and almost half had also introduced TQM. Yet none of these changes were related to post-acquisition performance. The sole exception was the introduction of group or teamworking, which was positively associated with sales performance. One reason why these operational and R&D changes did not consistently impact upon performance may be because they represented a managerial fashion—that of 'Japanization' (Oliver and Wilkinson 1992)—which was not necessarily applied with due care or knowledge.

A second widely adopted post-acquisition strategic shift bore a direct relation to performance in the case of one national group of acquirers only. The introduction of greater emphasis on price competitiveness was related to superior sales performance among Japanese-acquired but not among the other national groups. A likely reason for its generally low impact on performance is that most companies in the UK have been endeavouring to become more price competitive with the result that this strategy does not necessarily discriminate. Another possibility is that in a sufficient number of industries price *per se* is no longer as important a competitive advantage as the intrinsic worth of the product or service. One may recall that developing and offering unique products was the strategic change widely associated with superior performance in the present sample.

The widespread adoption of operational changes and the increased importance attached to price competition could have obscured the possibility that a few firms bucking these trends were below average performers. Examination of these cases, however, revealed that their performance levels were not significantly lower than those for the rest of the sample.

A third set of practices was not associated with post-acquisition performance, namely those concerned with organization structure: product-based or functional forms, levels in the hierarchy, and the number of specialized departments. The reason for this lack of relationship, however, is a different one as these organizational features generally changed very little following acquisition, either across the whole sample or among any of the national groups.

Conclusion

The competitive performance of companies has proved to be notoriously difficult to predict and explain. Accounting for performance is even more hazardous in the evolving situation that follows the trauma of acquisition. The management of organizations is a highly complex affair: many factors have a potential bearing on performance, with different lead-times and potential interaction effects. The presumption of this chapter was therefore that post-acquisition changes in management practice would be likely to have a positive impact on the performance of the acquired subsidiaries, but that this would probably be relatively modest. A second expectation, in the light of previously noted contrasts in the changes introduced by acquirers of different nationalities, was that such national groups might well pursue different paths towards the improvement of post-acquisition performance.

The conclusion emerging from our analysis of acquisitions in the UK is that changes in management practice do have a bearing on post-acquisition profitability and sales performance. These changes reflect an 'acquisition effect' and they also to some extent bear a 'nationality effect' as well. Acquiring companies, with relatively few exceptions, are reported to exert an influence over the changes that appear to impact upon the performance of their subsidiaries. The nationality effect has been evident in the form of certain national profiles—consistent tendencies for acquirers of different nationality to pursue somewhat different paths towards the improvement of subsidiary performance. This variation persists almost regardless of context.

Efforts to project the market image of the acquired company, and the development of new products and services, were the changes most consistently associated with a high level of profitability and sales performance vis-à-vis competitors. Moves towards engaging and developing the human resources of the acquired firm were also consistently associated with better performance. These included an opening up of the organization, in terms of shifts towards a more bottom-up culture and more open communications, more rapid promotion, and increased training. The bearing that these changes had on the performance of acquired companies was fairly consistent, if we take the sample as a whole.

These are, of course, the types of change that echo much of the advice offered in recent years to managers along the lines of strengthening a customer orientation, and developing human and organizational capabilities. It is particularly useful from the perspective of company policy to find that these positive changes for performance comprise a mutually reinforcing approach. Although they did not figure as strongly as single correlates of high performance, factor analysis suggests that moves towards a long-term planning horizon and decentralized operational decision-making often form part of the same positive package.

The picture is, however, complicated by other evidence suggesting that there may be more than one path to performance improvement. It appears that there is an Anglo-American path and a contrasting Japanese one. The two paths contrasted most clearly in the areas of strategy and decision centralization. The Anglo-Saxon acquisitions which achieved the best performance tended to have experienced a stronger product innovation strategy and decentralization, whereas their high-performing Japanese-acquired counterparts tended to have experienced a strengthening of a price-competitive strategy and greater centralization. With somewhat less certainty, one can discern a French path towards good post-acquisition performance which, counter to some characterizations of that country's managerial style, involves strengthening the company's market image, increasing cost control, more open and less formal communication, and decentralization. The German acquisitions did not present either a consistent or a strong pattern of connections between post-acquisition changes in management practice and performance.

It appears that the assets and competencies of UK companies can be harnessed through the stimulus of acquisition with good results, and that there are different paths to the achievement of good performance. The patterns of national distinctiveness in these paths deserve further investigation. Such investigation should endeavour to control for contextual factors, particularly sector, where it appears from our results that the distinction between high- and low-technology industries can have a bearing on the relation between changes in management practice and performance.

Summary

The key points arising from this chapter are:

- Acquisition is a lever for making changes aimed at company turnaround.
- Contextual factors—acquirer nationality, sector, size of acquired company, size of acquiring company, date of acquisition, and profitability of the subsidiary when acquired—do not impact directly on post-acquisition performance.
- Some post-acquisition changes are related to performance across a wide range of companies and without regard to acquirer nationality. They include strategic, marketing, and HRM changes.
- There appears to be more than one path towards post-acquisition performance improvement. The clearest contrast in this respect is between American and Japanese approaches.
- Certain areas of post-acquisition change have no direct relation to performance. They include operations management, R&D, and organization structure.

13

National Case Studies

This chapter introduces four case studies, one from each nationality of the foreign acquiring companies, and comments on their key characteristics. The purpose of these case studies is to provide illustrations of how post-acquisition management was handled by a selected company of each nationality.

1. US3: an American acquisition

US3, a major US-based parcel carrier, set about expanding into Europe in a major way in 1989, after over three-quarters of a century of growth mostly in the US domestic market. At the time the research was carried out it had acquired sixteen companies in Europe including four in the UK, bought in 1989 (two), 1990, and 1992. It proceeded to integrate these four UK acquisitions with its existing UK business, previously developed organically. This case study describes the absorption of the four UK acquisitions into the parent company. The case is both a very typical example of the characteristic approach by US multinational companies to the integration of overseas acquisitions, and also an example of the Haspeslagh and Jemison (1991) absorption approach to post-acquisition management of new subsidiaries. The informant was the UK local director of US3, who had been with the parent company eight years, and had 750 personnel reporting to him.

US3 was founded on the West Coast of the USA shortly after the beginning of the twentieth century by a visionary founder. It is a totally privately owned company with the stock in the hands of its managers. After growing steadily in the USA in the earlier part of the century, it began international expansion in the mid-1970s into Canada and then Germany, and in the 1980s began a world drive, with the result that it now operates in 200 countries in total. It bought its own airline to carry its freight, and currently has 550 aircraft and more than 350,000 employees. 'You get some idea of the scale of the company if you go to "Midsville" and see 100 US3 aircraft take off one after another.'

It is, however, still relatively small in the UK with only 4 per cent market share at the time that it began its UK acquisition plan, and had relied upon organic growth until it made the four acquisitions to be described in this case study. Each of the acquired companies was a UK SME (small or medium-sized enterprise).

Post-acquisition changes

As each of the companies purchased has been relatively small they have generally lacked specialist support functions, which US3 has been able to provide. Examples of the areas of support provided include industrial engineering, information services, accounts groups, and the US3 airline. US3 has carried out a general policy of leaving the pre-acquisition local MD in place to continue running the local operations, but now backed by US3 functional support, and operating within the very strong US3 corporate culture. Members of the acquired company either integrate and become US3 people, or they choose to leave. A US company executive said: 'We are very much a people company, and pay very well. Promotions are pretty rapid as growth is so fast. We have a policy book; it's a bit like a Mormon meeting sometimes. There is very high integrity and work ethic.'

Image projection is also an important integration factor. It is stressed that all US3 van drivers are always neat and tidy, and everyone is clean shaven, i.e. no beards. The 45,000 vehicles are washed every day, and the firm's advertising stresses these qualities.

Each divisional manager is responsible for developing his people. He cannot be promoted until he has trained someone to replace him. Therefore instead of people looking over their shoulders to prevent someone taking their job, they actively encourage it, so that they can move on upward. This is often very different from the culture of the acquired companies.

In US3, strategic decisions are centralized, and operational decisions decentralized. Although a top-down style of decision-making is strongly in evidence, bottom-up contributions are encouraged wherever possible. Many solutions to problems come from talking to people doing their jobs. However, US3 works to similar systems in all countries which affords considerable process scale economies, and enables rule by standardized procedures manuals to be achieved. Formal meetings have increased substantially as part of the big company culture, and formal planning up to four years ahead has been instituted. Communication has become more formal. However, there is some local adjustment: 'If you tell someone in North Yorkshire they are part of the Midlands division they won't like it! It took the Americans three or four years, a lot of money, and some quite painful decisions to realize things like this.'

High motivation is achieved through the US3 partnership philosophy, which makes managers into shareholders at an early age. They can become dollar millionaires in their forties with normal progress. The corporate culture is a somewhat strait-laced one, and although US3 is regularly in the *Fortune* list of the most admired companies in the USA and is AAA rated financially, employees have to embrace the corporate philosophy to survive and prosper in the company. Annual appraisal are of an 'up or out' nature where poor performers are 'let go'. To avoid negative language, those being appraised are described at 'people meetings' as best or 'least best' achievers!

It is stated that control is key to such a people-based service company. This was achieved after acquisition by US3 executives taking over the main positions and consciously integrating the new subsidiary into the parent group, so that there soon exists no 'them' and 'us'. As our informant tells us, complete absorption of new acquisitions is a cornerstone policy of US3: 'In a fully integrated company like ours the concept of the role of the subsidiary does not really apply, since the subsidiary ceases to exist and therefore parent and subsidiary are not meaningful terms.'

There is just one entity. Financial control systems are generally much tighter than they would have been previously in the acquired companies, and modern technology is used for such functions as billing and accounts receivable. US3 owns its own technology company to provide systems for this. TQM (total quality management) and other such techniques are widely used, and there are 'core groups' in each operations centre to solve local problems, the US3 equivalent of quality circles.

Absorption: the American approach to integration

US3 has carried out a very American approach to integrating a new acquisition or in this case four acquisitions. All functions are integrated into the organizational structure of the acquirer. The major positions in US3-UK are held by existing US3 members, i.e. CEO, finance director, sales and marketing director, R&D director and human resource management director. Only the operations director comes from one of the acquired companies. Central approval is required for all the major decisions on budgets, capital expenditure, new products, change in strategic direction, the formation of alliances or making of further acquisitions, although day-to-day operations are more decentralized.

An HRM strategy based on the strong corporate culture is a very important tool for the achievement of strategic and cultural change. Thus recruitment is on the basis of expected lifelong employment (although of course it does not always work out that way). Career development is carefully planned and regularly reviewed. Promotion can be rapid and a lot of young people are in positions of considerable authority, like our informant. Training is a very strong HRM component employed widely, generally through professional courses, and rewards systems are strongly performance oriented.

Sales and marketing are approached very professionally. Market intelligence is achieved through surveys, and image projection is strong both through advertising and by strong internal behaviour and personal presentation rules and standards.

Unusually for an American company the US3 financial time horizon is long term, consistent with the lifelong employment philosophy it has adopted. This is made possible by the fact that the company is in a worldwide expansion phase of development, and that the company's stock is owned by the employees, therefore avoiding the pressure for short-term financial results and dividend payments faced by US companies quoted on the stock market.

With regard to strategy, the fundamental philosophy of US3 is to place considerable emphasis on offering a unique service, rather than on just doing a job, and far greater emphasis on the development of new products and services, but at the same time far tighter cost control.

Company performance

US3 is expanding worldwide very fast and this applies also to the UK where it starts from a relatively low base in name recognition and market share. Local carriers like DHL still dominate the UK market. Each of the acquired UK companies was struggling to survive when US3 acquired it, so there was considerable cost involved in the turnaround and integration process. As a result, although sales have increased immensely, US3 was not yet in profit in the UK at the date when the research was carried out, although it was targeted to be in the next year, and in Europe generally by the year after that. The big company structure involves the addition of substantial overheads, which have to be added in before a real profit can be struck. So there are real costs involved in carrying out a root and branch integration strategy with companies that had previously survived by maintaining a very lean overhead structure.

Conclusion

In summary, the absorption of the four UK SMEs into the now global US3 will have led to very radical change for their employees. They will have been forced, if they were to survive, to adapt to a company with a very clear visionary philosophy and somewhat strait-laced code of conduct. They will have had to become more professional in their outlook, attitudes, and behaviour. They will have been faced with the opportunity to become a stockholder along with their colleagues in a firm with considerable financial stability, and a very aggressive approach to growth and development. They will have perceived US3's strong focus on quality and will have had to embrace it themselves. They will have been subjected to US3's very thorough systems of people appraisal and development, and they will have had to become more accustomed than previously to the use of IT routinely to assist in carrying out their duties. In short they will have had to adjust to working for a global company, but one with a very strong, even rather evangelistic, American culture, and to recognize that in the medium to longer term no excuses for substandard performance or commitment would be accepted.

2. J2: a Japanese acquisition

J2-UK was taken over by J2 in 1985 from a poorly performing diversified British engineering group. It was the acquiring company's first international venture outside Japan. The acquisition was motivated by the parent's desire to embark on international expansion and to base this on an inexpensive purchase of existing engineering facilities and skills. The case illustrates the relatively gentle approach to post-acquisition change that characterizes almost all of the Japanese cases we studied. It also highlights some of the difficulties that companies from one cultural milieu can face when they take over firms in a quite different national context. J2 went through a difficult learning process with its first foreign venture.

J2-UK has retained its original name and its own legal identity. It is a profit centre within the owning group. It continues to operate from the same site as before.

Our main informant for this case was the managing director of J2-UK. He was the company's quality manager at the time of the acquisition, and later became senior director before appointment to MD in April 1996.

Stages of post-acquisition management

There were three stages of post-acquisition management in J2-UK.

Stage 1
In the first stage, the then current MD stayed on together with his entire executive team. The Japanese parent let it be understood that it did not intend to change anything, that it would be 'business as usual'. It sent two people

over (both engineers by training), one at director level and the other at manager level. The two did not have any specific portfolio and the parent company indicated that their role was to act as a channel of communication between it and J2-UK and to advise J2-UK's management accordingly.

J2-UK's employment at acquisition stood at 650 people. This was slimmed down within a year to approximately 400. Part of the acquisition deal was that J2-UK would slim down to this size through buying some products from J2 which it had previously made in house.

Stage 2

The second stage of post-acquisition management began when the then current UK team of executive directors contacted the Japanese parent and requested the removal of the MD. J2 sent someone over with the backing of the parent company board and he fired the MD—nine months after the takeover. It is indicative of its low-profile stance that the parent company fired the local MD at the behest of the UK executive team, not because it was dissatisfied with him and wanted to do something about it.

J2 then promoted the sales director to be MD, and he stayed in that role for about two years. However, the relationship between the new MD and the Japanese parent became increasingly strained. Matters ultimately came to a head when the CEO of J2 came over and expressed dissatisfaction with J2-UK's performance. He demoted the MD to be 'senior operations director' and brought in a Japanese MD. The reason for the strain in relations was purely concerned with the subsidiary's poor performance. It was not due to any dissatisfaction by the parent that J2-UK was not making sufficient internal changes.

The new Japanese MD had been the manager of the parent's large domestic factory and was therefore expected to do quite well. But the relationship did not work. The senior operations director was then fired by the Japanese and the Japanese MD replaced by another Japanese MD. At this time, in 1990, J2-UK was beginning to experience a period of recession. The second Japanese MD went back to Japan after an eighteen-month standard tour of duty. He was replaced by an English-speaking Japanese MD, who stayed in that role for five years, all the way through the recession. The parent company had by now realized that there was a communication problem between the previous Japanese MDs (who had little English) and J2-UK's managers.

Stage 3

A third stage began in April 1996 when the current British MD was appointed. He is currently running the company with only two Japanese staff: the finance director and a graduate trainee. The finance director is not, however, from the head office, but was hired in the UK by J2. The new top management config-uration more or less coincided with J2-UK's emergence out of recession and re-entry into profit.

Post-acquisition changes

Some of the changes made after the acquisition of J2-UK were due to circum-stances and not primarily the result of initiatives or pressure from the Japanese parent company. One example is the reduction of employment beyond the original 400 target agreed at the time of the takeover. Another concerns changes made by British Steel on which J2-UK used to rely for all its steel supplies. When British Steel closed some of its mills and could no longer supply, J2-UK had to broaden its sources of supply. More recently, the Japanese parent in line with its international expansion has come to buy its steel on the world market from a range of sources and is now encouraging J2-UK to multi-source on an international basis.

Other changes were led by J2. These changes divide into two types. The first category consists of those changes initiated and promoted from Japan. J2 believed in them and wanted J2-UK to follow down that path. The most significant change directly promoted by the Japanese parent was the concept of having a management style based upon consensus. This was stressed by J2 right from the beginning of the post-acquisition period. The second, and related, major change involved the dismantling of the functional areas within the company in favour of addressing the processes that it needed to accom-plish. This was urged by J2 as early as 1986 and thus pre-dated the coming into vogue of the business process re-engineering concept. These were the two major positive changes introduced in J2-UK as a result of being taken over.

It took a long time to implement these changes and there were 'some serious casualties on the way'. They were initiated in 1986, shortly after the acquisition, and J2-UK only achieved a fully integrated structure by 1995. J2-UK had inherited a hierarchical bureaucratic structure from its former British parent company. In the words of the current MD:

We were hierarchical, with little boxes, everybody hiding behind the system, every-body working to a rigid system-type company with some directors in charge of that company whose attitudes were very different from the attitudes of the directors of the company today, and some of those directors lost their jobs in the process.

Whereas these organizational changes have had a positive effect, the third main change initiated directly by J2 had a negative effect. It concerns the parent company's attitude to marketing. Its policy was one of continual expansion and growth of sales. At the same time it applied marginal costing.

Expansion through the taking on of marginal business was therefore supposed to prove profitable. In practice, it contributed to serious losses at J2-UK.

The influence of the Japanese parent was less direct in the second category of Japanese-led changes. These occurred as a result of local circumstances which led J2-UK management to think that it would be a good idea to move in a certain direction. The moves accorded with a Japanese approach and J2 therefore encouraged them without specifically requesting or pressurizing J2-UK to make them. Only when the initiatives involved spending money was approval as well as advice sought from Japan. The adoption of TQM provides an example of this second type of post-acquisition change. Shortly after the acquisition, J2 had brought its practice of TQM and *kaizen* to the attention of J2-UK management, who largely ignored it. Later, when under pressure from growing competition and declining results, J2-UK management decided to implement TQM:

We took advantage of some of the earlier ideas that they'd given us and had further discussions and help from them about these things, which we had tended to ignore beforehand. So, we did get advice and help, but it had actually been there for us earlier, had we bothered to embrace it. (managing director, J2-UK)

According to J2-UK's managing director, the Japanese parent company made two major mistakes following its acquisition:

The first serious error they made was adopting a persuasive attitude, saying, 'We're not going to change anything, everything will be the same', and at the same time showing you lots of different things in the hope that you would grasp them. And in 1985, in UK industry, we didn't think anybody could tell us how to make fittings or how to do business thank you very much, and we had nice brick walls round everything and there was nothing we were going to do other than to pay total lip-service to anything they showed us—those guys over there. What they should have done, I think, is to come over and say, 'We are seriously interested in changing the way in which you operate; these are the reasons why; we want you to come on board with us; there's going to be a major redundancy; those that don't want to come on board with us please leave now.'

They then did the second big thing wrong, which was that they sent their second or third team over to help us change instead of sending their first team over and we ate them for breakfast and changed absolutely nothing.

So, they said we didn't have to change; they showed us some very inadequate people to try and persuade us to change; we didn't change. If they'd said, 'You've got to change', and sent enough of the right kind of people over to help us to do so and insist that we did so, then I think we would have been an entirely different company and an entirely different approach. And that would have shown, in my opinion, a maturity in dealing with overseas companies instead of a total lack of any experience in doing so.

When they came here, they were very Japanese. They are certainly not very Japanese now. They have now become an international company in the proper sense of the word. The experience has been expensive, but good for both of us.

The implementation of change

The moves towards consensus and process-oriented management were triggered and catalysed by the Japanese parent company, but they directly involved J2-UK's managers, some of whom were removed because they were unable to accept the change. The managing director stressed the role that individual managers played in a process that was initiated, but not wholly determined, by the acquiring parent company:

It is the individuals involved that actually make these changes. It is not a structure, or a system, or a command from headquarters. The first step in the change was basically a command from headquarters saying, 'Instead of you running that department, and you running that department, and you running that department, why don't you all get together and start running the business?' And almost forcing a weekly executive team meeting. Before, you got together with the managing director at the end of the month and he bollocked everybody for the fact that the results weren't right. What happened then was that the interdepartmental fights between executives continued within that team structure . . . Then TQM started a process where it became acceptable for people to poke their nose into the business of another department, which was totally unacceptable before within the hierarchy . . . There was a quantum culture change and I actually remember the meeting at which it took place, when somebody asked about somebody else's business and wanted to get involved, wanted to know why. And effectively that developed as a result of TQM and outside people saying, 'Come on, talk to each other, what are your company problems?' So that was the second step. The first step was setting up the structure and the second step was when we actually started to get involved in each other's business. The third step was when the people who wouldn't tolerate that were ejected from the company . . . but by the internal J2-UK structure not by the Japanese.

The parent company influence was at the beginning when they actually said, 'We want you to adopt a consensus management system'. And they have encouraged it all the way along. But they in no way could have sorted out the individual difficulties that I have talked about which were the steps on the way. Those had to be internal, and they were actually catalysed by the [Japanese] MD wanting to adopt an approach of harmony and being frustrated by the unwillingness of the directors on the board to actually be harmonious with each other.

The expansion-oriented marginal cost-based sales policy introduced by J2 was ultimately abandoned. This followed a study of J2-UK by Arthur Andersen who were brought in as a result of the company's serious losses during the early 1990s. There were two main prongs in Andersen's general message to J2. The first was that its marketing strategy was misguided; while this had been treated like a bible in Japan it was not suited to UK circumstances. The second was that J2 should permit J2-UK some autonomy in its approach to marketing. More specifically, Arthur Andersen recommended that the policy of sales without regard to profitability should be rejected in favour of discriminatory growth on the basis of net margin. J2 accepted this recommendation, coming as it did from a major consulting firm, even though J2-UK management had been arguing for it beforehand. It led to a major change in marketing policy, with J2-UK subsequently becoming profitable by the end of 1996.

The view was expressed within J2-UK that, with the benefit of hindsight, Japan Inc. was rather too patient in the process of inducing change in J2-UK. It might have achieved improvements faster if it had exercised more direction and active help in easing through the change. A policy of more steady intervention might also have made for a smoother progression over time rather than waiting to push through change until a crisis intervened. While this gentle low-profile approach does accord with the stereotype of Japanese management, in this particular case the explanation for it may lie as much with the fact that J2-UK was the Japanese parent's first overseas acquisition. In subsequent overseas ventures, J2 has taken a more active role, put more of its own people in, and asked for reporting information that has obliged people to work in a certain way in order to provide that information.

Preservation: the Japanese approach to integration

J2-UK preserves its own legal identity, has its own board of directors, and is run largely as a separate company. Two members of J2 sit on the J2-UK board. There is a third member from a large Japanese conglomerate which has a cross-shareholding with J2 and has a private shareholding in J2-UK. These three Japanese directors only attend the main meeting of the J2-UK board once a year. There are four UK directors who also attend other board meetings that are called ad hoc. No members of J2-UK sit on the J2 board or on any parent company committees.

All formal reporting from J2-UK to its Japanese parent is conducted via its managing director. The closest other relations are between the finance departments of J2 and J2-UK. The Japanese finance director comes over to talk with J2-UK's finance department on issues such as the cash flow for next year, but the meetings are always arranged via J2-UK's managing director. Just after the acquisition, the then British MD of J2-UK insisted on having all communication between Japanese staff in J2-UK and the parent translated for him to see. Now, there is sufficient trust within J2-UK for a great deal of direct communication between the Japanese financial director (who is also vice-president of J2-UK) and the headquarters office to take place with the current MD's blessing.

Following the acquisition, visits were arranged in the engineering and manufacturing areas. Two Japanese (one director and one manager) came to UK. There was then an exchange of foremen and key workers (including shop stewards) to learn each other's working practices; this continued for ten years after the acquisition. The exchange started with the quality area. Joint teams have also been formed on two occasions. The first was when J2 purchased large and complex manufacturing equipment from Sumitomo to install at J2-UK. The second was a joint working team on raw materials, which form a high percentage of J2-UK's costs. The only continuing direct relationship between J2-UK and J2 is in quality and engineering where information is exchanged frequently. This is, however, an information-sharing arrangement, not a reporting or hierarchical relationship.

J2-UK's management expressed general satisfaction with the relations it now has with J2. An important factor in this satisfaction lies in the parent company's consistent demonstration of support for J2-UK during its years of financial crisis. As noted below, there is a feeling that J2 stood by J2-UK in a way that an Anglo-Saxon parent might not have been willing to do.

The only serious conflict in the relationship was that between the second post-acquisition J2-UK MD and J2 over the former's determination to press on as before with his own style of organization. This was in part a clash of cultural styles. It was commented that the Japanese pursue ideas logically but naively because they ignore the local circumstances. This complication of issues was seen to have generated some conflict with J2-UK's management.

Resources from the parent company

By far the most important resource that J2 has provided to J2-UK has been financial. During the recession of the early 1990s, J2-UK's market prices dropped by 35 per cent. J2 covered all J2-UK's losses during this period. J2-UK's MD commented that:

The big thing they have done for us is to generate money for us to cover our losses. It's the only thing that kept this company going. And it's been never ending. It's come with a few moans, but they have never failed to support us financially. Whatever sacrifices they have had to make, and they had to make some, they have never failed to support us financially

He associated this level of support with a distinctively Japanese long-term corporate orientation: 'That support has been very, very large and I don't believe would have come from any American or British company. It's typically Japanese in terms of their long-term view of what the business is.'

In addition, J2 has injected over £2 million worth of equipment. This was seen as less helpful to J2-UK because reassembling it tied up an engineering resource for nearly two years. The equipment is not state of the art and does not give J2-UK a competitive edge. The prime reason why J2 sent the equipment was that it had been purchased from a competitor and was sent to the UK to take it off the Japanese market.

J2 has also offered technical support. J2-UK had a resident engineer from J2 for the first eight years after acquisition; he provided a channel for passing on improvements from J2 to J2-UK. Although the value of this technical support was limited by the fact that J2-UK is not a high-technology company, it was nonetheless perceived to have been useful at times.

Overall, the ideas and professional back-up offered by the Japanese parent were regarded as positive benefits from the acquisition. Japanese ideas on quality management, managing through consensus, breaking down departmental barriers, and job rotation were mentioned as among the more significant examples. On the other hand, a reluctance to assume individual responsibility and to challenge the system were seen as negative attributes of the parent company which J2-UK sought not to emulate.

Conclusion

The acquisition had a direct and fundamental impact of J2-UK's performance because of the parent company's willingness to provide financial support during the recession when J2-UK was losing money. This ensured J2-UK 's survival. In the words of its MD:

I have no doubt whatsoever that, had we not become part of a Japanese company, J2-UK would not be here today, and would not have been here for a number of years. If we'd stayed with MID [the former UK parent group], or if we'd had a management buyout, or if we'd gone to anybody without this long-term horizon, and without this impetus to change—because that's the big word, 'change': we never ever wanted or thought we could ever change or needed to change when we were part of MID—without that, J2-UK would have been part of the history of metal-bashing and blacksmithing in England.

Another positive impact on J2-UK's performance came from J2's requirement that J2-UK reduce fixed overheads in terms of people. This encouraged a dramatic fall in employment. J2-UK's ratio of direct to indirect workers has reduced since being taken over by an order of three. Total employment was cut from 650 to 187, and J2-UK is now much more efficient. Although manufacturing approximately 80 per cent of the tonnage being produced with 650 people, the company is now using less area (it has sub-leased off two of its warehouses), and is working on a faster turnaround and with lower stocks. This improvement in performance has not been due to new equipment or automation—this is virtually the same as at the time of acquisition. It has been due to a change in practices: 'Organizational changes, management changes, changes in the way in which we measure ourselves, changes in the contracts of employment we have, and the way in which we look at our work-force and they look at us, and changes in working practices.'

Contracts of employment now incorporate multi-skilling and multi-flexibility. These developments were prompted by the Japanese parent asking why J2-UK needed so many people, and why it organized its workforce as it did.

As noted earlier, the moves towards consensus management and the shift from functional to process orientation also contributed to J2-UK's improved performance. They were initiated and encouraged by J2.

The main performance downside of the acquisition lay in the parent company's imposition of its marketing policy of growth at all cost.

Acquisition therefore brought a combination of positive and negative contributions to J2-UK's performance, and at considerable cost to the parent company which had to sustain several years of loss incurred by its new subsidiary. However, at the time this case was written, J2-UK was into its second post-recession year of profit and was enjoying increased sales.

3. F1: a French acquisition

F1 is a major French aeronautics and defence contractor, not unlike British Aerospace in the UK. It is 50 per cent owned by the French government, and has 60 per cent of its sales in defence aircraft and avionics and 40 per cent in civil aircraft sales. Until 1990 F1 had been a very French company. However, in the late 1980s it made a conscious decision to internationalize and gain a major presence in world markets as a 'domestic' manufacturer, i.e. one that is recognized as belonging to the country in which it operates. In the UK for example Ford is thought of as a British company by the 'man in the street'. As a result F1 carries out a policy of extremely low image projection lest its very Frenchness become too obvious to the public. It has adopted a policy of expanding into a new market by acquiring already existing national com-panies. Thus it has been on the acquisition trail for the last decade. In the UK it bought a loss-making link trainer company in 1990 and added a further similar acquisition in a complementary field in 1993. It then merged the two UK acquisitions by moving the operations of the first acquisition to the site of the second. It has also bought other small UK companies in the industry as they sought to exit the defence market.

F1 is organized into five divisions: (1) Aerospace and Equipment; (2) Communication and Command; (3) Detection and Missile Systems; (4) Sextants; (5) Information Technology. Our informant was the director of corporate development of the UK company. He is English by nationality.

Post-acquisition changes

All the UK acquisitions have been integrated into the existing French structure. The UK acquisitions are now in F1 Training and Simulation, which is part of the Aerospace division. Organizationally the levels in the hierarchy have increased, as a new level of French management has been inserted into the organization structure. The company is run on a global basis, and the UK is global headquarters for F1 Training and Simulation, so a layer of French management has been moved to the UK on top of the UK management. At the same time there have been substantial redundancies in the UK companies in an attempt to pull them into profit. We are informed that more managers have been appointed, whilst many workers have been made redundant. 'We now have people who believe their job is to run F1-France, people who believe their job is to run F1-UK, and people who believe their job is to coordinate the two.'

On an operational basis the heads of F1 subsidiaries have considerable autonomy to run things the way they want to, but promotion is generally slow. Although a long-term strategic approach rather than a short-term financial one exists in the company, morale is low and a very top-down culture of management persists with all strategic decisions being taken at the centre, in effect in France. Specific key decisions retained by the foreign company are in the areas of budgeting, capital expenditure, appointment and termination of senior personnel, formation of alliances, all major contractual agreements, any change in scope of the company or the development of new products.

People fight for their reserved space in the car park to the detriment of the customers. There is a whole history of people trying to protect their own back, and hold on to their territory. The two companies were merged but personnel still identify with one or other of the companies. Then the French arrived and moved into what is referred to as the French wing. They are slightly detached. They don't go down on the shop floor often, and they commute to France at weekends. So that is where the 'them and us' attitude comes from . . . Things are decided informally amongst Frenchmen to the exclusion of British middle management.

On the other hand F1 has introduced more high-tech production techniques than existed previously (especially TQM), scientific staff have increased in number, and the French have introduced a new generation of very high-tech simulators into the product range. The company has been successfully integrated from a product and technology perspective, and has become more product based than functionally organized, but it has not been successfully integrated from a cultural or people point of view.

Colonization: the French approach to integration

Apart from the organizational integration described above, there have been attempts to achieve some cultural integration by setting up 'common efficiency teams' company-wide. UK managers take part in these teams, but attendance by the British is not good, as the meetings tend to be run in French. The rules of the company are that if there is a non-French-speaking person in the room, the language to be spoken in meetings is English. However, this does not tend to happen. 'It doesn't help me if I go to a meeting in France and insist on the meeting being conducted in English.'

In terms of reporting relationships, the CEO of F1 Training and Simulation is French, and theoretically based in the UK, although in practice he is as much located in France as the UK, spending much of his time commuting. All UK personnel report to him. 'If informal, social, and organizational contacts were plotted on a grid pretty well all of them would be between the French.'

In the refashioned post-acquisition company, all management systems have changed and of course all trademarks are now F1. New product design has also been contributed by the acquirer. In terms of the level of integration the acquisition comes into the partial integration category, in that it has not been totally absorbed in US style but rather 'colonized' in French style.

Although there is a reduction in the incidence of formal meetings, due probably to the French tendency to decide things in corridors, there is nonetheless a considerable increase in the imposition of formal planning systems.

Performance

Post-acquisition performance has not been deemed satisfactory from the viewpoint of either the acquirer or the acquired company. As a result the British management has been changed three times since 1990. The British management have also been unhappy about being colonized, and the promotion limitations of the so-called 'glass ceiling'.

Being part of F1 does not seem to have helped the UK subsidiary in terms of sales. Total sales have declined since the takeover, but the overall size of the market has declined too. Also, being a French company has now caused problems in achieving US defence industry sales. However, had the acquisitions not taken place, the UK stand-alone companies would certainly not have survived, and the new access to technology and product development and to sources of finance has given the companies a future, although it is doubtful whether much strategic thought has been given to the question of the strategic integration of the UK companies into a coherent global group.

The French connection has been a problem for the British and internal cultural tensions have developed. The initial French management waved the tricolour around and showed a total misunderstanding of how to do business in the UK . . . Where French expats have been appointed to run the British business, they have behaved like French expats not like international businessmen.

Conclusion

In the case of the acquisition of principally two UK flight simulator companies by the major French multinational defence contractor F1, a very French approach to the post-acquisition of the companies was adopted. This involved a French 'colonial' mindset and type of behaviour to the extent that all major strategic decisions were taken by and between French executives, with only minimal consultation with the British. This has had a strong negative effect on the morale of the UK management.

Thus, although the French acquisitions saved the British companies from almost certain bankruptcy, the acquirers caused bad feeling through the creation of a 'them' and 'us' feeling in the newly configured company. To be a British executive was to be a second-class citizen. F1 brought with it finance, technology, new product development, and the promise of a future within a fast-globalizing group, yet at the time of the research internal morale was poor, and the acquired company executives were by no means committed to their new masters, and would no doubt have been eminently susceptible to offers from the competition. Clearly national attitudes and behaviour, where they are excluding, can and do have a significant effect on company morale and motivation.

4. G10: a German acquisition

G10, a German privately owned company, acquired G10-UK in the early 1990s. G10-UK had been formed as a result of an MBO and prior to the acquisition had grown rapidly and made several acquisitions itself. Amongst these acquisitions was another German private company, which was a major competitor of G10. This acquisition had come about in part as a result of the excellent personal links between the main board members and similarities between the businesses. At the same time the company was one which G10 too had been interested in acquiring for some time. By the end of the 1980s, though, whilst business was booming there were signs that the road ahead might be less rosy for G10-UK. As a result, when G10 approached G10-UK with a view to acquiring it at a reasonably generous price G10-UK readily agreed. The generous price might in part reflect G10's inordinate desire to acquire G10-UK's German subsidiary. Following the acquisition of G10-UK, whilst G10 had achieved its objective of acquiring its German competitor, its expectations regarding G10-UK were not fulfilled and eventually G10-UK was sold. The informant in this case study was the British MD of G10-UK who had been with the company since its formation. The names and industries of the companies involved have been disguised.

Post-acquisition changes

Following the acquisition G10-UK's MD described several major areas of change which occurred. First, communication became more formalized; secondly, decisions became more decentralized; and, thirdly, the company became more specialized and product based than before.

Communication

The first difference to strike G10-UK's MD was the change to an almost consensual form of management:

I think the overriding influence I found was that there was a rather strange non-hierarchical way of running the company. There was a board of directors formed from G10 which was the immediate parent, and there were four members, myself and three Germans. We were all called *Geschäftsführer*. All MDs which was slightly strange. None of us had seniority over the others except that one was known as *Der Sprecher*—the spokesman for the board. But the others of us recognized Manfred as the *Führer* as well as *Der Sprecher* because clearly there had to be someone to determine the agenda of the matters for discussion. We found that consensual board decision-making seemed like a very cosy way to run a company, but that at the end of the day you need a focus for someone to say let's do this. So there was a de facto election of *Der Sprecher* to *Der Führer*.

This was felt in part to reflect the aims of the main board directors of G10, whose influence was felt indirectly through the operation of the company's supervisory board. The MD of G10-UK said:

I was surprised at the lack of dynamic influence coming down from the top. We would have these board meetings which were operational meetings [and there was a] supervisory board on top of that with a number of advisers brought in from the Group HQ and independent consultants. . . . I found that the whole thing was done in an almost a club-like atmosphere. It lacked what I'd been used to under American and British management—the cut and thrust of the need to achieve objectives—it was all rather leisurely.

An associated aspect of the acquisition was that the UK managers found the accounting disciplines to be surprisingly less severe than they had been used to compared to either the UK company or US companies.

Decentralization

Following the merger the MD of G10-UK was told that he was to be put in charge of the G10-UK product range across the entire group. In his opinion this did not, however, extend to being given the authority to pursue those aims. This again to his mind illustrated the problem that 'the pervasive private company long-term comfort level that the Germans seemed to want to operate their business within tended to act in a claustrophobic way'.

In contrast to this the MD also found that the management style was in general one of imaginative delegation of authority wherever possible. As he put it:

Here are the assets you have at your disposal, here are the responsibilities you have for achieving the results we require, go forth and do it and we'll leave you alone. There was no doubt whatsoever that they weren't too fussed how the business was run.

The end result of this delegation was a form of 'benign neglect' of the company. In the MD's opinion the acquisition needed a plan to integrate the companies and to use resources on the Continent to further the business of the UK company. This simply did not happen and as a result the company under German ownership retreated and lost its way. This was accentuated by the fact that the MD of the G10-UK subsidiary had his salary determined more by overall group results than by those of the subsidiary he was in charge of and, as a result, G10-UK did not perhaps receive the attention it deserved. In addition, the MD of G10-UK found that people tended to be more sectional in their interests. The other board members each had an area of responsibility but each tended to look after their own area without thinking of the business as a whole. As a result, the MD said that he would 'never again advocate that form of leadership unless it was coordinated by a strong guiding person at the helm of the operation'.

It is also interesting to note that, throughout the time that G10 owned G10-UK, there was also very little in the way of visits by G10 managers to G10-UK. This contrasted with US parent companies which the MD saw as being much more prepared to intervene.

More generally, the MD saw that there were some aspects of being owned by a German company which did not help communication between parent and subsidiary. On the one hand at the technical level the links between the companies were quite good. In particular, the MD found that there was good communication regarding product and technical development but that again this was quite dependent on the personalities involved. On the other hand, communication from Germany was found to be slowed down by 'their very strange and arcane attention to the hierarchy', especially the need within the company for joint signatures on letters. The MD commented that: 'If one wanted some trivial bit of information one often found that one couldn't get the information because the person sending it couldn't get a countersignature from his boss because he was away on holiday.'

In the MD's mind these 'quaint rituals' characterized a formality which is reflected in the whole German societal structure. The bigger the company, the more these hierarchical rituals were attended to, and that, he felt, was an impediment. The result in this case was that there was little attempt to integrate people and G10 was seen to be rather stand-offish, with only rather slow communication being possible below board level.

Specialization
Following the acquisition G10-UK became primarily product driven and the four board members were each given responsibility for a main product area. However, this coincided with the decline in markets foreseen by G10-UK and, in the UK at least, a decline in profitability, and a need to save costs resulted in some other subsidiaries being absorbed into G10-UK and the MD becoming responsible for other products than those dealt with by G10-UK itself. This, in the MD's opinion, signalled the 'beginning of the end and the board structure broke down from that point on'.

Two factors that were seen as responsible for the failure of the product-driven strategy were, first, that there was a duplication of effort where companies were independently structured because of the need to keep products in separate divisions. This in effect acted against any attempt to search for possible synergies or areas for cooperation, for example in information systems. The decline in profitability also meant that there was no possibility of continuing to support the higher overheads that were necessary with this arrangement. Secondly, when the MD of G10-UK, having been given group-wide responsibility for the G10-UK product area, began to introduce G10-UK products into the German company's distribution system, there was resistance to it. As the MD said, 'There was an inbuilt reaction to that, a closing of ranks, a hostility toward any foreign intervention. What is this British product being imposed upon us? Why should we sell this when we don't like it?'

At the same time as this specialization and hindrances to cooperation were occurring, there was also some attempt to manage some areas functionally across the company. Financial controllers of the subsidiary companies including G10-UK communicated directly with the financial manager on the G10 board. There was also a move to appoint a group manufacturing director. However, the attempt to influence the subsidiary's manufacturing on a matrix management basis was eventually overtaken by events and the sale of G10-UK, and so had little effect.

A lack of consistency: the German integration story

In some senses, the lack of long-term success regarding the relationship between the two companies might be ascribed to the set of skills possessed or not possessed by the members of the board. The UK board member was unable to speak German, the leader of the main board was relatively inexperienced and a key manager in the German company was fired. Added to this, the acquisition of G10-UK was driven in large part by G10's desire to acquire G10-UK's German subsidiary rather than G10-UK itself, even though G10 felt at first able to justify retaining G10-UK. All these factors could be said to have had a negative impact on the combined company. It would be unfair, however, to ignore the considerable effect of external events in the surrounding business environment which the managers involved were powerless to do anything about. These as much as anything could be said to have contributed to the eventual sale of G10-UK by G10 and to the financial and other pressures which caused the breakdown in the consensual management style.

However, there were also some positive sides to the relationship between G10 and G10-UK. The most significant area in this respect was that concerning finance and attitudes to investment. The MD's overall opinion was that:

The greatest support was finance. The company would not have survived had it not been for a very supportive parent. The financial support the company had was quite substantial and it had to be, to be quite frank, over that period of time [early 1990s]. The other thing was that they were more supportive of their capital expenditure programmes than the owners we had had previously. We found that the Germans were capable of taking long-term views and actually backing a judgement, even if the figures didn't look as though they would support investment in a new piece of machinery. If they warmed to your belief that this was a good investment for other than financial reasons then they would support you.

This may have been in part due to the private ownership structure of G10. The MD pointed out that there is a higher level of freehold ownership of factory buildings by German companies. The MD of G10-UK's German subsidiary said that, even after twenty-five years, he was doubtful about the company's success and still wanted to have the security of things and buildings around him. This perhaps results in a higher propensity to invest in machinery and buildings than an analysis that concentrates on high utilization rates would suggest. The aim was thus long-term stability and durable assets, perhaps the more so among that generation of managers who had experienced the aftermath of the last war in Germany.

The end result is that G10-UK benefited substantially from investment and support from G10 throughout the period in the early 1990s when business conditions might otherwise have led to the failure of the company as a whole. It is thus hard to fault the decision to sell the company to G10 in terms of preserving G10-UK. Looking at G10's point of view, the acquisition of the G10-UK subsidiary was successfully achieved but the key criticism that might be made of its handling of G10-UK was one of a lack of direction, in some senses exemplified by the consensual management style and 'benign neglect' of the company. Whilst this was in some senses to G10-UK's benefit it was said that:

It was a feeling that nobody actually cared much about us. It was almost a failing of the Germans to be as supportive as they were. So it was a lack of leadership from the top and thus strategic planning and the British management really didn't rise to the occasion because what we should have done was fill that gap and done it for ourselves.

It is interesting to wonder whether acquisition by a company from another country would have produced different results. Of course, one can never make direct comparisons because of differences over time in the surrounding business environment. However, the MD of G10-UK had experienced US management styles and commented that:

If I was to say what is the lesser of the two evils—is it the benign neglect of the Germans and their avuncular style of management, or the helter-skelter dynamics of the Americans?—I would go for the American style quite frankly because, at the end of the day, you can temper people but . . . if you're trying to wake someone up from a slumber it's extremely difficult.

Conclusion

G10 and a number of other cases point to the conclusion that two of the key aspects of post-acquisition management are the provision of finance to the acquired company and whether the new parent company takes a long- or short-term financial view. For an acquisition to be a success, there has not only got to be financial support from the parent company but also some clear idea about its long-term strategic direction and thus how that continuing support is going to be used. Just one or the other is insufficient.

14

Conclusion

In this book, we have examined the management of international acquisitions from the perspective of the changes introduced and their impact on the performance of the acquired company. We have paid particular attention to the role of the acquiring companies in introducing changes to management practice, to their approach towards integrating the acquired company, and to HRM issues.

The research from which we have drawn examined the outcomes from acquisitions of UK companies by four of the world's major acquiring countries: the USA, Japan, France, and Germany. A set of domestic acquisitions made by other UK companies was also included in the research sample in order to assist in the identification of distinctively national patterns of post-acquisition management. The research procedures combined a lengthy survey questionnaire with a smaller number of on-site visits each focusing around a key interview. The questionnaire covered a wide range of management practice dimensions applied to 201 acquisitions. The areas and forms of practice to be investigated were identified from previous research and the general management literature. Their relevance was confirmed through a pilot study. Visits were subsequently made to forty acquisitions during which a key informant who had experienced the post-acquisition process was interviewed in a semi-structured manner. These visits uncovered insights into post-acquisition changes and ways in which the acquisition was integrated into the parent company.

Although the survey was focused and structured so as to permit an examination of general trends across a large number of acquisitions, its broad coverage of different areas of management allowed for unanticipated and sometimes unusual findings to emerge. This prompted the further compilation of individual case studies in the second phase of the research, some of which have been summarized in preceding chapters. At this second stage of the research, we were seeking to understand more specific contexts and processes underlying the changes that the questionnaire survey had allowed us to profile in broad terms. Much interesting information emerged from both stages of the research; certainly enough to prompt further studies that may choose to test hypotheses on selected aspects of the subject and/or extend investigations to other locations.

One set of questions arising from the research concerns the *content* of management practice. For instance, do the post-acquisition changes introduced by companies of different nationality bear witness to an international convergence of management practice? Are there some changes that generally lead to better post-acquisition performance? Or does the relationship to performance depend on specific circumstances such as acquirer nationality or the type of industry in which the acquisition is located? Another set of questions has more to do with the *process* of post-acquisition management. These include how changes are introduced following an acquisition, and how the acquired unit is integrated to its new parent company. Both content and process raise the question as to whether there is an optimum way to manage acquisitions.

This chapter reviews our key findings on these issues, in order both to provide a platform for future research and to draw out implications for policy.

Convergence?

Much current management thinking holds that we live in an era of rapidly increasing globalization in tastes, supply chains, products, and technologies. This is not to say that goods and services produced for local needs or tastes are disappearing, but rather that global products are growing in number and range, and that competition has increasingly crossed national borders. In addition, comparative surveys suggest there is some convergence of consumer preferences and work values, at least in the world's major conurbations which are accounting for a steadily increasing proportion of the world's population.

In such circumstances, management policies and practices might also be expected to converge worldwide, in response to a homogenization of the people at which they are directed as both consumers and employees. This is consistent with the thesis that MNCs are becoming more polyethnic and 'transnational' in the policies and practices they adopt. The research reported in this book provides some evidence to support this theory. Companies from all the nations investigated tended to adopt or strengthen a number of similar policies within the companies they acquired. Such policies include developing and offering differentiated products and services, enhancing the acquired company's image, relating pay to performance, increasing training, opening up communications, introducing more teamwork into product development and work organization, and emphasizing quality and continuous improvement in operations.

All five national groups of acquirers also tended to control the strategic decisions of their new subsidiaries rather than treating them as purely portfolio investments. They generally reserved for themselves at least five out of eight key decisions, including the financial ones of budgeting and capital expenditure approval. So although there was some national variation in parent companies' policies on integrating acquisitions, they normally established strong top-down control over the acquisitions' strategic decisions.

Other aspects of post-acquisition management differed according to the acquiring company's nationality. These differences were apparent in the strategic (versus financial) orientation of policy, the extent that acquirers appointed new senior managers to the acquired company, the formalization of communications and meetings, and the use of financial control systems. Our evidence does not therefore lend unqualified support to the thesis that management practices are converging. Rather it points to a combination of divergent and standardizing tendencies. Contemporary management literature is increasingly emphasizing the need for multinationals to learn from their local units and environments (e.g. Doz et al. 2000), and this speaks for local autonomy and variation within the scope of their organization. Nevertheless, the control of far-flung diversified operations remains of critical concern to MNCs and this, together with the belief that they have evolved a set of internationally best practices, is an important motivation for MNCs to evolve standardized practices and to apply these to their core operations.

Integration and control

Companies of all nationalities tend to strengthen strategic control in their acquisitions, to decentralize or make little change in operational control, and to pursue different approaches towards their integration. For this reason, there is a general lack of correlation between integration, on the one hand, and strategic or operational control on the other.[1] The two concepts, integration and control, are empirically distinct. Integration need not necessarily involve control, nor vice versa. In the two instances where integration is correlated with control, the form of control differs. Integration correlates with strategic control among German acquisitions and with operational control among American acquisitions. This points to a significant contrast in

---

[1] As indicated in Chapter 10, the measure of integration used in the survey and referred to here is based on the number of key positions in the acquired company, from a list of seven, which were held by parent company appointees. In the case studies, it was possible to assess integration on a broader basis in terms of acquired companies' reporting lines to their parent companies and the extent to which their departments had been absorbed into those of the parent.

how German and American acquirers view the way to exercise leadership over their acquisitions.

There is, in fact, a noticeable difference between the degrees of integration and strategic and operational control by nationality. American and UK subsidiaries were significantly more integrated than companies with German or French parents; Japanese companies tended to fall in the middle. French, UK, and German acquirers decentralized operational control, whereas there was little overall change among companies with American or Japanese parents. Furthermore all companies showed a tendency towards increasing top-down control over the subsidiaries' strategies compared with pre-acquisition, but this was most pronounced in American and French companies. Overall, American acquirers introduced most direction over the policy of their acquisitions with a combination of high integration and a centralization of the subsidiary's strategic decisions. At the other end of the continuum, German acquirers tended neither to integrate highly nor to increase strategic control very much.

The present research confirms that sometimes a need for organizational autonomy and a need for strategic interdependence among acquisitions can both be regarded as critical. There were several German-acquired companies, such as the G1 case described in Chapter 10, where the new parents wished to keep their subsidiary intact partly in order to preserve and learn from its special competence; in this case the ability to produce and market generic pharmaceutical products very effectively. By contrast, there were also companies such as the American-acquired freight company (US3) where absorption was total leaving almost no trace of the subsidiary's former independent exitence.

Other factors also affect the degree of integration to be pursued. Haspeslagh and Jemison (1991) point to acquired company quality and acquisition size. The present research has identified as further important factors the control methods and systems adopted by the parent, methods of communication, and philosophy concerning management of subsidiaries. As we have seen, the key contextual category of this study, nationality, was also significant.

Organizationally embedded capabilities requiring the protection of the acquired company's boundaries for their preservation are no less important strategically than others which require the boundary-less conditions of absorption to maximize their benefits. The overall choice to be made is one of the degree of integration to be adopted. The key factor to be assessed is whether, following acquisition, integration of the two companies will enhance or damage the capabilities of the subsidiary. Our case studies suggest that it is relevant to assess this issue in terms of a scale of integration, ranging from not integrated, through partially integrated, to fully integrated where the subsidiary organization is no longer distinguishable within the parent company. This scale is more broadly based than the measure of integration used in the survey (see n. 1 above).

The research showed that US subsidiaries tended to be significantly more integrated in terms of this scale than other nationalities and German and Japanese subsidiaries significantly less integrated than others, with French subsidiaries somewhere in between. The case study interviews also showed that, while the degree of integration differed, the means of control used were common, if not all applied to the same degree. Key examples were financial controls related to investment, but the more common cost controls were also involved as well. The use of advisers and or informal controls in Japanese and German subsidiaries contrasted with the stricter financial controls of US companies. The way in which parents communicated with their subsidiaries also showed distinct differences between the four nationalities studied, with the main parameters being the degree of formality versus informality, the degree of openness versus a limited 'need-to-know' approach, and the extent to which communication is explicit versus implicit. As expected, Japanese companies operated more on a need-to-know basis and with an implicit communication style. American companies were open but formal, and French companies tended to adopt a more autocratic top-down style. German companies, which the cultural stereotype suggests will be highly formal, were found to be upwardly formal in dealing with their parent but downwardly very informal in communicating with their subsidiary.

There are several lessons to be learned from these findings. First, while there are some similarities between acquisitions taking a broad view, there are also substantial differences in the specific approaches adopted by acquiring companies of different nationalities. Secondly, communication is critical in building links between parents and subsidiaries but words must be backed by consistent actions if credibility is to be maintained. Linguistic and cultural problems with communication deserve more attention than they usually receive. Thirdly, a range of control styles is possible, ranging from the very strict financial controls favoured by many American parents to the more *laissez-faire* style of Japanese parent companies and even some German companies.

In Chapter 10, we compared these findings with those of Goold and Campbell (1988) who draw attention to three main approaches to managing subsidiaries, strategic planning, strategic control, and financial control, depending on the degree of control and planning by the corporate centre that is involved. The present research shows that strategic and financial control and planning are important elements of managing an acquisition. However, it also shows that many other elements are involved and equally important to the success of the acquisition, not least the issues relating to the differing cultures of the acquiring and acquired companies and communication between them, as well as the overall level of integration. This again emphasizes the multi-dimensional nature of post-acquisition integration and control.

Human resource management is a critical but often neglected area of management, providing subtle but potentially effective control mechanisms through which the parent can influence the subsidiary. It can aid organizational learning by both parent and subsidiary, through providing staff and training to make the most of knowledge transfers. HRM can also facilitate smooth integration of the new subsidiary into the parent group by creating an appropriate identity for it and spreading the parent culture and an understanding of the parent's strategic intent.

Each of the five nationalities studied approached the issue of HRM policies differently in certain respects. The Americans and the British often used it as a very conscious integration tool, and one in which the new subsidiary was taught the 'way we do things around here'. The Japanese were subtler in their approach, using HRM to convey their business philosophy which generally included a long-term perspective, concern for people, and a relatively slow and considered approach to promotion as well as to decision-making in general. The French used HRM in a 'modern' way, introducing for instance performance-related pay and career development paths, but did so without losing their distinctly French national character. Finally, German acquirers approached HRM policies in a less clear and purposive way. This was part and parcel of their more hesitant approach to post-acquisition integration.

It is worth recalling that, despite the distinct national approaches to managing the control and integration of subsidiaries, no one country's acquisitions were overall significantly more successful than any other. This leads to the conclusion that it is not so much how companies control, communicate with, or integrate new subsidiaries that impacts upon performance but the conviction that they apply to the process. Conviction and consistency in introducing new management practices are important as well as the intrinsic quality of the practices themselves. One has to bear in mind that integration and control are but means to the end of providing effective leadership to acquired firms.

Performance

As just mentioned, there were no significant differences in average post-acquisition performance levels across the five national groups of acquirers. Within each national category, most acquiring companies were able to improve the performance of their new subsidiaries. The most distinctive performance profile was found among Japanese acquisitions, which tended to report below-average levels of profitability but somewhat above-average levels of sales growth. This deviation accords with the known tendency of Japanese companies to have pursued strongly growth-oriented policies, at least up to the mid-1990s.

Perhaps the most significant conclusion to be drawn from our research is that post-acquisition management does have an impact on the performance of acquisitions. First, certain policies and practices were clearly associated with improved performance among acquired companies. Second, with only a few exceptions, the acquiring companies exerted an influence over the changes that impacted upon the performance of their subsidiaries. In other words, as parent companies, they played a definite role in performance improvement.

Some of the performance-related changes characterized companies regardless of parent nationality; others were specific to that nationality. A number of identifiable policies were conducive to above average post-acquisition performance across the board. Efforts to project the market image of the acquired company, closely followed by the development of new products and services, were the changes most consistently associated with a high level of profitability and sales performance vis-à-vis competitors. Moves toward engaging and developing the human resources of the acquired firm were also consistently associated with better performance. These included an opening up of the organization in terms of shifts towards a more bottom-up culture and more open communications, more rapid promotion, and increased training. The bearing that these changes had on the performance of acquired companies was fairly consistent, if we take the sample as a whole.

These changes echo much of the advice offered in recent years to managers to strengthen their customer orientation and develop their human resources. Insofar as the levels of performance achieved through acquisition will in time separate out the winners from the losers in international business, we can see here another process leading towards convergence in management practice.

The picture is, however, complicated by other evidence suggesting that there may be more than one path towards performance improvement. An Anglo-Saxon path and a contrasting Japanese path were particularly apparent. The two paths contrasted most clearly in the areas of strategy and decision centralization. The American and British acquisitions which achieved the best performance tended to have experienced a stronger product innovation strategy and greater decentralization, whereas their high-performing Japanese-acquired counterparts tended to have experienced a strengthening of a price-competitive strategy and greater centralization. Although less clear-cut, there also appears to be a French path towards good post-acquisition performance which, counter to some characterizations of that country's managerial style, involves strengthening the company's market image, increasing cost control, more open and less formal communication, and decentralization. The German acquisitions did not show a consistent or strong connection between post-acquisition changes in management practice and performance.

There are also some national differences in the relationship between integration and acquisition performance. Only in companies acquired by other British firms was higher integration associated with better profitability and sales growth. Integration did not relate to performance among other acquirer nationalities, except for a negative correlation between integration and profitability among the American cases. The reasons for this contrast are not clear, but it suggests a number of possibilities. For instance, the lack of national cultural differences in UK–UK acquisitions may assist the acceptability and ease of achieving effective integration, whereas the rather aggressive American style of integration may be counter-productive in a British setting. Evidence from the case studies points to a third possibility, namely that American companies adopt a particularly vigorous approach to integrating acquisitions that require a turnaround in performance. This means that the level of performance may itself be a factor influencing the acquiring company's approach to integration.

The picture for control over acquired companies is likewise complicated. A high level of strategic and operational control over subsidiaries was generally associated with inferior performance in the case of American, British, and French acquisitions, but it was associated with better performance among German and Japanese acquisitions. The processes whereby integration and control have a bearing on post-acquisition performance obviously require closer examination in future research. The potential influence of cultural distance between acquirer and acquired company deserves exploration, while an investigation that is sensitive to the nuances of control and integration may uncover some of the subtleties in their relationship. Detailed case studies appear to be the most appropriate vehicle for this further investigation.

The conclusion emerging from our study of acquisitions in the UK is that changes in management practice do have a bearing on post-acquisition profitability and sales performance. These changes reflect both an 'acquisition effect' and a 'transfer of national practice effect'. Most of the acquisitions were 'hands on', with the acquiring company providing an impetus for change, some of which was similar in nature across the board. A nationality effect was, however, also evident in the form of contrasting national profiles—consistent tendencies for acquirers of different nationality to pursue somewhat different paths towards the improvement of subsidiary performance. This national contrast persisted almost regardless of context. It therefore appears that the assets and competencies of UK companies can be harnessed through the stimulus of acquisition with good results, and that there are different paths to the achievement of good performance.

American parent companies achieved success while adopting a short-term, very financially oriented philosophy, but they did so with considerable consistency and ruthlessness. The fact that Japanese companies were able to turn around even failing companies they acquired in the British engineering sector attests to the success of another consistently followed strategy. It must be said, however, that we are here judging performance from the standpoint of the acquired unit, and not taking into account the costs to the parent which in the case of Japanese companies were sometimes considerable. The German acquisitions presented the least consistent set of post-acquisition policies, and the case studies of German acquisitions in fact uncovered several examples where this lack of consistency and commitment on the part of the parent company had had deleterious consequences for the acquired company.

The most general conclusion to be drawn from a combination of our survey and case study evidence is that self-confidence in one's approach, allied to strong financial support and a willingness to take a long-term strategic view, is a good recipe for successful acquisition. The best advice to an acquiring company is to show both commitment and resolve towards its new acquisition. Self-confidence and the reconstruction of a new identity for the acquired company, otherwise described as 'leadership' (cf. Olie 1994), on the part of the acquirer are perhaps the most important factors. This transfers to the subsidiary a belief that it is in the hands of a 'winner' and leads to an enhanced motivation and ultimately performance.

This conclusion recalls the true story of a Hungarian army detachment that became lost in the Alps during military manoeuvres. It snowed for several days and the soldiers despaired of escaping from the frozen wilderness. Then suddenly one of the soldiers found a map in his pocket, he and his colleagues took heart, and they marched confidently out of the mountains. It was only later that they discovered the map was of the Pyrenees, some 400 miles away (Weick 1990). It was their collective belief that had given them the confidence to move out of danger, rather than the specific information that it contained.

Joan Woodward, a pioneer of the contingency approach to management based on comparative investigations, once expressed a similar view. She was concerned that the very approach she had helped to develop, with its recommendation to fine-tune practices to suit the situation, might have a paralysing effect on the resolve of managers to take sufficiently decisive actions. A lack of decisiveness on the part of an acquiring company is likely to exacerbate the nervousness of staff in the acquired unit, encouraging the best to leave and the others to adopt defensive behaviours. In other words, the confidence to pursue a consistent post-acquisition policy, based on a clear vision that can be informed by national preferences, may be the most important requisite for success, especially when that policy is in tune with basic business common sense regarding customer awareness and the breaking down of organizational inefficiencies.

This is not to conclude that contingencies can be ignored, but rather to suggest that they should not be factored in to the extent that they lead to hesitant or inconsistent post-acquisition policies. It is a well-recognized problem that different contingencies, such as size, workforce competencies, culture, and competitive environment, can speak for different accommodations: this is a basic dilemma of management (Child 1984; Tushman and O'Reilly 1996). Our survey indicated that these contingent contrasts were most evident when comparing acquisitions in high-technology and low-technology manufacturing sectors. Among the high-tech acquisitions, changes towards a bottom-up style and culture, and less use of cost and financial control, were associated with superior profitability and sales performance. By contrast, among the low-tech manufacturing acquisitions moves towards greater cost and financial control were important predictors of better performance. The low-tech companies also evidenced a connection between emphasis on developing and offering unique products and superior profitability and sales performance, especially the latter. It appears that in high-technology firms moves towards freeing people up from financial restrictions and encouraging their participation favour high performance, whereas the performance of low-technology acquisitions benefits when they move towards both greater product differentiation and financial control.

This finding among the high-tech acquisitions accords with the recommendations of writers on the conditions that favour knowledge creation in companies (Nonaka and Takeuchi 1995). It points to the necessity of motivating the creative people whom a company adds to its pool of human competencies through an acquisition, and of encouraging the organizational conditions under which they can best contribute to its competitive performance as an innovation-seeking company. The contrasting finding among low-tech acquisitions suggests that the more important contingencies these tend to face concern their ability to exploit market niches and offer value-for-money products.

The process of post-acquisition management

The survey research has shown that there are different paths to the achievement of good post-acquisition performance, albeit that these are combined with certain fundamental 'good practices'. The forty case studies indicated that there are also different approaches to the processes of integrating and controlling acquired subsidiaries, which varied quite strikingly according to the nationality of the acquiring parent company and certain contingent conditions.

Haspeslagh and Jemison's (1991) taxonomy of acquisition methods fits to a considerable degree with the various national styles. American acquirers tended to prefer an *absorption* approach. The preference among Japanese acquirers tended towards *preservation,* or, where advantage could be clearly seen, towards *symbiosis.* The French acquirers, however, had their own distinctive style which we have called *colonial.* The German companies in our sample ranged between all the identifiable approaches, without a clear preference save for that of avoiding absorption.

The way in which individual acquirers went about their post-acquisition management did not depend just on their nationality, but also on two other factors. One was the condition of the acquired company at the time of purchase; the other was the acquirer's previous experience. When an acquired company was in crisis, a more interventionist approach was adopted than in the case of a company making acceptable profits. In addition, acquirers with little international experience tended, as might be expected, to be more tentative in their actions than acquirers who were major MNCs with extensive prior experience of integrating acquisitions into their group and dealing with employees from different countries.

Methods of post-acquisition integration varied widely, however, and Hunt's (1988) claim that most acquisitions are 'hands on' in the first year was certainly not confirmed. Many were distinctly 'hands off'. However, there were discernible differences between the approaches adopted by companies of different nationalities, irrespective of the international experience of the acquirer or the economic condition of the subsidiary.

Among the case study firms, the American acquirers made the most effort to ensure that their acquisitions were profitable at the time of purchase. They were interested in quick returns rather than in gaining a new asset that would pay off only in the longer term. They then tended to absorb their new acquisitions into the parent company systems and to demand a rapid achievement of high financial performance. One way or the other, the Americans' absorptive style usually achieved high performance in their subsidiaries. At the time of visiting the ten American case studies, only two of them were still making a loss and it was believed that these were destined for imminent drastic action by their parents.

Japanese companies were less concerned to buy companies that were making a profit at the time, since their aims were more long term than those of American companies. They tended to be gentler in the treatment of their acquisitions, often playing the role of catalyst or exemplar rather than of controlling owner. The Japanese were the only nationality to appoint 'advisers' to monitor events in the new subsidiary rather than new senior managers with executive powers. On the whole, the results achieved by Japanese acquirers were no worse than those of American companies. This was remarkable, given their relative lack of international experience. Considering the generally better initial condition of the American acquisitions, this cooperative and catalytic style of post-acquisition change has to be acknowledged as a successful alternative.

The French approach to post-acquisition management tended to be centralist and 'colonialist'. French acquirers either appointed a new French managing director who took decisions after prior discussions in France, or they left the local team in day-to-day charge of operations but decided high-level strategy at the French headquarters. This contrasts somewhat with Calori, et al.'s (1994) experience that the French tend to exercise high-level formal control of both strategy and operations. Overall, the approach was also found to be quite effective.

Although the performance of the German companies as reported by survey respondents matched the levels of other national categories, the ten detailed case studies revealed a less convincing picture. These German companies were less successful or certain in their post-acquisition approaches. There was no discernible German method of change-making. Their actions varied from appointing a new managing director with a brief to give orders, to leaving well alone and hoping for the best. This eclectic, apparently unfocused, and largely non-interventionist approach failed to achieve any turnarounds in the troubled acquisitions but maintained profitability in the healthy ones. The reasons for this variable pattern are not clear. They may be due partly to the lesser experience of acquisition, both international and domestic, among German companies. They may also be due to institutional factors in which the dual board system inhibits executive leadership. As noted in Chapter 6, others have pointed to a lack of distinctiveness, or at least transition, in present-day German management practice, and this was carried over to many of German acquisitions in the UK. The hesitancy and lack of clarity regarding intentions apparent in some of the German cases created uncertainty in acquired firms that were in need of guidance as to how to turn around.

Implications

When companies of different nationalities buy UK companies, they tend to introduce a series of changes over time, sometimes incrementally rather than dramatically. Sometimes the trigger for such change lies in a deteriorating performance position of the acquired subsidiary, as we saw in the case of the J2 company. Any impact that changes in management practice have on performance may in any event take several years to manifest itself. It is therefore extremely difficult to be sure about causality. In reaching our judgements, we have relied partly on the reports of events over time provided in our site visits, partly on interpretations offered by our survey and case study respondents, and sometimes on our own common sense. But they remain judgements nonetheless. We can, and have, reported co-relationships between post-acquisition changes and performance trends. Their interpretation, however, has to be shared with our readers.

It is also difficult to be sure that nationality is the key factor to isolate when investigating the changes that come about after an acquisition. We were guided by the emphasis it has received in previous discussions to design our research so as to isolate the nationality factor, while at the same time taking care to guard against the various forms of bias that are likely to enter into studies of this kind. As a result, we have a substantial degree of confidence in stating that there are different national approaches to undertaking post-acquisition management, especially in regard to integration and control. There are also some important similarities among acquirers.

The results of the research give rise to a number of policy implications for the management of international acquisitions.

First, it is important to decide on a mode of integration and control of the acquisition that accords with the strategic objectives of the purchase and which recognizes the relative competencies between the parent and subsidiary companies. There is no one method of integration and control that can be prescribed a priori. There were clear national differences in the approaches taken to integration and control, which reflect the national styles of management that have been characterized by previous research. A complication lies in the fact that these national differences tended to parallel the degree of international experience enjoyed by the acquiring companies. On the whole, the Japanese and German companies studied had less experience of managing international subsidiaries. Such experience is an important relevant competence, which an acquirer should take into account when deciding how to manage post-acquisition change. A highly interventionist approach aimed at total integration could prove disastrous for an inexperienced parent company.

Second, there are certain practices that are consistently favourable for the performance of acquired companies. These centre on efforts to project the market image of the acquired company, to assist its development of new products and services, and to engage and develop the human resources of the acquired firm which were all consistently associated with better performance. Favourable HRM policies include an opening up of the organization in terms of shifts towards a more bottom-up culture and more open communications, more rapid promotion, and increased training. It should therefore normally be a priority to introduce or strengthen these practices in a company that has been taken over.

Third, the introduction into acquired companies of greater involvement and more open communication, and the creation of a generally less restrictive atmosphere, is particularly important as a key to success in knowledge-based sectors. It is essential to retain and motivate the creative people whom a company adds to its pool of human competencies through an acquisition, and to encourage the organizational conditions under which they can best contribute to its competitive performance as an innovation-seeking company. Cisco Systems illustrates this point, as we saw in Chapter 1. It has expanded through many acquisitions and has been outstandingly successful in securing the commitment of its newly acquired staff through carefully planned, positive HRM policies.

Fourth, some areas of management practice relate differentially to levels of post-acquisition performance according to the nationality of parent companies. This indicates that an optimum approach to post-acquisition performance requires a blend of general 'best practice' with other practice reflecting the acquirer's national traditions. Acquiring companies need to combine the positive customer and human resource orientation that is generally beneficial to performance with other practices that have a positive impact because they are consistent with the companies' own traditions. It is unreasonable to expect an acquiring company to make a success of introducing practices with which it is neither experienced nor comfortable. The practices that acquirers introduce and the way they tackle the process of post-acquisition change is therefore path dependent. Their capacity to undertake these tasks is conditioned by their existing capabilities and previous experience.

The recommendation to blend both the general and the nationally specific stems from the findings of our research. It is also consistent with the way successful international companies are learning to combine certain global 'best practices' with other policies that reflect their own specific situations, including their cultural heritages at both corporate and local levels. This combination is not an easy one to achieve, but it does appear to offer the key to successful transnationality in business whether this is pursued through acquisitions, mergers, or organic expansion.

Summary

The key points this chapter makes are:

- Parent companies can play a significant role in improving the performance of their acquisitions.
- The optimum approach to post-acquisition performance requires a blend of international 'best practice' with other practices reflecting the acquirer's national traditions.
- Acquisitions are vehicles for standardization in some aspects of management practice and for reproducing national differences in others.
- Convergence is therefore apparent in some areas of management, especially cost control, operations, and HRM.
- An approach to integrating and controlling the acquisition should be identified that accords with the strategic objectives of the purchase and that recognizes relative competencies between the parent and subsidiary companies.
- Open communication, staff involvement, and the creation of a generally non-restrictive atmosphere are especially important as keys to success in managing knowledge-based acquisitions where human capabilities are particularly vital.
- The clear communication of intentions towards change in an acquisition is preferable to an approach that is unclear or hesitant and hence generates uncertainties, especially in situations requiring a turnaround in performance.
- The single most important requirement for acquisition success may be the confidence to pursue a consistent post-acquisition policy, based on a clear vision that can be informed by national preferences, especially when that policy is in tune with basic business common sense regarding customer awareness and the breaking down of organizational inefficiencies.

REFERENCES

ABEGGLEN, J. C., and STALK, G. (1985). *Kaisha: The Japanese Corporation.* New York: Basic Books.

ABO, T. (ed.) (1994). *Hybrid Factory: The Japanese Production System in the United States.* New York: Oxford University Press.

ADAMS, J. S. (1965). 'Injustice in Social Exchange', in L. Berkowitz (ed.), *Advances in Experimental Social Psychology.* New York: Academic Press.

ADLER, N., DOKTER, R., and REDDING, S. G. (1986). 'From the Atlantic to the Pacific Century: Cross-Cultural Management Reviewed', *Journal of Management*, 12: 295–318.

ADSIT, D. J., LONDON, M., CROM, S., and JONES, D. (1997). 'Cross Cultural Differences in Upward Ratings in a Multinational Company', *International Journal of Human Resource Management*, 8: 385–402.

AGRAWAL, A., JAFFE, J. F., and MANDELKER, G. N. (1992). 'The Post-Merger Performance of Acquiring Firms: A Re-examination of an Anomaly', *Journal of Finance*, 47: 1605–21.

ALDEN, V. R. (1987). 'Who Says You Can't Crack Japanese Markets?', *Harvard Business Review*, Jan.–Feb.: 52–6.

ALSTON, J. P. (1989). *The American Samurai: Blending American and Japanese Managerial Practices.* Berlin: De Gruyter.

ANGWIN, D. N. (1999). 'Post-acquisition Management of Corporate Take-overs in the United Kingdom', unpublished Ph.D. dissertation, Warwick Business School, University of Warwick.

—— and SAVILL, B. (1997). 'Strategic Perspectives on European Cross-border Acquisitions: A view from Top European Executives,' *European Management Journal*, 15/4: 423–35.

ANSLINGER, P. A., and COPELAND, T. E. (1996). 'Growth through Acquisitions: A Fresh Look', *Harvard Business Review*, 74/1: 126–36.

APPLEGATE, L. M. (1995). 'Designing and Managing the Information Age Organization', Boston: Harvard Business School Note No. 9–196–003.

BARSOUX, J.-L., and LAWRENCE, P. (1990). *Management in France.* London: Cassell.

BARTLETT, C. A., and GHOSHAL, S. (1989). *Managing across Borders: The Transnational Solution.* Boston: Harvard Business School Press.

BERLE, A. A., Jr., and MEANS, G. C. (1932). *The Modern Corporation and Private Property.* New York: Macmillan.

BIGGART, N. W. (1997). 'Explaining Asian Economic Organization: Toward a Weberian Institutional Perspective', in M. Orru, N. W. Biggart, and G. G. Hamilton (eds.), *The Economic Organization of East Asian Capitalism.* Thousand Oaks, Calif.: Sage.

—— and GUILLḯN, M. F. (1999). 'Developing Difference: Social Organization and the Rise of the Auto Industries of South Korea, Taiwan, Spain and Argentina', *American Sociological Review*, 64: 722–47.

BLAUNER, R. (1964). *Alienation and Freedom.* Chicago: University of Chicago Press.

BLEEKE, J., and ERNST, D. (1991). 'The Way to Win in Cross-Border Alliances', *Harvard Business Review*, Nov.–Dec.: 127–35.

—— —— (1995). 'Is your Strategic Alliance Really a Sale?', *Harvard Business Review*, Jan.–Feb.: 97–105.

Boisot, M. (1986). 'Markets and Hierarchies in Cultural Perspective', *Organization Studies,* 7: 135–58.

—— (1995). *Information Space: A Framework for Learning in Organizations, Institutions and Culture.* London: Routledge.

Bond, M. H., and Smith, P. B. (1996). 'Cross-cultural Social and Organizational Psychology', *Annual Review of Psychology,* 47: 205–35.

Botti, H. F. (1995). 'Going Local: The Hybridization Process as Organizational Learning', paper presented to the Workshop on the Production, Diffusion and Consumption of Management Knowledge in Europe, IESE, Barcelona, Jan.

Bower, J. L. (1986). *Managing the Resource Allocation Process.* Boston: Harvard Business School Press.

Bowman, C., and Ambrosini, V. (1997). 'Using Single Respondents in Strategy Research', *British Journal of Management,* 8: 119–32.

Brewster, C., and Tyson, S. (1991). *International Companies in Human Resource Management.* London: Pitman.

Brooke, M. Z., and Remmers, H. L. (1972). *The Multinational Company in Europe.* London: Longman.

Brush, Thomas H. (1996). 'Predicted Change in Operational Synergy and Post-acquisition Performance of Acquired Businesses', *Strategic Management Journal,* 17: 1–25.

Buckley, P. J., and Casson, M. (1976). *The Future of the Multinational Enterprise.* London: Macmillan.

—— and Ghauri, P. N. (1999). *The Internationalization of the Firm: A Reader.* 2nd edn. London: International Thomson Business Press.

Buono, A. F., and Bowditch, J. L. (1989). *The Human Side of Mergers and Acquisitions.* San Francisco: Jossey-Bass.

—— —— and Lewis III, J. W. (1985). 'When Cultures Collide: The Anatomy of a Merger', *Human Relations,* 38: 477–500.

Caligieri, P. M., and Stroh, L. K. (1995). 'Multinational Corporations' Management Strategies and International Human Resource Practices: Bringing IHRM to the Bottom Line', *International Journal of Human Resource Management,* 6: 494–507.

Calori, R., and De Woot, P. (eds.) (1994). *A European Management Model.* Hemel Hempstead: Prentice-Hall.

—— Lubatkin, M., and Very, P. (1994). 'Control Mechanisms in Cross-border Acquisitions: An International Comparison', *Organization Studies,* 15: 361–79.

Carrington, C. A. (1997). 'Hurdles to Clear when Investing in Latin America', *Mergers & Acquisitions,* May–June: 41–5.

Castells, M. (1996). *The Rise of the Network Society.* Cambridge, Mass.: Blackwell.

Chakrabarti, Alok K. (1990). 'Organizational Factors in Post-Acquisition Management', *IEEE Transactions in Engineering Management,* 37: 259–68.

Chandler, A. D., Jr. (1977). *The Visible Hand: The Managerial Revolution in American Business.* Cambridge, Mass.: Harvard University Press.

—— (1986). 'The Evolution of Modern Global Competition', in M. E. Porter (ed.), *Competition in Global Industries.* Boston: Harvard Business School Press.

—— (1990). *Scale and Scope: The Dynamics of Industrial Capitalism.* Cambridge, Mass.: Harvard University Press.

Child, J. (1972). 'Organization Structure and Strategies of Control: A Replication of the Aston Study', *Administrative Science Quarterly,* 17: 163–77.

—— (1973). 'Strategies of Control and Organizational Behavior', *Administrative Science Quarterly*, 18: 1–17.

—— (1981). 'Culture, Contingency and Capitalism in the Cross-national Study of Organizations', *Research in Organizational Behavior*, 3: 303–56.

—— (1984). *Organization : A Guide to Problems and Practice.* London: Harper & Row.

—— (1997). 'Strategic Choice in the Analysis of Action, Structure, Organizations and Environment: Retrospect and Prospect', *Organization Studies*, 18: 43–76.

—— (2000). 'Theorizing about Organization Cross-nationally', *Advances in Comparative International Management*, 13: 27–75.

—— and ELLIS, T. (1973). 'Predictors of Variation in Managerial Roles', *Human Relations*, 26: 227–50.

—— and FAULKNER, D. O. (1998). *Strategies of Co-operation.* Oxford: Oxford University Press.

—— FAULKNER, D. O., and PITKETHLY, R. (2000). 'Foreign Direct Investment in the UK 1985–1994: The Impact on Domestic Management Practice', *Journal of Management Studies*, 37: 141–66.

—— FORES, M., GLOVER, I., and LAWRENCE, P. (1983). 'A Price to Pay? Professionalism and Work Organization in Britain and West Germany', *Sociology*, 17: 63–78.

—— and KIESER, A. (1979). 'Organization and Managerial Roles in British and West German Companies: An Examination of the Culture-Free Thesis', in C. J. Lammers and D. J. Hickson (eds.), *Organizations Alike and Unlike.* London: Routledge.

—— and LOVERIDGE, R. (1990). *Information Technology in European Services.* Oxford: Blackwell.

—— and RODRIGUES, S. B. (1996). 'The Role of Social Identity in the International Transfer of Knowledge through Joint Ventures', in S. R. Clegg and G. Palmer (eds.), *Producing Management Knowledge.* London: Sage.

—— and YAN, Y. (2001). 'National and Transnational Effects in International Business: Indications from Sino-foreign Joint Ventures', *Management International Review* (forthcoming).

—— PITKETHLY, R. and FAULKNER, D. (1999). 'Changes in Management Practice and the Post-Acquisition Performance Achieved by Direct Investors in the UK', *British Journal of Management*, 10: 185–198.

CHU, W. (1996). 'The Human Side of Examining a Foreign Target', *Mergers & Acquisitions*, Jan.–Feb.: 35–9.

COOPERS & LYBRAND (1992). *A Review of the Acquisitions Experience of Major UK Companies.* London: Coopers & Lybrand.

CROZIER, M. (1964). *The Bureaucratic Phenomenon.* London: Tavistock.

DANBOLT, J. (1998). 'An Analysis of Target Company "Cross-border Effects" in Acquisitions of Listed United Kingdom Companies', unpublished paper, Department of Accountancy and Finance, Heriot-Watt University, Edinburgh.

DANIELS, J. D., and RADEBAUGH, L. H. (1992). *International Business.* 6th edition. Reading, Mass.: Addison-Wesley.

DATTA, D. K. (1991). 'Organizational Fit and Acquisition Performance: Effects of Post-acquisition Integration', *Strategic Management Journal*, 12: 281–97.

—— and GRANT, J. H. (1990). 'Relationships between Type of Acquisition, the Autonomy Given to the Acquired Firm, and Acquisition Success: An Empirical Analysis', *Journal of Management*, 16: 29–44.

—— and PUIA, G. (1995). 'Cross-border Acquisitions: An Examination of the Influence of Relatedness and Cultural Fit on Shareholder Value Creation in U.S. Acquiring Firms', *Management International Review*, 35: 337–59.

DAVID, K., and SINGH, H. (1993). 'Acquisition Regimes: Managing Cultural Risk and Relative Deprivation in Corporate Acquisitions', *International Review of Strategic Management*, 4: 227–77.

DICKEN, P. (1998). *Global Shift: Transforming the World Economy*. London: Paul Chapman.

D'IRIBARNE, P. (1994). 'The Honour Principle in the "Bureaucratic Phenomenon"', *Organization Studies*, 15: 81–97.

DJELIC, M.-L. (1998). *Exporting the American Model: The Postwar Transformation of European Business*. Oxford: Oxford University Press.

DOSI, G., and KOGUT, B. (1993). 'National Specificities and the Context of Change: The Coevolution of Organization and Technology', in B. Kogut (ed.), *Country Competitiveness: Technology and the Organization of Work*. New York: Oxford University Press.

DOUGLAS, S., and WIND, Y. (1987). 'The Myth of Globalization', *Columbia Journal of World Business*, 22: 19–29.

DOZ, Y., SANTOS, J., and WILLIAMSON, P. (2000). *The Metanationals*. Boston: Harvard Business School Press.

DRUMMOND, A., Jr. (1997). 'Enabling Conditions for Organizational Learning: A Study in International Business Ventures', unpublished Ph.D. thesis, University of Cambridge, Feb.

DUNNING, J. H. (1958). *American Investment in British Manufacturing Industry*. London: Allen & Unwin.

—— (1993a). 'The Governance of Japanese and U.S. Manufacturing Affiliates in the U.K.: Some Country-Specific Differences', in B. Kogut (ed.), *Country Competitiveness: Technology and the Organization of Work*. New York: Oxford University Press.

—— (1993b). *Multinational Enterprises and the Global Economy*. Wokingham: Addison-Wesley.

EASTERBY SMITH, M., MALINA, D., and LU YUAN (1995). 'How Culture Sensitive is HRM? A Comparative Analysis of Practice in Chinese and UK Companies', *International Journal of Human Resource Management*, 6/1: 31–58.

EBSTER-GROSZ, D., and PUGH, D. (1996). *Anglo-German Business Collaboration*. Basingstoke: Macmillan.

The Economist (1999). 'Foreign Investment: Ruling the Merger Wave', 23 Jan.: 29.

—— (2000). 'Business This Week', 13 May: 5.

EDSTROM, A., and GALBRAITH, J. R. (1977). 'Transfer of Managers as a Coordination and Control Strategy in Multinational Organizations', *Administrative Science Quarterly*, 22: 248–63.

EDWARDS, P., FERRER, A., and SISSONS, K. (1996). 'The Conditions for International Human Resource Management: Two Case Studies', *International Journal of Human Resource Management*, 7: 20–40.

ELGER, T., and SMITH, C. (eds.) (1994). *Global Japanization?* London: Routledge.

ELTIS, W. (1996). *The Political Economy of United Kingdom Foreign Direct Investment*. London: Foundation for Manufacturing and Industry.

EMPSON, L. F. (1998). 'Mergers between Professional Services Firms: How the Distinctive Organizational Characteristics Influence the Process of Value Creation', unpublished Ph.D. thesis, London Business School.

FAULKNER, D. O. (1999). 'Balancing Trust and Control in Alliances', *FT Mastering Management Review*, Aug.: 34–7.

—— and JOHNSON, G. (eds.) (1992). *The Challenge of Strategic Management*. London: Kogan Page.

—— PITKETHLY, R., and CHILD, J. (1998). 'Change Processes in Acquisitions: National Comparisons', unpublished working paper, Said Business School, University of Oxford.

FERNER, A., and QUINTANILLA, J. (1998). 'Multinationals, National Business Systems and HRM: The Enduring Influence of National Identity or a Process of "Anglo-Saxonization"', *International Journal of Human Resource Management*, 9: 710–31.

Financial Times (2000). 'Foreign Investment Flows Hit a Record on Strong M&A Activity', 9 Feb.: 5 (Far Eastern edition).

FIRTH, M. (1996). 'The Diffusion of Managerial Accounting Procedures in the People's Republic of China and the Influence of Foreign Partnered Joint Ventures', *Accounting, Organizations and Society*, 21: 629–54.

FLIGSTEIN, N. (1990). *The Transformation of Corporate Control*. Cambridge, Mass.: Harvard University Press.

FOWLER, K. L., and SCHMIDT, D. R. (1988). 'Tender Offers, Acquisitions, and Subsequent Performance in Manufacturing Firms', *Academy of Management Journal*, 31: 962–74.

FRANKS, J. R., BROYLES, J. E., and CARLETON, W. T. (1985). *Corporate Finance: Concepts and Applications*. Boston: Kent Publishing.

FRAYNE, C. A., and GERINGER, J. M. (1990). 'The Strategic Use of HRM Practices as Control Mechanisms in International Joint Ventures', *Research in Personnel and Human Resource Management*, supplement 2: 53–69.

FREEMAN, C. (1988). 'Introduction', in G. Dosi, C. Freeman, R. Nelson, G. Silverberg, and L. Soete (eds.), *Technical Change and Economic Theory*. London: Francis Pinter.

FRUIN, W. M., and NISHIGUCHI, T. (1993). 'Supplying the Toyota Production System: Intercorporate Organizational Evolution and Supplier Subsystems', in B. Kogut (ed.), *Country Competitiveness: Technology and the Organization of Work*. New York: Oxford University Press.

FULK, J., and DESANCTIS, G. (1995). 'Electronic Communication and Changing Organizational Forms', *Organization Science*, 6: 337–49.

GALL, E. A. (1991). 'Strategies for Merger Success', *Journal of Business Strategy*, 12: 26–9.

GALLIE, D. (1983). *Social Inequality and Class Radicalism in France and Britain*. Cambridge: Cambridge University Press.

GANNON, M. J. (1994). *Understanding Global Cultures: Metaphorical Journeys through 17 Countries*. Thousand Oaks, Calif.: Sage.

GARNSEY, E., ALFORD, H., and ROBERTS, J. (1992). 'Acquisition as Long Term Venture: Cases from High Technology Industry', *Journal of General Management*, 18: 15–34.

GATES, S. R., and EGELHOFF, W. G. (1986). 'Centralization in Headquarters–Subsidiary Relationships', *Journal of International Business Studies*, 17: 71–92.

GERINGER, J. M., and HEBERT, L. (1989). 'Control and Performance of International Joint Ventures', *Journal of International Business Studies*, 20: 235–54.

GERLACH, M. L. (1992). *Alliance Capitalism: The Social Organization of Japanese Business*. Berkeley and Los Angeles: University of California Press.

GHOSHAL, S., and WESTNEY, E. D. (eds.) (1993). *Organization Theory and the Multinational Corporation*. New York: St Martin's Press.

GILL, R., and WONG, A. (1998). 'The Cross-cultural Transfer of Management Practices: The Case of Japanese Human Resource Management in Singapore', *International Journal of Human Resource Management*, 9: 116–33.

GLAISTER, K. W., and BUCKLEY, P. J. (1994). 'UK International Joint Ventures: An Analysis of Patterns of Activity and Distribution', *British Journal of Management*, 5: 33–51.

GLUNK, U., WILDEROM, C., and OGILVIE, R. (1997). 'Finding the Key to German-Style Management', *International Studies of Management and Organization*, 26: 93–108.

GOOLD, M., and CAMPBELL, A. (1988). 'Managing the Diversified Corporation: The Tensions Facing the Chief Executive', *Long Range Planning*, 21/4: 12–24.

GOVINDARAJAN, V., and GUPTA, A. (1998). 'Setting a Course for the New Global Landscape', *Financial Times Mastering Global Business*, Part 1, Feb.

GRAY, S. J., and McDERMOTT, M. C. (1985). 'International Mergers and Takeovers: A Review of Trends and Recent Developments', *European Management Journal*, 6: 26–43.

GRINYER, P. H., MAYES, D. G., and McKIERNAN, P. (1988). *Sharpbenders*. Oxford: Blackwell.

—— and SPENDER, J.-C. (1979). *Turnaround: Managerial Recipes for Success: The Fall and Rise of the Newton Chambers Group*. London: Associated Business Press.

GUILLⁱN, M. F. (2001). 'Is Globalization Civilizing, Destructive or Feeble? A Critique of Six Debates in the Social-Science Literature', *Annual Review of Sociology*, 27 (forthcoming).

HALL, E. T., and HALL, M. R. (1990). *Understanding Cultural Differences*. Yarmouth, Me.: Intercultural Press.

HALL, P. D., and NORBURN, D. (1987). 'The Management Factor in Acquisition Performance', *Leadership and Organization Development Journal*, 8: 23–30.

HAMPDEN-TURNER, C., and TROMPENAARS, F. (1993). *The Seven Cultures of Capitalism*. London: Doubleday.

HANDY, C., GORDON, C., GOW, I., and RANDLESOME, C. (eds.) (1988). *Making Managers*. London: Pitman.

HARRIGAN, K. R. (1986). *Managing for Joint Venture Success*. New York: Lexington Books.

HARRIS, C. (1999). 'On Course to Topple the Record', *Financial Times Survey on International Mergers & Acquisitions*, 22 Sept.: I.

HARZING, A.-W. K. (1999). *Managing the Multinationals: An International Study of Control Mechanisms*. Cheltenham: Edward Elgar.

HASPESLAGH, P. C., and JEMISON, D. B. (1991). *Managing Acquisitions: Creating Value through Corporate Renewal*. New York: Free Press.

HAWLEY, J. P., and WILLIAMS, A. T. (1996). *Corporate Governance in the US: The Rise of Fiduciary Capitalism—a Review of the Literature*. Report to OECD, Jan.

HEDLUND, G. (1986). 'The Hypermodern MNC: A Heterarchy?', *Human Resource Management*, 25: 9–35.

HENNART, J.-F. (1993). 'Control in Multinational Firms: The Role of Price and Hierarchy', in S. Ghoshal and D. E. Westney (eds.), *Organization Theory and the Multinational Corporation*. London: Macmillan.

HICKSON, D. J. (ed.) (1993). *Management in Western Europe: Society, Culture and Organization in Twelve Nations*. Berlin: De Gruyter.

—— HININGS, C. R., McMILLAN, C. J., and SCHWITTER, J. P. (1974). 'The Culture-Free Context of Organization Structure: A Tri-national Comparison', *Sociology*, 8: 59–80.

—— and PUGH, D. S. (1995). *Management Worldwide: The Impact of Social Culture on Organizations around the Globe*. London: Penguin.

HITT, M., HARRISON, J., IRELAND, R. D., and BEST, A. (1998). 'Attributes of Successful and Unsuccessful Acquisitions of US Firms', *British Journal of Management*, 9: 91–114.

HODGETTS, R. M., and LUTHANS, F. (1990). 'International Human Resource Management: Motivation and Leadership Dimensions', in A. Nedd (ed.), *International Human Resource Management Review* (Singapore), 1: 61–74.

HOFSTEDE, G. (1980a). *Culture's Consequences: International Differences in Work-Related Values*. London: Sage.

—— (1980b). 'Motivation, Leadership and Organization: Do American Theories Apply Abroad?', *Organization Dynamics*, Summer: 42–63.

—— (1991). *Cultures and Organizations: Software of the Mind*. Maidenhead: McGraw-Hill.

—— (1996). 'Riding the Waves of Commerce: A Test of Trompenaars' "Model" of National Cultural Differences', *International Journal of Intercultural Relations*, 20: 189–98.

—— and BOND, M. H. (1988). 'The Confucius Connection: From Cultural Roots to Economic Growth', *Organizational Dynamics*, 16: 4–21.

HOROWITZ, J. H. (1978). 'Management Control in France, Great Britain and Germany', *Columbia Journal of World Business*, 13: 16–22.

—— (1980). *Top Management Control in Europe*. London: Macmillan.

HUAULT, I. (1996). 'French Multinational Companies' Strategies and Co-ordination Mechanisms: The Role of Human Resource Management in Europe and Nigeria', *International Journal of Human Resource Management*, 7: 572–84.

HUNT, J. (1988). 'Managing the Successful Acquisition: A People Question', Stockton Lecture, London Business School.

—— LEES, S., GRUMBAR, J. J., and VIVIAN, P. D. (1986). *Acquisitions: The Human Factor*. London: London Business School and Egon Zehnder International.

INKSON, J. H. K., SCHWITTER, J. P., PHEYSEY, D. C., and Hickson, D.J. (1970). 'A Comparison of Organization Structure and Managerial Roles: Ohio, U.S.A. and the Midlands, England', *Journal of Management Studies*, 7: 347–63.

IRELAND, J. (1991). 'Find the Right Management Approach', *China Business Review*, Jan.–Feb.: 14–31.

JACOBS, M. T. (1991). *Short-Term America: The Causes and Cures of our Business Myopia*. Boston: Harvard Business School Press.

JAMIESON, I. (1980). *Capitalism and Culture*. Aldershot: Gower.

JOHANSON, J., and VAHLNE, J.-E. (1977). 'The Internationalization Process of the Firm: A Model of Knowledge Development and Increasing Foreign Market Commitments', *Journal of International Business Studies*, 8: 23–32.

JOHNSON, B. T., HOLMES, K. R., and KIRKPATRICK, M. (1998). 'Freedom is the Surest Path to Growth', *Asian Wall Street Journal*, 1 Dec.: 14.

JONES, G. (1993). 'Foreign Multinationals and British Industry before 1945', in G. Jones (ed.), *Transnational Corporations: A Historical Perspective*. London: Routledge.

KESSLER, I. (1996). 'Payment Systems', in M. Warner (ed.), *International Encyclopedia of Business and Management*. London: Routledge.

KITCHIN, J. (1974). 'Winning and Losing with European Acquisitions', *Harvard Business Review*, Mar.–Apr.

KNIGHTS, D., and MURRAY, F. (1994). *Managers Divided: Organisation Politics and Information Technology Management*. Chichester: Wiley.

KOGUT, B. (1988). 'Joint Ventures: Theoretical and Empirical Perspectives', *Strategic Management Journal*, 9: 319–32.

—— and SINGH, H. (1988). 'The Effect of National Culture on the Choice of Entry Model', *Journal of International Business Studies*, 19: 411–33.

KOTLER, P. (1985). 'Global Standardization—Courting Danger?', Panel Discussion, 23 American Marketing Association Conference, Washington.

KPMG (1997). *Corporate Finance Survey*. London.

LANE, C. (1989). *Management and Labour in Europe: The Industrial Enterprise in Germany, Britain and France*. Aldershot: Edward Elgar.

—— (1995). *Industry and Society in Europe*. Aldershot: Edward Elgar.

—— (1997). 'The Governance of Interfirm Relations in Britain and Germany: Societal or Dominance Effects?', in R. Whitley and P. H. Kristensen (eds.), *Governance at Work: The Social Regulation of Economic Relations*. Oxford: Oxford University Press.

LAWRENCE, P. (1996a). *Management in the USA*. London: Sage.

—— (1996b). 'Through a Glass Darkly: Towards a Characterization of British Management', in I. Glover and M. Hughes (eds.), *The Professional Managerial Class*. Aldershot: Avebury.

—— (1996c). 'Management in Europe', in M. Warner (ed.), *International Encyclopedia of Business and Management*. London: Routledge.

—— and EDWARDS, V. (2000). *Management in Western Europe*. Basingstoke: Macmillan.

LAZONICK, W., and O'SULLIVAN, M. (1996). 'Organization, Finance and International Competition', *Industrial and Corporate Change*, 5: 1–49.

LEVITT, T. (1983). 'The Globalization of Markets', *Harvard Business Review*, May–June: 92–102.

LINCOLN, J. R. (1993). 'Work Organization in Japan and the United States', in B. Kogut (ed.), *Country Competitiveness: Technology and the Organization of Work*. New York: Oxford University Press.

LINDGREN, U., and SPANGBERG, K. (1981). 'Management of the Post-acquisition Process in Diversified MNCs', in Lars Otterber (ed.), *The Management of Headquarters–Subsidiary Relationships in Multinational Corporations*. Gower: Aldershot.

LOCKE, R. R. (1989). *Management and Higher Education since 1940: The Influence of America and Japan on West Germany, Great Britain and France*. Cambridge: Cambridge University Press.

LODERER, C., and MARTIN, K. (1992). 'Postacquisition Performance of Acquiring Firms', *Financial Management*, 21: 69–79.

LORANGE, P., and ROOS, J. (1992). *Strategic Alliances: Formation, Implementation and Evolution*. Oxford: Basil Blackwell.

LUBATKIN, M. (1988). 'Value-Creating Mergers: Fact or Folklore?', *Academy of Management Executive*, 2/4: 295–302.

McGAUGHEY, S. L., and DE CIERI, H. (1999). 'Reassessment of Convergence and Divergence Dynamics: Implications for International HRM', *International Journal of Human Resource Management*, 10: 235–50.

MACINTOSH, N. B. (1994). *Management Accounting and Control Systems*. Chichester: John Wiley & Sons.

McMILLAN, C. J. (1996). *The Japanese Industrial System*. 3rd edn. New York: De Gruyter.

MAKHIJA, M. V., KIM, K. and WILLIAMSON, S. D. (1997). 'Measuring Globalization of Industries Using a National Industry Approach: Empirical Evidence Across Five Countries and Over Time', *Journal of International Business Studies*, 28: 679–710.

MARKIDES, C., and OYON, D. (1998). 'International Acquisitions: Do They Create Value For Shareholders?', *European Management Journal*, 16: 125–35.

MARKS, M. L., and MIRVIS, P. H. (1992). 'Rebuilding after the Merger: Dealing with "Survivor Sickness"', *Organizational Dynamics*, 21/2: 18–32.

MARR, R. (1996). 'Management in Germany', in M. Warner (ed.), *International Encyclopaedia of Business and Management*. London: Routledge.

MARSH, D. (1995). 'Contact between Cultures. Germany and the UK: Learning from Each Other', *Financial Times*, 29 May: 15.

MASLOW, A. H. (1943). 'A Theory of Human Motivation', *Psychological Review*, 50: 370–96.

MAURICE, M., SORGE, A., and WARNER, M. (1980). 'Societal Differences in Organizing Manufacturing Units: A Comparison of France, West Germany and Great Britain', *Organization Studies*, 1: 59–86.

MELLOAN, G. (1999). 'Corporate Marriages are not Made in Heaven', *Asian Wall Street Journal*, 5 Jan: 8.

MILES, G. L. (1995). 'The Trials of Two Acquirers', *International Business*, Feb: 34–46.

MINTZBERG, H. (1994). *The Rise and Fall of Strategic Planning*. New York: Prentice-Hall.

MOROSINI, P., and SINGH, H. (1994). 'Post Cross-border Acquisitions: Implementing "National Culture-Compatible" Strategies to Improve Performance', *European Management Journal*, 12/4: 390–400.

MORRIS, J., and WILKINSON, B. (1996). 'The Transfer of Japanese Management to Alien Institutional Environments', *Journal of Management Studies*, 32: 719–30.

MORTON, G., and BEAUMONT, P. (1998). 'Diffusing "Best Practice" in Multinational Corporations', *International Journal of Human Resource Management*, 9: 671–95.

NAHAVANDI, A., and MALEKZADEH, A. R. (1988). 'Acculturation in Mergers and Acquisitions', *Academy of Management Review*, 13: 79–90.

NAKAMOTO, M. (1997). 'Death of the Salaryman', *Financial Times Weekend*, 17 May: I.

NAPIER, N. K. (1989). 'Mergers and Acquisitions, Human Resource Issues and Outcomes: A Review and Suggested Typology', *Journal of Management Studies*, 26: 271–89.

NGO, H. Y., TURBAN, D., LAU, C. M., and LUI, S. Y. (1998). 'Human Resource Practices and Firm Performance of Multinational Corporations: Influences of Country Origin', *International Journal of Human Resource Management*, 9: 632–52.

NICHOLSON, N., and WEST, M. (1988). *Managerial Job Change: Men and Women in Transition*. Cambridge: Cambridge University Press.

NOBLE, D. F. (1977). *America by Design: Science, Technology, and the Rise of Corporate Capitalism*. New York: Knopf.

NONAKA, I., and TAKEUCHI, H. (1995). *The Knowledge-Creating Company*. New York: Oxford University Press.

NORBURN, D., and SCHOENBERG, R. (1994). 'European Cross-border Acquisition: How Was it for You?', *Long Range Planning*, 27/4: 25–34.

OHMAE, K. (1990). *The Borderless World: Power and Strategy in the Interlinked Economy*. New York: Free Press.

OLIE, R. (1994) 'Shades of Culture and Institutions in International Mergers', *Organization Studies*, 15: 381–405.

OLIVER, N., and WILKINSON, B. (1992). *The Japanization of British Industry: New Developments in the 1990s*. 2nd edn. Oxford: Blackwell.

ORRU, M., BIGGART, N. W., and HAMILTON, G. G. (eds.) (1997). *The Economic Organization of East Asian Capitalism*. Thousand Oaks, Calif.: Sage.

OUCHI, W. G. (1981). *Theory Z*. Reading, Mass.: Addison-Wesley.

PABLO, A. L. (1994). 'Determinants of Acquisition Integration Level: A Decision-Making Perspective', *Academy of Management Journal*, 37: 803–36.

PASCALE, R. T., and ATHOS, A. G., (1981). *The Art of Japanese Management*. New York: Simon & Schuster.

PAULY, L. W., and REICH, S. (1997). 'National Structures and Multinational Corporate Behavior: Enduring Differences in the Age of Globalization', *International Organization*, 51: 1–30.

PERLMUTTER, H. (1969). 'The Tortuous Evolution of the Multinational Corporation', *Columbia Journal of World Business*, 4: 9–18.

PETERS, T., and WATERMAN, R. H. (1982). *In Search of Excellence: Lessons from America's Best-Run Companies*. New York: Harper & Row.

POOLE, M., and JENKINS, G. (1997). 'Developments in HRM in Manufacturing in Modern Britain', *International Journal of Human Resource Management*, 8: 841–57.

POORTINGA, Y. (1992). 'Towards a Conceptualization of Culture for Psychology', in S. Iwawaki, Y. Kashima, and K. Leung (eds.), *Innovations in Cross-cultural Psychology*. Amsterdam: Swets & Zeitlinger.

PORTER, L. W., and LAWLER, E. E. (1968). *Managerial Attitudes and Performance*. Homewood, Ill.: Irwin.

PORTER, M. E. (1985). *Competitive Advantage: Creating and Sustaining Superior Performance*. New York: Free Press.

—— (1987). 'From Competitive Advantage to Corporate Strategy', *Harvard Business Review*, May–June: 43–59.

PRAHALAD, C. K., and HAMEL, G. (1985). 'Strategic Intent', *Harvard Business Review*, May–June: 63–76.

PUCIK, V. (1988). 'Strategic Alliances with the Japanese: Implications for Human Resource Management', in F. J. Contractor and P. Lorange (eds.), *Cooperative Strategies in International Business*. New York: Lexington Books.

PUGH, D. S., HICKSON, D. J., HININGS, C. R., (1969). 'An Empirical Taxonomy of Structures of Work Organization', *Administrative Science Quarterly*, 14: 115–26.

—— —— ——, MACDONALD, K. M., TURNER, C., and LUPTON, T. (1963). 'A Conceptual Scheme for Organizational Analysis', *Administrative Science Quarterly*, 8: 289–315.

QUELCH, J. A., and HOFF, E. J. (1986). 'Customizing Global Marketing', *Harvard Business Review*, May–June: 59–68.

REECE, R. (1996). 'Easing the Transition During a Merger or Acquisition', *Banking Marketing*, 28/8: 38–42.

ROBERTS, K. H. (1970). 'On Looking at an Elephant: An Evaluation of Cross-cultural Research Related to Organizations', *Psychological Bulletin*, 74: 327–50.

RUGMAN, A. (2000). *The End of Globalization*. London: Random House.

RUIGROK, W., and VAN TULDER, R. (1995). *The Logic of International Restructuring*. London: Routledge.

SALES, A., and MIRVIS, P. (1984). 'When Cultures Collide: Issues of Acquisition', in J. R. Kimberly and R. E. Quinn (eds.), *Managing Organizational Transition*. Homewood, Ill.: Irwin.

SAMUELSON, R. J. (2000). 'Globalization's Double Edge', *International Herald Tribune*, 4 Jan.: 1, 3.

SCHOENBERG, R., and REEVES, R. (1999). 'What Determines Acquisition Activity within an Industry?', *European Management Journal*, 17/1: 93–8.

SCHUMPETER, J. (1943). *Capitalism, Socialism and Democracy*. London: Allen & Unwin.

SCHWEIGER, D. M., IVANCEVICH, J. M., and POWER, F. R. (1987). 'Executive Actions for Managing Human Resources before and after Acquisition', *Academy of Management Executive*, 1/2: 127–38.

—— and WEBER, Y. (1989). 'Strategies for Managing Human Resources during Mergers and Acquisitions: An Empirical Investigation', *Human Resource Planning*, 12/2: 69–86.

SEBENIUS, J. K. (1998). 'Case Study: Negotiating Cross-border Acquisitions', *Sloan Management Review*, 39/2: 27–41.

SHADUR, M. A., RODWELL, J. J., and BAMBER, G. J. (1995). 'The Adoption of International Best Practices in a Western Culture: East Meets West', *International Journal of Human Resource Management*, 6: 735–57.

SHELTON, L. M. (1988). 'Strategic Business and Corporate Acquisition: Empirical Evidence', *Strategic Management Journal*, 9: 279–87.

SHLEIFER, A., and VISHNY, R. W. (1997). 'A Survey of Corporate Governance', *Journal of Finance*, 52: 737–83.

SHRIVASTAVA, P. (1986). 'Postmerger Integration', *Journal of Business Strategy*, 7: 65–76.

SIMONIN, BERNARD L. (1997). 'The Importance of Collaborative Know-how', *Academy of Management Journal*, 40: 1150–74.

SKAPINKER, M. (2000). 'Marrying in Haste', *Financial Times*, 12 Apr.: 14.

SLATTER, S. (1984). *Corporate Recovery: A Guide to Turnaround Management*. Harmondsworth: Penguin.

SMITH, K. W. (1997). 'Mercer on Management: Post-deal Management is Vital to M&A Success', *Management Review*, 86: S4.

SORGE, A. (1982). 'Cultured Organization', *International Studies of Management and Organization*, 12: 106–35.

—— (1993). 'Management in France', in D. J. Hickson (ed.), *Management in Western Europe: Society, Culture and Organization in Twelve Nations*. Berlin: De Gruyter.

SPARROW, P. R. (1995). 'Towards a Dynamic and Comparative Model of European Human Resource Management: An Extended Review', *International Journal of Human Resource Management*, 6: 935–53.

—— SCHULER, R. S. and JACKSON, S. E. (1994). 'Convergence or Divergence: Human Resource Practices and Policies for Competitive Advantage Worldwide', *International Journal of Human Resource Management*, 5: 268–99.

STEWART, R., BARSOUX, J.-L., KIESER, A., GANTER, H.-D., and WALGENBACH, P. (1994). *Managing in Britain and Germany*. Basingstoke: Macmillan.

SUDARSANAM, P. S. (1995). *The Essence of Mergers and Acquisitions*. Engelwood Cliffs, NJ: Prentice-Hall.

SVELICIC, M., and ROJEC, M. (1994). 'Foreign Direct Investment and the Transformation of Central European Economies', *Management International Review*, 34: 293–312.

SZARKA, J. (1996). 'Management in France', in M. Warner (ed.), *International Encyclopaedia of Business and Management*. London: Routledge.

TAYEB, M. (1994). 'Japanese Managers and British Culture: A Comparative Study', *International Journal of Human Resource Management*, 5: 145–66.

—— (1998). 'Transfer of Human Resource Management Practices across Cultures: An American Company in Scotland', *International Journal of Human Resource Management*, 9: 332–58.

TJOSVOLD, D. (1991). *Team Organization: An Enduring Competitive Advantage*. Chichester: Wiley.

TOFFLER, A. (1971). *Future Shock*. London: Pan Books.

TOLBERT, P. S., and ZUCKER, L. G. (1996). 'The Institutionalization of Institutional Theory', in S. R. Clegg, C. Hardy, and W. R. Nord (eds.), *Handbook of Organization Studies*. London: Sage.

TROMPENAARS, F. (1993). *Riding the Waves of Culture*. London: Economist Books.

TUSHMAN, M. L., and O'REILLY, C. A. (1996). 'The Ambidextrous Organization', *California Management Review*, 38: 8–30.

ULRICH, D., CODY, T., LAFASTO, F., and RUCCI, T. (1989). 'Human Resources at Baxter Healthcare Corporation Merger: A Strategic Partner Role', *Human Resource Planning*, 12: 87–103.

United Nations Conference on Trade and Development (UNCTAD) (1995). *World Investment Report 1995*. New York: United Nations.

—— (1996). *World Investment Report 1996*. New York: United Nations.

—— (1999). *World Investment Report 1999*. New York: United Nations.

—— (2000). *World Investment Report 2000*. New York: United Nations.

VERY, P., LUBATKIN, M., and CALORI, R. (1996). 'A Cross-national Assessment of Acculturative Stress in Recent European Mergers', *International Studies of Management and Organization*, 26: 59–86.

WALSH, J. P. (1988). 'Top Management Turnover Following Mergers and Acquisitions', *Strategic Management Journal*, 9: 173–83.

WARNER, M., and CAMPBELL, A. (1993). 'German Management', in D. J. Hickson (ed.), *Management in Western Europe*. Berlin: De Gruyter.

WEICK, K. E. (1990). 'Cartographic Myths in Organizations', in A. Huff (ed.), *Mapping Strategic Thought*. London: Wiley.

WEVER, K. S. (1995). 'Human Resource Management and Organisational Strategies: German and US-Owned Companies', *International Journal of Human Resource Management*, 6: 606–25.

WHITLEY, R. D. (1992a). *Business Systems in East Asia*. London: Sage.

—— (ed.) (1992b). *European Business Systems: Firms and Markets in their National Contexts*. London: Sage.

WHITTAKER, D. H. (1993). 'New Technology and the Organization of Work: British and Japanese Factories', in B. Kogut (ed.), *Country Competitiveness: Technology and the Organization of Work*. New York: Oxford University Press.

WHYTE, W. H. (1956). *The Organization Man*. New York: Simon & Schuster.

WILLIAMSON, O. E. (1970). *Corporate Control and Business Behavior: An Enquiry into the Effects of Organizational Form on Enterprise Behavior*. Englewood Cliffs, NJ: Prentice-Hall.

—— (1975). *Markets and Hierarchies*. New York: Free Press.

—— (1985). *The Economic Institutions of Capitalism: Firms, Markets, Relational Contracting*. New York: Free Press.

WOODWARD, J. (1965). *Industrial Organization: Theory and Practice*. London: Oxford University Press.

YIP, G. S. (1992). *Total Global Strategy: Managing for Worldwide Competitive Advantage*. Englewood Cliffs, NJ: Prentice-Hall.

YONEYAMA, E. (1994). 'Japanese Subsidiaries: Strengths and Weaknesses', in R. Calori and P. De Woot (eds.), *A European Management Model: Beyond Diversity*. New York: Prentice-Hall.

ZUBOFF, S. (1988). *In the Age of the Smart Machine*. New York: Basic Books.

Index